ASSESSING THE 1984 *ULYSSES*

The Princess Grace Irish Library Series
ISSN: 0269–2619
General Editor: C. George Sandulescu

ASSESSING
THE 1984 *ULYSSES*

edited by
C. George Sandulescu and Clive Hart

Princess Grace Irish Library: 1

1986
COLIN SMYTHE
Gerrards Cross, Bucks

BARNES & NOBLE BOOKS
Totowa, New Jersey

Foreword © 1986 by Anthony Burgess
All other contributions copyright © 1986 by
The Princess Grace Irish Library

First published in 1986 by Colin Smythe Limited,
Gerrards Cross, Buckinghamshire

British Library Cataloguing in Publication Data

Assessing the 1984 Ulysses. – (Princess
Grace Irish Library, ISSN 0269-2619; 1)
1. Joyce, James *1882-1941*. Ulysses
I. Sandulescu, Constantin-George
II. Hart, Clive   III. Series
823' .912   PR6019.09U6

ISBN 0–86140–243–x

First published in the United States of America by
Barnes & Noble Books, Totowa, New Jersey 07512

Library of Congress Cataloguing in Publication Data

Assessing the 1984 'Ulysses'.
(The Princess Grace Irish Library series, ISSN 0269-2619)
1. Joyce, James, 1882-1941. Ulysses—Criticism,
Textual—Congresses.   I. Sandulescu, Constantin-George.
II. Hart, Clive.   III. Title.   IV. Series.
PR6019.09U58   1986   823' .912   86-17493
ISBN 0–389–20635–0

Produced in Great Britain
Set by Grove Graphics, Tring, Hertfordshire
and printed and bound by Billing & Sons Ltd.
Worcester

A BRIEF NOTE ABOUT THIS BOOK

An invitational conference on the topic A *FINNEGANS WAKE APPROACH TO ULYSSES* was organized by The Princess Grace Irish Library in Monaco in late May 1985. Her Serene Highness Princess Caroline said in her inaugural speech that this was the first in a series of annual international conferences devoted to Irish studies to take place there.

The sole purpose of this first conference was to achieve a collective assessment of the three-volume *Ulysses* by James Joyce, edited by H. W. Gabler & team, and published by Garland of New York on Bloomsday 1984. This book contains the proceedings of that conference.

The Editors

CONTENTS

Contents

A *FINNEGANS WAKE* APPROACH TO *ULYSSES*

In the early summer of 1985 a number of distinguished Joyce scholars travelled to the Principality of Monaco to discuss *Ulysses*. Some of these thought they were travelling to Monte Carlo, which is merely a suburb of Monaco, for the great world, which includes the French railway system, inverts topography and includes the greater in the lesser. This may be regarded as Irish and a good augury for a scholarly Joyce convention but, facetiousness apart (though it can never properly be apart when Joyce is on the scene), the question may be asked: Why choose Monaco for yet another symposium dedicated to the enigmatic Irish master? Joyce visited the Côte d'Azur, but the only reference he makes in his work to the princely enclave is in a wholly facetious connection. In the Cyclops episode of *Ulysses* he admits the Man Who Broke the Bank at Monte Carlo in the pantheon of Irish heroes. Why then should Monaco be received into the comity of locales which – Dublin, Trieste, Zurich and Paris in the lead – were blessed or cursed by the Joyce presence?

The answer lies in the Irish affiliation established by the late and powerfully missed Princess Grace. She was of Philadelphia Irish stock, and, like many Americans domiciled in Europe, became strongly aware of her European ancestry. Her devotion to Ireland took many forms, some of them convivial – the celebration of St Patrick's Day in Monaco was, under her aegis, always a great occasion – and some of them artistic and scholarly. She amassed a considerable library of Irish literature, history and folklore, and this, after her death, formed the nucleus of the Princess Grace Irish Library, a wholly appropriate memorial. It is, in terms of wide scholarship and extensive amenity, as yet a mere infant, but it will grow. As a venue for the meeting of scholars of Irish literature it is already established, but here again it will grow.

One of Joyce's sardonic extra-literary aims was to keep the professors busy. No modern writer has attracted so much scholarly attention as he, and biennial Joyce symposia in the cities where he lived are a feature of the continued inquiry into the meaning and method of his books. Some of these conventions are on a large scale and sussurate with the rustle of many learned papers. The 1985 meeting at the Princess Grace Irish Library in Monaco was intimate and almost arcane. It dealt not with narratology or semiotics but with the narrower problems of textuality. It was occasioned by the fruit of mainly German scholarship that had just resulted in the publication of a three volume edition of *Ulysses* for which final authenticity was claimed.

The contesting of this claim was one of the activities of the symposium. The overall title may seem Joyceanly wayward, but it indicated accurately enough the spirit of the approach. It is possible to see *Ulysses* not primarily as a great avant-garde book, more of a codex than a novel, but as a triumph of narration much in the tradition of Sterne, Fielding and even Dickens. A characteristic of great orthodox novels (and the fundamental orthodoxy of *Ulysses* is becoming more and more apparent) is their capacity to be transferred to a region of discourse where their verbal structure is subordinated to their content. In other words, it has been found possible to adapt *Ulysses* to such extra-literary media as stage and film and even (I must cite my own *Blooms of Dublin* here) musical comedy. Bloom and Stephen Dedalus can be separated from the text, as can also the factual elements of the *récit* in which they move, act, speak and think. With Joyce's other great book, *Finnegans Wake*, it is virtually impossible to divide substance from form. This work, for all the arguments of the more rarefied scholars in support of its quasi-musical self-referentiality, does contain characters in the manner of *Ulysses*, but these are so firmly embedded in their mode of presentation that it would be dangerous to release them from their verbal ambience and make them walk Dublin, or Chapelizod, as identifiable citizens. The multiguity of character, speech, action and narrative technique forbids our seeing them as personages in the traditional sense.

In other words, *Finnegans Wake* can be approached only as

a text. To transpose the purely textual treatment to *Ulysses* entails concentration on the words and on those words as they add up to the structure we call a book. But in a book there are more than words. There is their arrangement on the page, always important in Joyce, who was not blind to the new influence of journalistic techniques on literature, and there is the apparently irrelevant element of pagination. One approach to *Finnegans Wake* is not verbal at all but arithmological. Indeed, Joyce believed that the importance of number in that book would draw the unliterary scientific to it.

Numerical symbology is essential to *Finnegans Wake*, which has to hold the shifting patterns of a dream down to countable solidities. In *Ulysses* it is not so important. But the magician in Joyce could not resist drawing the accidents of pagination into the text. The number at the head or bottom of a page had to be granted sly significance, and the form in which the book was originally published by Shakespeare and Company in Paris represented to Joyce a structure as immutable as that of a painting. So, at least, some argue. Joyce, who could never leave well alone, was still working on *Ulysses* in its page-proof stage. It was only the ultimatum of publication on his birthday – 2 February – that forced him to release his text in the form we know it or think we know it. Paul Valéry said that poems are never finished, only abandoned. *Ulysses* is a sort of poem.

The three-volume allegedly authentic edition of the work is a kind of palimpsest in which a variety of readings are presented, along with a final text acceptable to the editors if not to all Joyce scholars. Certainly, the pagination has no more sly symbolism in it. The pages we look at are not the pages Joyce reluctantly let go in response to the urgent signals of his publisher and printer. Certain readings, rescued at last from the morass of uncorrected misprints, add depth and erase puzzles. We know, for instance, that Bloom thought of mitey, not mighty, cheese. But certain scholars fear that, while something is gained much is lost. This was one of the contentions of the Monaco symposium.

I forfeited my right to Joyce scholarship many years ago. Novelists ought not to be scholars, and I gave my allegiance to the fictional art as I practise it in my own way, not in Joyce's. But I deeply admire the analytical skill and unremitting labour, to say nothing of the humour and humanity, exemplified in the papers presented here. This collection is a most valuable addition to the multitude of Joyce lucubrations that are beginning to oppress those of us who retain a nostalgia for scholarship, as well as those who are already domesticated into it. It is also a production that comes out of Monaco, obliquely honours its late great princess, and will serve to remind the world that brains as well as roulette wheels spin in it. There is no phrase more egregiously improper for Joyce studies than *rien ne va plus.*

Monaco, 29 January 1986

Anthony Burgess

ACKNOWLEDGEMENTS

The publishers are most grateful to the Bodley Head Ltd. and to Random House Inc. for permission to quote extracts from James Joyce's *Ulysses*. The death mask of James Joyce that appears on the dust jacket is reproduced by courtesy of Robert Nicholson, Curator of the James Joyce Tower, Sandycove, Co. Dublin.

ABBREVIATIONS AND CONVENTIONS

Quotations from *Ulysses* are drawn either from James Joyce, *Ulysses: A Critical and Synoptic Edition*, ed. Hans Walter Gabler with Wolfhard Steppe and Claus Melchior, 3 vols (New York and London: Garland Publishing, Inc., 1984), or from *Ulysses*, corrected and reset edition (New York: Random House, Inc., 1961), or from both. Where two references are given, the first is to the Garland edition, the second to Random House. Garland references take the form suggested by Hans Gabler: an episode/line number; Random House references are made by means of a page number preceded by *U*. Page references to editorial matter in Garland are preceded by G.

The following additional symbols are used in the notes and in references given in-text:

Ellmann	Richard Ellmann, *James Joyce*, new and revised edition (New York, Oxford and Toronto: Oxford University Press, 1982).
FW	James Joyce, *Finnegans Wake* (New York: Viking Press, 1939; London: Faber and Faber, 1939).
JJA	*James Joyce Archive*, ed. Michael Groden and others (New York: Garland, 1978).
JJQ	*James Joyce Quarterly*, ed. Thomas F. Staley (Tulsa, Oklahoma, 1963—).
Letters I, II, III	*Letters of James Joyce* I, ed. Stuart Gilbert (1957), reissued with corrections (New York: Viking Press, 1966; London, Faber and Faber, 1966); II, III, ed. Richard Ellmann (New York: Viking Press, 1966; London: Faber and Faber, 1966).
P	James Joyce, *A Portrait of the Artist as a Young Man* (1916), ed. Chester C.

Anderson and Richard Ellmann (New
York: Viking Press, 1964).

R   *Ulysses, A Facsimile of the Manuscript,*
ed. Clive Driver, 2 vols (New York:
Octagon Books & Philadelphia: Rosenbach
Foundation, 1975).

SH   James Joyce, *Stephen Hero,* ed. John J.
Slocum and Herbert Cahoon (New York:
New Directions, 1944, 1963).

THE EDITIONS OF *ULYSSES*

(First Edition)   *Ulysses* by James Joyce (Paris: Shakespeare and Company, 1922).

(Second Edition)   *Ulysses* by James Joyce (Paris: Shakespeare and Company, 1926).

(Third Edition)   *Ulysses* by James Joyce (Paris: Shakespeare and Company, 1927).

(Fourth Edition)   *Ulysses* by James Joyce. Two volumes. (Hamburg, Paris, Bologna: The Odyssey Press, 1932).

(Fifth Edition)   *Ulysses* by James Joyce (New York: Random House, 1934).

(Sixth Edition)   *Ulysses* by James Joyce. With an Introduction by Stuart Gilbert and Illustrations by Henri Matisse. (New York: The Limited Editions Club, 1935).

(Seventh Edition) *Ulysses* James Joyce (London: John Lane, The Bodley Head, 1936).

(Eighth Edition)   *Ulysses* James Joyce (London: The Bodley Head, 1960).

(Ninth Edition)   *Ulysses* by James Joyce (New York: Random House, 1961).

(Tenth Edition)   James Joyce, *Ulysses* (Harmondsworth: Penguin Books, 1968).

(Eleventh Edition) *Ulysses,* James Joyce. Three Volumes. A Critical and Synoptic Edition prepared by Hans Walter Gabler with Wolfhard Steppe and Claus Melchior. (New York & London: Garland Publishing, Inc., 1984).

HOW THIS PARTICULAR
FUNFORALL CAME ABOUT

Disagreement proves to be more productive than agreement.
– Roman Jakobson

1. The 1984 *Ulysses* is an impressive but vulnerable achievement: many have so far stressed how impressive it is; few have emphasized its vulnerability.

In calling an International Conference in Monaco to analyse this scholarly achievement of 'Monaco di Baviera', I assumed that the right balance would be struck between these two poles. Now it is up to the reader of this volume to see whether this has indeed been the case. For it is only when the right balance is obtained between agreement and disagreement that such a gathering could be considered to have been a success.

2. As a Conference Convener, I owe the Joyce community of scholars a word of explanation. The International Meeting which took place in Monaco in late May of 1985 arose out of a deep sense of frustration which I first experienced at the 1984 Joyce symposium held in Frankfurt. On a precedent largely created in 1979 in Zurich, I went to Frankfurt-am-Main almost obsessed, and one might even say saddened, by the idea that the whole conference would be literally monopolized by the publication of the new *Ulysses*. Nothing of the kind!

I was so blinded by my obsession that upon arrival I went straight to the Conference bookstand with the firm intention of getting hold of a copy: for I could not bear the thought of facing the discussion of a book that I had not even seen. I was bluntly told that the three-volume achievement was not yet available: they were certainly hoping to get a few copies before the conference was half way through! Desperately, I went through the programme in order to spot the sessions which I should definitely avoid, deprived of the book as I was . . . I only found that there were no sessions devoted to the new book. Except the last! Except the very last!

After the publicity that the book had already been given in all the dailies, from the low-brow London *Telegraph* and *Nice-Matin* to the high-brow unmentionables, I was downright flabbergasted at the Joyceans' indifference. It took me quite a few hours to realise that there was something deliberate about it. And corridor gossip only contributed to strengthening an intuition. Then half way through the Conference the book arrived; and I was further astonished to find that Joycean colleagues were not even offered the slightest discount on that $200 bagatelle . . .

Of course I did not buy it, of course next to nobody bought it, and of course a very low sales figure had been envisaged as but few copies were made available. It was when I got back home that I was even more astonished: my New York book club, *The Readers' Subscription*, was offering it to all its members at a 15 per cent discount . . . It was then that I was less surprised by the two parallel monologues of Stephen Joyce and Richard Ellmann on Saturday 16 June 1984 as part of the publication ceremony. I had first thought, in my naïve mind, that publication day *happened* to be Bloomsday – instead of 2 February – and, in its turn, Bloomsday *happened* to be the very last day of the Ninth International James Joyce Symposium, Frankfurt, 11–16 June 1984. In retrospect, such sheer coincidence appeared genuinely Joycean . . . The way all his birthdays and all his art had always been: with a touch of cunning to it. The only difference was that Joyce's cunning never led to frustration.

3. Later that autumn I was asked by one of the editors of *Etudes Irlandaises*, published in Lille, to write an account of what had happened at Frankfurt for that journal, the way I had already done for the Centenary Symposium in Dublin in 1982. I started piecing my information together and decided on making it as factual as is humanly possible, but then I realised that insincerity is a grave sin and dropped the idea of writing an account about Frankfurt altogether. However, it was at that moment that the thought dawned upon me, epiphany-like, that the New 1984 *Ulysses* was badly in need of collective scholarly discussion. In consequence, I then restricted the topic of the Monaco Seminar which I had announced on the very same Bloomsday in the very same hall to the very same

public to that one book, by cutting its title in half. John Kidd's visit to Monaco on Epiphany Day of 1985 in order to attend the lecture Anthony Burgess was giving on 'Joyce and the Wake' in the premises of the Princess Grace Irish Library only strengthened my by now deep-seated conviction that the 1984 *Ulysses* was very urgently in need of collective assessment. The readiness and interest with which more than forty outstanding Joyceans responded to the invitations sent on behalf of the newly set-up Library in Monaco was further solid evidence along that line.

4. In addition to the choice of topic, another word of explanation may be needed about two other choices – that of the date, and that of the invitees.

Mid to late May is indeed the best time of the year to have a scholarly gathering in Monaco: neither the wave of heat nor the big crowds of tourists have yet arrived. Also, it is a fairly convenient date for academics on both sides of the Atlantic, and it has the advantage over late August and early September that it does not clash with many other conventions. I insist on the date for the simple reason that the Whitsun weekend will remain a permanent choice for all the international gatherings to be sponsored by the Princess Grace Irish Library in the years to come, be they on Yeats, or on Beckett, or – why not? – on *Finnegans Wake*. Their Proceedings will all be issued in the present series, which this volume inaugurates.

The choice of participants seemed at the start, and in theory, equally simple and straightforward: in addition to the parties concerned – Publisher (Garland), Editor (Gabler and team), Advisors (Ellmann and Hart) –, one simply needed a representative cross-section of the Joyce Symposia habitués. In other words, I aimed at a mini-Symposium audience, worked out on premises which were analogous to population samples in a Gallup poll. After all, professional merit conjoined with symmetric geographical spread are criteria which are very much there even for the awarding of the Nobel Prize for literature . . . Five participants from the United States and, say, five from France would be a fair balance . . . and five from Britain would balance the five from the German-speaking area of central Europe. Then, Switzerland would balance Belgium, and Scandinavia would balance Monaco. I was painfully aware, at the time the invitations were being sent out, that I was the first in Europe ever to organize an invitational conference on James Joyce closely, minutely, and deliberately patterned on the communicative gimmicks of the Chomsky-type think-tank-cum-brain-storm at M.I.T.

Then the trouble seemed to be starting: Garland Publishers never even bothered to reply to the invitation. Hans Walter Gabler wrote to me saying in as many words that I was 'to a considerable degree falling victim to the strange operations of Dr John Kidd', and the French, with one exception – that of Jacques Aubert, who acted as observer (and is not present in this volume) –, decided that they were unavailable for the Monaco event, as they had their own Gablerian *funforall* at the Sorbonne anyhow.

At first sight, these were insurmountable difficulties, but in the long run they turned into clear advantages of objectivity and homogeneousness. The objectivity was generated by the absence of both Hans Walter Gabler and John Kidd; for by now the *Washington Post* splash article had been published, and the Kidd-Gabler New York duel had taken place (in spite of my attempts at U.N. neutrality, all three texts were going round like hot cakes among the Monaco participants). Homogeneousness meant an emphasis on Ireland, and an increase in the English-speaking contingent, which led to very heated and very spontaneous debates in the centre of which was more often than not the ebullient and all too resourceful David Norris of T.C.D.

5. Speaking of spontaneous debates . . . They have not vanished into thin air: they have all been recorded on tape, have by now become part of the archives of the Princess Grace Irish Library, and in the centuries to come inquisitive Joyce scholars will have the opportunity to study the birth of Gablerisms, or how opinions may vary from one day to another, or from the spoken to the written medium. At one time Clive and I even envisaged including the tapescripts, given in full, in the body of this volume. But on account of strict limitations of space, that will have to wait for another book.

6. Finally, speaking of the spoken medium . . . Not all the

papers contained in the present volume were read in session in the shape they are in now. Some were not read at all.

Bernard Benstock was invited to the Monaco Seminar, but could not attend: he sent a paper instead, which did not arrive in time to be read and discussed in session. On the other hand, Wilhelm Füger, Michael Patrick Gillespie, and Charles Peake did attend the Seminar, though they did not read formal papers at the time; Professor Peake was particularly active throughout the Seminar discussions. After their return home, all three of them sent in their respective papers at the end of the summer. Suzette Henke, Richard M. Kain, Ira B. Nadel, and Donald Phillip Verene read out their respective papers in session in almost exactly the same shape in which they are printed in this volume. During the summer, Richard Ellmann slightly strengthened the argumentation of the original version of his paper. All the others spoke from notes in the Seminar sessions and submitted their definitive texts some time afterwards.

7. The First Monaco International Seminar on Joyce was hailed in the media as an outstanding success: In a B.B.C. interview, somebody even tagged to me the label 'remarkable academic impressario', and Fritz Senn, thinking of the Seminar as a whole, kindly jotted 'one of the best ever' in the Library's *Livre d'Or* on his departure.

But organizational success is not enough: it is merely a stepping stone towards something else. The first step is to provide a forum for genuinely unbiassed and free discussion; but the real goal is to provide an accurate, explicit, concise, and lasting assessment of the 1984 *Ulysses*. And in that respect, though I now leave the reader to decide entirely for himself, I personally express the conviction that there is still a tremendous lot to be done.

8. It took the Gabler team just about as long to fish this fictional man-made mountain out of the water as Joyce himself had initially needed to throw it in. And one is never quite sure whether this mountain-size fish now out of the water in three-volume format does not indeed feel like a fish out of water . . . John Kidd has so far made a few very strong points in favour of a return to the 1922 *Ulysses*, and there are a few other points to be made in the same direction. As Gabler himself has so far brushed aside all these points, and as the

Monaco Conference, with the exception of philosopher Verene (in this volume), did not have much time to deal with them, a satisfactory assessment of the 1984 *Ulysses* is by no means finished: it is, on the contrary, barely starting to take shape. What is the cause of the slow start? you may ask.

9. Before, during, and after this memorable conference devoted to the man who broke the back (sic!) of Monte Carlo, I had literally been haunted by a statement (partially quoted as an epigraph to this account) made in 1958 by linguist Roman Jakobson[1] at an analogous conference which was being held at the University of Indiana:

Fortunately, scholarly and political conferences have nothing in common. The success of a political convention depends on the general agreement of the majority or totality of its participants. The use of votes and vetoes, however, is alien to scholarly discussion where DISAGREEMENT GENERALLY PROVES TO BE MORE PRODUCTIVE THAN AGREEMENT. Disagreement discloses antinomies and tensions within the field and calls for novel exploration. Not political conferences but rather exploratory activities in Antarctica present an analogy to scholarly meetings.

Joyce scholars might wish not only to give extra thought to the above memorable statement but also to remember that the assessment of the 1984 *Ulysses* attained in Monaco in May of 1985, and only imperfectly mirrored in this little book, is but the tip of the iceberg. For Gabler has by now effectively proved that anything dealing with Joyce's *Ulysses* must be at least *twice its size* in order to begin to make sense . . . genetically.

Monaco, 2 February 1986

C. George Sandulescu
Director,
Princess Grace Irish Library.

ULYSSES: HOW MANY TEXTS ARE THERE IN IT?

BERNARD BENSTOCK

> The most beautiful book that has come out of our country in my time. One thinks of Homer. (9.1164–65)

The search for a perfect *Ulysses* began when James Joyce complained that the first edition published by Shakespeare and Company contained so many errors needing correction; he undertook it for a while, but eventually lost interest as other concerns preoccupied him more. The low point in seeking perfection came in 1934 when Random House arranged to publish the first American edition, using the text from the pirated Samuel Roth version, at a time when Joyce was preparing the terrain for an imperfect text of *Finnegans Wake*. (An odd by-product of the first American edition was the *Word List* prepared by Miles Hanley, with us still, where available.) Joyce lived to see various editions of *Ulysses* (Shakespeare, Egoist, Random House, Bodley Head) and whatever concerns he had early on regarding misprints and lost lines have since been inherited by Joyce commentators, at times with fanatical zeal. For decades Joyceans wondered whether they would ever live to see an edition of *Ulysses* uncorrupted by errors, and assumed that such an ideal was worth striving and waiting for. Hans Walter Gabler, his team and his advisors and his computers, dedicated themselves to that ideal; and in 1984 the Critical and Synoptic Edition of *Ulysses* was published by Garland Press.

The exoteric ideals to which almost all Joyce scholars gave lip service were silently accompanied by esoteric and oddly personal behaviour practised by most *Ulysses* scholars: choosing for oneself a preferred text from those already extant and silently emending as the obviousness of an error suggested itself. When Gabler unveiled his sleek new model, three of the antiquated models were still being assembled and mass produced, and most of us had one of those held together by

1

rubber bands and scotch tape, and road-worthy only in the hands of the owner-driver. When you have memorized the page numbers for hundreds of bits and pieces in your personal and corrupt copy, you may not be as quick to welcome an uncorrupted *Ulysses*, newly repaginated and looking very foreign, no matter how enthusiastic you claimed to have been about waiting for Gabler. To have produced a perfect *Ulysses* – if that is indeed what Gabler has done – only to find that the world is somewhat reluctant to beat a path to your door – if indeed the world is reluctant – must be frustrating to a textual editor who had undertaken in good faith to provide what was always assumed to have been wanted.

The accusation of ingratitude cannot be ignored, even if the subliminal causes for retaining a firm hold on one's 'afflicted' copy of an old *Ulysses* become apparent. What cannot fail to come into question is the nature of authority, not just the credentials of the editor of the new edition but the right of anyone to determine the fixed form of Joyce's *Ulysses* other than James Joyce. For most of us the idea of a plodding textual editor, trained in bibliographic method and with the requisite scrupulosity, reconstructing the text along purely scientific lines (should that actually have been possible given the scattered condition of the necessary documents) is probably repugnant: *Ulysses* should not be placed in the hands of someone without intellectual involvement with it as a work of literary art. On the other hand, each of us, assuming the role of literary critic, promptly admits that without the technical training one could not hope to accomplish an accurate text of *Ulysses*. Although no one appointed or elected Hans Gabler, his voluntary undertaking seemed in most ways a perfect compromise, since he has credentials both as a textual editor and a Joyce scholar. Yet, as we attempt to read his explanations for choices made in his new edition, a discrepancy between the two halves of his expertise seems to present itself. When, as an editor, he paints himself out on to a gangplank, as a critic he quickly turns around and walks on water. It is essentially because we as Joyce scholars grant a knowledgable editor the prerogative to make judicious choices where definitive evidence cannot be dredged up that we also reserve the right to make judgements along our own lines of preference.

Ulysses: *How Many Texts Are There In It!*

Evidence, as Dr Gideon Fell once remarked, is like a stick – it points two ways. And in reconstituting *Ulysses* into the 'Synoptic and Critical Edition' Hans Gabler had to contend both with the lack of a definitive piece of textual evidence (missing typescripts) and an *embarras de richesses* (too many drafts). In the decision to bring every indented piece of dialogue flush with the lefthand margin he has physically altered the reading text into something new and strange, an act of alteration that took great courage and could not have been made without careful deliberation. We have always been aware that Joyce sought to revolutionize the printed page, not just with the displacement of inverted commas with the French *tirets*, but also for a while with concluding dashes to signal the close of spoken material. That he toyed with fully boxing in paragraphs by eliminating the indentation before the opening *tirets* seems consistent with this experimentation, but if that had been his decision prior to the publication in 1922 he could easily have directed Maurice Darantière that those were his wishes. Even as an afterthought within the next few years it could have been arranged, yet Joyce let edition after edition of *Ulysses* come off the presses and pass before his eyes without ever having been as audacious in this regard as Gabler has now been. As was to be suspected, Gabler reincorporated the *tirets* in instances where they were lost (every reader has done the same in his own copy since the necessity of designating speech usually makes itself obvious), and in so doing he must have been aware of how easy it is to lose that slight mark of indication; yet bringing them all forward to the margin makes them even more vulnerable to the carelessness of printers. He need only have looked at a copy of *A Portrait of the Artist as a Young Man* printed in Stockholm in 1945 by the Continental Book Company to see how unaesthetic it is and how dangerous to confuse the eye so frequently. More timid editors would probably have insisted on a telegraphic message from Joyce before proceeding in that particular direction.

Barring the imprimatur of such Higher Authority the editor assumes authority for himself and invests the edition with an ineffable claim to authority, and whereas reviewers may challenge particular items among the 5000 or so changes (or even throw up their hands in horror at solidified lefthand margins), they rarely challenge the authority (only the selectivity) of the editor. That challenge came almost inadvertently, and silently (in the form of that old standby, the silent emendation), when an Italian edition was published which based itself religiously on the corrected *Ulysses* but did not accept the unindented dialogue. There is no indication anyway in the textual apparatus of the Synoptic and Critical Edition that the changes incorporated are anything but a monolithic mass of changes, that all of them are part of the whole, that a perfected means of determining what should and should not now be included in the 'real' *Ulysses* has produced this 'definitive' text. No one – or almost no one – would want to scrap the edition entirely, but very few of us will ever accept an edition on an all-or-nothing basis, and there is no reason to assume that Hans Gabler would insist on such absolute allegiance to authority although there is a precedent in such insistence coming from Gabler's predecessor, whose authority is frequently cited in the new edition, and at times rather uncritically. Surely the only authority any of us actually recognizes is that of Joyce himself, who – despite a tendency toward full control of his material – was subject to changes of mood and perspective and creative reassessment. The 'packaging' of Joyce's creativity was artificially determined by his 40th birthday on 2 February 1922, and despite Paul Valéry's comment that a work of art is never finished, only abandoned, Joyce's *Ulysses* was neither finished nor abandoned – a poor lookout for any textual editor.

Ulysses itself is not a monolithic structure. As we handle it, bits and pieces occasionally fall out, just as pages in our ancient copies tend to detach themselves mysteriously through constant handling; some pieces get lost, most are returned but not always in the original place. The text undergoes changes as we read it just as it had undergone changes when it was being written, and what we now know from having a 'definitive' text presented to us that we never could have known before is that no such thing as a definitive text can ever exist. When Gabler restores phrases and passages to *Ulysses* which never were part of any printed text that passed though Joyce's hands, he is providing us with marginalia rather than with the entelechy, the form of forms.

There were no blank spots in existing text(s) insisting on being filled in, as in Sapphic verses, no empty chair at the table for the awaited spirit. The text – such as it was – constantly closed in upon itself (for better or worse) to form its own form, into which an informed editor like Hans Gabler is certainly permitted to intrude what he finds on the cutting room floor – yet without ever fulfilling an 'intended' design. When 'called out' replaces 'called up' on the first page of *Ulysses*, most of us breathe a sigh of relief: something now makes literal sense when it hadn't before, although occasionally we hear murmurs of regret that the connotation of conjuring up has now been lost. When 'Nother' replaces 'Mother' we smile with delight at Joycean cleverness and at the accident of typographical 'correction' that verifies Joyce's views on accidentals and correctives. But when the Love passage is inserted (or restored or intruded) into Scylla and Charybdis, it must give us pause, even if we are willing to accept its placement there – *especially* if we accept the restoration. As it now stands, *pace* Gabler, the answer to the question posed in Circe has already preceded the question (not an intolerable condition *chez* Joyce, and one that could provide some interesting speculative interpretation, although none has yet appeared in print). But the nagging thought that the same hand that wrote on wall may also have erased the writing on the wall needs to have some serious attention paid to it. We have many texts of *Ulysses* (several more than the ten Gabler acknowledges) that do not contain the Love passage, and now, taking its place alongside them, is an edition that does contain the passage. We are the richer for having it, but not necessarily the wiser.

Now that we are faced with the possibility that *Ulysses* contains more than the sum total of its parts, more than is dreamed of in the philosophy of textual editing or floating among the intangibles in computers, that more than one *Ulysses* text has always existed (including 'yours and mine and of all for a bare shilling and her luckpenny'), we are also confronted by two ancillary problems. The need for a corrected word index to *Ulysses* has existed for decades, but the assumption has been that there was little value in having it geared to a corrupt text. A concordance based on the new edition is now available, yet a reference tool which does not cross-reference the existing standard texts endows it with an authority that we may not be granting to the Synoptic and Critical Edition. Also hovering in the wings is the spectre of an imperfect *Finnegans Wake*, like a patient not yet etherized upon a table but waiting to learn about the success of the *Ulysses* surgery before undergoing a similar process. When James Blish tried to solicit 'corrections' that could be appended to the existing text (a formative stage that might have been considered for *Ulysses* as well), pitifully few suggestions were offered and the project was abandoned. What, then, is our collective thinking on revisions for *Finnegans Wake* on the basis of our experience with the revised *Ulysses*? Both of these projects need careful consideration, even if such words as 'perfect' and 'definitive' are losing credence for us; but then, no one ever expected a perfect or definitive mousetrap, only a better one.

JOYCE THE SCRIBE AND
THE RIGHT HAND READER

ROSA MARIA BOLLETTIERI BOSINELLI

I have been engaged in Joyce studies for many years now, during which time I have become acquainted with Joyce the Author, Joyce the Creator, Joyce the Artist, Joyce the Man (the husband, the father, the brother, the son), Joyce the Exile, Joyce the Political Person. I could go on: at different times, in the course of different readings, one figure or another became the focus of my attention. The path I followed shifted from a mainly biographical interest to an increasing need to concentrate on the product rather than on the producer, in other words, to grant privilege to the text, rather than to its originator.

Therefore, the idea of a corrupted text, particularly for *Ulysses*, a text full of mistakes, misreadings, mistypings, misunderstandings, misprints, misplacements was rather disturbing. On the other hand, when, nearly twenty years ago, Jack Dalton started calling attention to Joyce's corrupted texts, and, as far as *Ulysses* is concerned, proclaimed the existence of 'well over 2,000 corruptions which went back to the manuscripts, things that had never been printed correctly,'[1] the problems posed by a critical edition appeared to be so challenging that no solution seemed possible, at least in the short term.

Hans Walter Gabler has now shown us that the 'imperfection' we have had to accept so far consisted of at least 5,000 points in need of correction. Indeed, every step of the textual reconstruction is traceable and open to comment, or, as the case might be, to criticism. By looking at the synoptic text on the left hand page, scholars who can cope with its at first confusing layout may agree or disagree with the decisions taken by Gabler and his team: all the cards seem to be on the table.

As to myself, I will only consider two consequences, two

7

side effects, so to speak, of the Garland edition: the introduction of two new characters into the field of Joycean criticism, the scribe and the right hand reader.

I will start with the scribe. There are mistakes in the current printings of *Ulysses* that originated with Joyce himself, words that he did write, but, in the light of Gabler's research, did not intend to write. It was this kind of corruption that mostly interested me when I read the 'Afterword' in the third volume: the corruption that occurred in the process of Joyce's hand-copying his text from one draft to the next, the corruption that asks for critical judgement as to its nature more than other kinds of errors, the corruption that puts into doubt the very notion of 'error'.

When talking, for example, about the Eumaeus chapter, Gabler discusses the process of the author's fair-copying his text on the Rosenbach manuscript from a previous draft (Draft V.A.21, later in the 'Afterword' referred to as P–E). In comparison with this draft there are lacunae in the Rosenbach manuscript that pose the question: 'do they represent authorial commissions or indeed scribal omissions?' (G 1867). According to Gabler (G 1865), 'attention to the mechanical act of copying can become deflected by the writer's concentration on the continuing creative development of the text'. That is certainly true, and it has produced, as a consequence, a kind of corruption that has led Gabler to emendation of the Rosenbach manuscript. As he says (G 1865) 'such emendation restores the text of Joyce, the author, that was impinged on by Joyce, the scribe. Significantly, it repeatedly anticipates authorial repair in proof or typists' corrections'. And here is the first consequence I mentioned above: besides giving us the critical, restored text of *Ulysses*, Gabler has introduced a new character into the multi-faced gallery of Joyce's portraits, Joyce the scribe, who now has his place authorially secured alongside those of Joyce the writer, Joyce the narrator, Joyce the arranger, Joyce the creator and so on. And, not surprisingly, Joyce the scribe is no more reliable than Joyce the narrator, to pick just one from the list; one, by the way, whose existence or importance has become a controversial issue among Joyceans.[2] Joyce the scribe is a corruptor of words in the best tradition of the Joyce canon.

Just as there is no reading without misreading, so Joyce the scribe tells us that there is no copying without miscopying. Or should I say no writing without miswriting? Is the distinction between the scribe and the writer always possible? If the scribe and the writer, unlike the mediaeval copyist, are the same person, wouldn't it be possible for even involuntary omissions or corruptions perpetrated by Joyce the scribe against Joyce the writer to have become, at some later stage, accepted and legitimized by the author while re-reading, checking, reviewing his text? In other words, couldn't we accept Joyce the scribe as a creator of meaning? Couldn't the reviser be a creator of meaning?

Consider, for instance, what Richard Brown has to say about the restoration of an omitted fragment in Proteus, during Stephen's long monologue:

> Wilde's love that dare not speak its name. *His arm*:
> *Cranly's arm*. He now will leave me . . . (3.451–52)

The sequence here given in italic did not appear in previous editions. According to Brown[3] this 'is another example of an important passage restored to the reading text of *Ulysses* though not discovered for the first time by its editors.' He is referring to the well known restoration of the sequence about 'love' in the Scylla and Charybdis episode[4] (9.429–31) that derives from the Rosenbach manuscript, which, as Brown says, 'has been widely available in Clive Driver's photographic facsimile edition since 1975'. His polemical point is that 'the novelty is, strictly, in Gabler's inclusion of these items into the new text'. I do not agree with Brown. Gabler's restoration is very important, because, despite the fact that the existence of the omitted sequence had been pointed out by Harry Levin in the introduction to Driver's facsimile, very few had noticed it or fully understood its implications.

To go back to Proteus, Brown claims, and here I agree with him, that

the phrase, in its context, clearly implies a suspicion of homosexual attachment between Stephen and Cranly. Levin observed that the occurrence of the phrase in inverted form and in a different context in 'Telemachus' (which appears in all editions of *Ulysses*) carried no such implication. Levin's suggestion that, in revising, Joyce was

9

conscious of leaving this small but contentious hint out of his book is surely no less plausible than Gabler's rather curt and threateningly capitalized labelling of this omission as an EYESKIP.[5]

The problem of revision and miscopying is a highly debated one in philological studies. Cesare Segre[6] has made an important contribution to the subject. As Pugliati[7] points out in reviewing Segre's work, he has called attention to such textual problems as the notion of 'the text as a layered matrix of information about the contexts of composition; the relationship between sender and receiver, both expressing their respective intentionality (and, in the case of philological reconstruction/restoration of texts, the necessity of defining the interference between two different – linguistic and stylistic – systems: that of the author and that of the copyist or editor)'.

In talking about the interference of different systems and in discussing the problems posed by the collation of mediaeval manuscripts, Segre introduces the notion of *diasystem*. This is defined as 'the result of the linguistic compromise deriving from the encounter of two different tendencies present in the mediaeval copyist (that of respecting the original manuscript and that of introducing his own linguistic habits).'[8] Thus the notion of *diasystem* affects that of '*reconstruction of the relations* holding together the systems of variants' (*ibidem*).

It seems to me that this concept can cast new light on the relationship between Joyce the scribe and Joyce the writer. It stresses the importance of the synoptic text because it points in the direction of a plurality of texts rather than a granting of privilege to the 'original'. In other words, if we accept the notion of diasystem as fruitful, we must agree with Segre when he says:

This standpoint puts in a different light the manuscripts which we use to reconstruct the text. Traditional philology considered the various transcriptions preserved in manuscripts as the effect of a movement which was seen as centrifugal to a central datum, the original. According to this notion entropy is continually at work in it. With the concept of diasystem one discovers on the contrary a series of no less centripetal forces: those holding together the diasystems realized in every manuscript. At the centre of this tension is no longer

10

the original text but every time – and every time differently – the text resulting from the compromise between systems.[9]

We may limit the application of the notion of diasystem only to the interplay of Joyce the scribe and Joyce the author. If we extended it to all the materials that have led to the critical edition we would have various consequences: 1. we would have to assimilate the French typists and printers to the mediaeval copyist mentioned above, which may not be an accurate parallel; 2. we would have to negate the legitimacy of Gabler's text as 'the' critical text, and so confine it to the role of just one text among others, which is a possibility that might be taken into account.

But what I want to do here is merely to call attention to the figure of the scribe that emerges from Gabler's afterword; it is a figure that makes us ponder the complex, intriguing, mysterious paths through which a work of art comes to light.

I am ironically reminded of what Edgar Allen Poe had to say in 1846 about 'The Philosophy of Composition':

I have often thought how interesting a magazine paper might be written by any author who would – that is to say who could – detail, step by step, the process by which any one of his compositions attained its ultimate point of completion. Why such a paper has never been given to the world, I am at a loss to say – but, perhaps, the authorial vanity has had more to do with the omission than any other cause. Most writers – poets in special – prefer having it understood that they compose by a species of fine frenzy – an ecstatic intuition – and would positively shudder at letting the public take a peep behind the scenes, at the elaborate and vacillating crudities of thought – at the true purposes seized only at the last moment – at the innumerable glimpses of idea that arrived not at the maturity of full view . . . at the cautious selections and rejections – at the painful erasures and interpolations – in a word . . . at the cock's feathers, the red paint and the black patches which, in ninety-nine cases out of a hundred, constitute the property of the literary *histrio*.[10]

Poe then proceeds to give an apparently detailed reconstruction of the steps that brought him to the composition of 'The Raven'. Despite his explanations, the experience of reading the poem does not have much to do with all this. Is the literary *histrio* at play here, too? Or is there an intrinsic inexplicability of the work of art, whose magic

11

quality is reaffirmed, reinforced the very moment that the act of writing is presented as a matter-of-fact business, with nothing mysterious or ecstatic about it? A similar question can be posed about the appearance of the critical edition of *Ulysses*: does it modify in any way our reading experience? Yes, it does, but neither substantially nor for everybody.

Thanks to this edition, we now know how a great number of imprecisions, corruptions, and inexplicable phrases came to be printed; we know a great deal more about the problematics of textual reconstruction; and some new circumstances under which the text was composed have been made clear. But we still do not know everything about this text. The text is not 'definitive'.[11]

I do not consider this a fault since I do not believe in any method that doesn't lead one to the seriousness of the provisional. I therefore disagree with any harsh criticism of this edition as a whole.[12] My suggestion is that this, as well as other previous editions of *Ulysses* is, and can only be, provisional, though certainly far less 'provisional' than the others. It is nevertheless mainly a pre-text, the text that comes before the performance of reading – a pretext for interpretation, just as the different editions of Shakespeare's plays can be viewed as pretexts for the performance on the stage.

In fact, some of the other points that have been debated in this seminar were based not so much on philological arguments as on a kind of resistance to accepting Gabler's emendations because they would 'betray' previous readings, consolidated by about sixty years of scholarship, including the loved and cherished marginal notes and glosses that every Joycean has inscribed in his own copy over the years. This attitude is summarised by a sentence I have often heard in the last few days: 'Although I approve of the principle I am sorry to see this word/phrase/passage modified'.

I would like to turn to the second consequence of the critical edition: the introduction of a right hand reader as opposed to the left hand one. The coexistence of the two texts – the synoptic and the reading text – makes the comparison legitimate. Ira Nadel has called the two pages the 'time text' (left) and the 'space text' (right), and Fritz Senn has spoken of a 'Shem side' and a 'Shaun side' plus a third text compressed between the two, even mentioning the 'sinister' connotations of the left hand page.

There are, in fact, readers who are not particularly interested in the historical development of the text: to them, the synoptic page looks quite frightening, full as it is of diacritic signs and mysterious references. These readers will concentrate on the right hand page and happily ignore the left hand one. At least two attitudes are possible: they may trust the editors' choices and consider the very existence, if not the use, of the left hand page as a guarantee of the reliability of textual accuracy in the right hand one. Or the right hand reader may decide not to care about textual accuracy as he had to do before the appearance of a critical edition; he may decide freely to enjoy the seduction of Joyce's writing and to trust his own competence as a reader of the macrotext to be a cooperative reader, so used to creating meaning, his own meaning, even where none appears to exist, that he doesn't care about commas, single words, single sentences. This reader is not offended if textual scholars consider him unscrupulous and inaccurate; he is convinced that, despite the impressive figure of 5,000 emendations, the really important changes are comparatively few.

I tend to sympathise with the right hand reader, although his boldness may be irritating at times. I tend to stand by his side, mainly because I am convinced that at least some of the corruptions that made current texts of *Ulysses* obscure and nonsensical had already been emended by this cooperative reader before the appearance of the critical edition. Here is an example that was first signalled by Jack Dalton: in the first episode, Stephen is haunted by obsessive memories of his mother. At the climax of the scene he silently cries out 'No, mother. Let me be and let me live'. The 1960 printers left out the comma after 'No', a comma which was omitted in later editions.

As Jack Dalton[13] says: 'without the comma, Stephen speaks not to the mother but to himself, saying that he will have no mother. "Only" a comma, you see, but its presence or absence determines the grammar of "mother", determines the syntax of the sentence, controls the meaning and tone of an intense page-long scene and has considerable significance for a scene almost 600 pages away' (Circe). My point is that there are very few readers of *Ulysses* who would not mentally supply that comma; there are few readers who would interpret the passage as an assertion of orphanage on the part of Stephen. That passage possesses a dramatic power that is made up of a number of textual markers, explicit and implicit. It is clearly a piece of interior monologue, which in turn becomes dramatised in an ideal dialogue with the mother, evoked and invoked independently of the presence or absence of the comma. The 'grammar of mother', i.e. Stephen's relationship to her, goes beyond the graphic sign: it is supplied by the cooperative reader on the basis of a wealth of textual clues.

Another example in support of the right hand reader can be found in a quotation given by Fritz Senn in a paper first delivered in Cesena, July 1982. Senn, illustrating the notion of dislocution that he was to develop later,[14] called attention to the sequence:

Curious mice never squeal (4.28)

which appears at the beginning of the first Bloom chapter, as Bloom is looking at his cat. The sequence of words might make the naive reader wonder as to how the curiosity of mice makes them behave in one way, whereas lack of curiosity, by implication, should make them behave differently. Senn[15] comments: 'the miracle is that we, at least we late readers, do hardly fall into this misreading any more, though we might have done . . . We do in fact process the Joycean shorthand into a variant of "(it is) curious (that) mice never squeal" '. I'd like to add that what we really do here is to insert a comma (or a colon) after 'curious', just as in the 'No, mother' example given above. But this time the missing comma has not appeared in the critical edition, because it has never been there.

It is because of this and similar considerations that I shall conclude this paper with one last word in favour of the right hand reader, who establishes a pact with Joyce the scribe based on reciprocal tolerance, acceptance and enjoyment; the reader who wants to ignore the steps of textual reconstruction, following perhaps the biblical command: 'do not let your left

14

hand know what your right is doing; your good deed must be secret, and your Father who sees what is done in secret will reward you' (Matthew 6. 3–4).

TYPOGRAPHY UNDERRATED: A NOTE ON AEOLUS IN GABLER'S EDITION

GIOVANNI CIANCI

The experimental character of the avant-garde movement requires, at least in some cases, that the critical edition of their works pay due attention not only to the linguistic text but also to the formal, typographical aspect of that text. In the case of *Ulysses* there were good reasons to believe that a critical edition aspiring to being the definitive one would take into special consideration the formal problems posited by the episode that critics have unanimously recognised as the beginning of the experimental Joyce, i.e. the Aeolus chapter given over to the world of the daily press.

As is well known, after its publication in *The Little Review* in 1918, the chapter underwent modifications and was subjected to considerable revisions and additions, above all in the final phase of 1921–22[1]. Aeolus, which first presented itself as a narrative *continuum*, in this phase now takes on the aspect of a narrative broken up into sections, each preceded by a showy journalistic headline. The experimentation which was introduced into the text by these late modifications was not only made up of rhetorical amplifications (the addition of the famous thirty-two windy metapors etc.). Judging from the first edition of *Ulysses*, there was also the formal, visual and spatial lay-out of the page in which a different type of typographical character (the boldfaced headlines in capital letters) stood out producing a contrasting play of black and white. Far from being a secondary aspect of the chapter, it jumped to the foreground, given that the attention of the reader is most probably caught first by the iconic effect of the words as signs and afterwards by their meaning as words. One can say that it is the visual effect of the chapter, that is, the way in which it presents itself to the reader, that announces its experimental structure. Besides, at the centre of this episode is the newspaper,

16

including its actual production which consists not only of the deafening 'language' of the printing press, but also of its iconicity, the non-verbal communication which results from handling typographical characters and their spatial arrangement in the line and in the frame of the page. One remembers that this visual aspect of the words on the page is emphasised on the occasion when the foreman, in the section ORTHOGRAPHICAL, checks that there are no misprints in the proofs given to him by the typesetter:

It is amusing to view the unpar one ar alleled embarra two ars is it? double ess ment of a harassed pedlar while gauging au the symmetry with a y of a peeled pear under a cemetery wall. Silly, isn't it? Cemetery put in of course on account of the symmetry. (7.166–70)

It was therefore logical to expect from the new edition at least an explanatory note about the choice of typographical characters used in the headlines of Aeolus. But in the critical apparatus there is no indication of this. Hence the legitimate doubt that the editor never thought of the problem. Yet it is clear that even if this is so, the editor has in fact made a choice, which is the one appearing in the typographical characters of his edition. No reasons being given, the choice seems arbitrary. One has the impression that the editor has behaved as a person who had to choose the colour or quality of the paper to be used and left these details to his own personal taste and discretion.

Another consequence of an insensitivity to the iconic dimension of Aeolus is seen in the critical apparatus. Even if it is well-documented on the genesis of the text and its transmission, it says nothing about the printing history of the other editions of *Ulysses*. It does not, therefore, record the divergences from, and similarities to, the typography of the other editions of Aeolus. This seems to me a serious omission in a critical edition that aspires to having a complete critical and informative apparatus. Let me say right away that I think the typography of the Aeolus of the 1922 edition superior to that of Gabler's. I believe the reason for my preference, and therefore of my reservations about the Garland edition in this connection, is supported by historical and critical considerations.

Anyone who is familiar with the original texts of modern-

17

ism, from Cubism to Futurism, Vorticism and Dadaism, knows how important the revolution created in the field of typography was. The manipulation of the characters, from their subversive dynamism to their gigantic enlargement on the page, was one of the ways in which the avant-garde sought to *épater le bourgeois* and to bring themselves to the attention of the public. Destroying the order and harmony of the page was a way of challenging the age-old conventions of the printed page. In Joyce's decision to fragment the narration into anonymous sections preceded by flashy headlines one feels a continuity with the gusto and experimental charge of the typographical adventure of the avant-garde. We must not forget that the Futurist and Vorticist revolution of the pre-war years (in manifestos, in the journals *Lacerba* (Florence) and *Blast* (London) etc.) continued after the war in the Dadaist journals in Zurich and Paris (Tzara's *Dada*, Picabia's *391* etc.) – just those years in which Joyce worked on the last revisions and additions. It is true that Joyce's pages do not present themselves in such disarray as those of the Futurists or the Dadaists. In fact his pages keep the linearity observed by the Vorticists. But even if the typographical appearance of the 1922 edition in preserving the alignment of characters did not aim to activate visually what the Futurists called 'the leaps and bursts of style'[2], it is nevertheless true that the headlines, when reproduced boldfaced as in the first edition, are nearer to the intentions – to quote once again the Futurists – of grasping pieces of news brutally and 'hurl(ing) them in the readers's face'[3]. That was part of the shock-tactics used by the newspapers and manifestos that Joyce wanted to reproduce. It is not important here to ascertain if Joyce's intention was objectively to document the presence of an essential instrument of the mass media in the new industrial society, or if he wanted to use it for parody of – most probably – both at the same time. Aeolus in the 1922 edition succeeds in recreating the aggressive euphoric, adventurous climate of those years. The Garland edition, by toning down the showy effects, makes the page aseptic, compromising the scandal and the disruptive effects. In short, the page is 'normalized'. It seems to me that this normalization betrays the essential character of Aeolus which is bound up with the feverish and audacious temper of early Modernism. The typographical experiment of Joyce, forming part of its time, to the point of being a 'period piece', should have been respected. Moreover, one must not forget, in order to understand better the climate in which Joyce's experiments took place, the journalistic headlines, newspaper fragments and large eye-catching characters then in vogue in the Cubist and Futurist canvases, from the *papiers collés* to the *collages* etc.[4]

Criticism of Aeolus has often dwelt on the rich rhetorical modulations of the chapter, discussing the insistence of the windy metaphors and the ostentatious display of the art of rhetoric (the deliberative, forensic and epideictic forms).[5] But in this episode 'the art of rhetoric' – to use the words of the schema Joyce sent to Linati – does not at all exclude those visually persuasive effects achieved by the boldface of the headlines. In the newspapers, manifestos and avant-garde reviews, the verbal devices of the old rhetoric are often updated and transformed into the visual devices of experimental typography. And so to take no notice of the novelty of the boldface type of the headlines means ignoring an aspect which is no less important in the rhetorical strategy of the chapter. How can we miss the suggestion that the boldface print was put there to break the monotony of the typographical character of the narration in order to produce astonishment and estrangement? In terms of classical rhetoric, the boldface character serves the purpose of lifting *taedium* by means of the unexpected. Hence the effect of surprise of the boldface type. There is nothing merely decorative in the boldfaced headlines. Diminishing their effect, surreptitiously introducing criteria of propriety, amounts to ignoring their function. This function is directly connected with the theme of the chapter, which is the world both of the press and of the city. The attempt objectively to render on the page the rich and complex experience of the metropolis in its new mechanical aspects, of which the area of the newspaper is well-known to be a central aspect for all the avant-garde, stimulates Joyce to set up an experimental poetic whose principal characteristic is its inclusiveness. By using every possible device, Joyce incorporates not only sounds, noises, smells, etc., but also the sense of being bombarded by visual messages which in the form of newspapers, manifestos

19

and bright advertisements, come from every corner of the *ville tentaculaire*. From Baudelaire on, and above all thanks to the sensitivity created by the Futurists, the word, shouted out and printed in gigantic characters, stands out as an essential ingredient of metropolitan modernity. Critics commenting on the rôle of Bloom as an adman rightly praise the mastery with which Joyce renders and creates publicity slogans. He seems to have been aware of all the devices of the advertising industry and its techniques of production, as can be seen in over one hundred references scattered throughout *Ulysses*[6]. This makes critically questionable any edition which undervalues the typographical expression of Joyce's sensitivity, so careful in documenting the visual and spectacular side of this industry in billboards, sandwichmen etc. If it is true that the headlines share the nature of advertisements in so far as their purpose is to catch the reader's attention, then one should take into account that – to quote from another passage in *Ulysses* – the headlines as a horizontal advertisement will need to be 'of maximum legibility'. And it is clear that the boldface amplifies the legibility of the headlines. To reduce the visual impact of Aeolus is critically disputable as is any attempt to render less cacophonous the onomatopoeic language with which Joyce tries his best to make the printing press speak. Hugh Kenner has noted that the rhythms of Aeolus 'have grown more abrupt, the tempi more barbaric' and that 'the note of vitality, extending even to the author's incentive to find expressive devices, is unmistakable'[7]. Thus there is the need to conserve the visual aggressiveness and vivacity of the boldfaced headlines if we want to keep intact the sense of the intrusiveness of the new metropolitan environment. It is an environment which shows off its signs and publicity posters and shouts its slogans in a way that increases enormously its expressive codes in order to catch the attention of the most distracted passer-by. As the Linati schema confirms, the colour which sets the tone of the chapter is red, a showy colour that imposes itself. Just as it is not permissible to tone it down, so it is not permissible to reduce the visibility of the headlines. Aeolus is an episode which aspires to transform the reader into a spectator who is involved in the 'theatrical' event of the page, in its 'confusion and formal extravaganza'[8]. We must not reduce the typographical assertiveness of the headlines in order not to compromise the clash of the expressive modalities of the new urban civilization that Joyce aims to reproduce in their totality. To judge from the insistence with which Joyce painstakingly oversaw the printing of the full-stop that finishes the last sentence of Ithaca, giving instructions to the typographer Darantière a good three times,[9] we can conjecture that Joyce was not at all insensitive to the typographical appearance of the text. If the most experimental parts of the work did not find their correspondingly faithful typographical expression there was a risk that the innovative message of the text might be lost. It was not for nothing that the link between the avant-garde writers and their printers was always a tight one. Giovanni Papini, who in 1914 was a Futurist and took part in the movement which inaugurated the most advanced stage of typographical revolution, had sent to *Lacerba* a 'Declaration to the Printer' calling him the writer's confidant, friend and brother, a 'hidden and necessary accomplice of every delight and crime of mine'.[10]

By eliminating the boldface type we inevitably reduce the stylistic contrasts between headlines and sections achieved by typography. We diminish the 'work's presentational capacity' if it is true that the page in Aeolus 'imitates to a certain extent the appearance of a newspaper'.[11] Recent criticism has outlined the visual nature of the episode, its discontinuity, the 'process of stylistic deformation' introduced by the newspaper headlines. Marilyn French has commented on Aeolus as providing 'the first major break in decorum'[12] and Karen Lawrence has pointed out that 'the disturbance created by the headings is stylistic and tonal as well as visual'.[13] Judging from the editions I have succeeded in laying my hands on it is not difficult to realize that since the 1922 edition, with a few exceptions,[14] we have lost the sense of the importance of the typographical aspect of Aeolus. I am afraid the Garland edition does nothing to recover it.

21

ON MONDADORI'S *TELEMACHIA*

CARLA DE PETRIS

In September 1983 Mondadori published a new volume in the *Biblioteca Classica* series, namely *Ulysses – Telemachia*, edited by Giorgio Melchiori, and containing the first three episodes of the novel. The book was the result of two years' work. Though it was limited to the first three episodes only, this book was the first genuinely bilingual and fully annotated edition of Joyce's *Ulysses* ever to be published in Italy. Personally I provided the notes to the Telemachus episode, Miranda Melchiori did the same for the Nestor episode, and Carlo Bigazzi for the Proteus episode.

In a sense our work marked a new point of departure in the field of the Italian editions of James Joyce's works. As Giovanni Cianci pointed out in his book *La fortuna di Joyce in Italia*[1], the works of Joyce were translated into Italian rather early – some during the author's life, some by the author himself. As we all know, Joyce himself provided his own Italian version for two passages of *Anna Livia Plurabelle*[2]. Until now the Italian reader was not able to compare Giulio de Angelis' excellent translation of *Ulysses*, published in 1960 by Mondadori, with the original. Italian publishers celebrated Joyce's centennial anniversary in 1982 with a final attempt at completeness: they issued Melchiori's first bilingual edition of the *Epiphanies*[3], as well as Luigi Schenoni's bilingual translation/transversion of the first hundred pages of *Finnegans Wake*[4]. Our *Telemachia* was started under the same stimulus.

In fact the idea of the *Telemachia* book was Joyce's own, as expressed in a letter of 1918, long before the novel itself was completed:

If *The Little Review* continues to publish it regularly, he [the American publisher Huebsch] may publish as a cheap paperbound book the *Telemachia*, that is, the first three episodes – under the title *Ulysses I*[5].

22

In the following I will try and explain how our team took shape, and how we developed a 'method' of reading *Ulysses* which is derived from the consideration that *leggere* 'to read' is both *elegere* 'to choose' and *legare* 'to link'. Bearing in mind the circular structure of *Ulysses*, and its strictly triadic disposition, as suggested by the Linati scheme, Giorgio Melchiori wanted a different editor for each episode. He himself acted as general editor, and contributed a new introduction to the whole of *Ulysses*, but apart from that there was little 'team co-ordination' among the three of us. This may seem strange, but our method of work derived directly from the fact that each episode forms a whole and autonomous unit. Even the choice of episode was not the individual editor's own, but rather each episode was assigned to one editor or another by the drawing of lots in order to avoid any possible spiritual or cultural affinity and preference.

Though having constant access and permanently referring to other works of the same sort already published, such as Thornton's *Allusions*[6], Gifford and Seidman's *Notes*[7], and the unpublished Vreeswijk notes that Fritz Senn most kindly sent us, we deliberately worked in a sort of void, so that each of us might have the impression or illusion of making new discoveries, or at least of having traced one's own thematic recurrences which are specifically Joycean. Our main purpose was to achieve a new virginity as readers, notwithstanding the vast amount of critical material available to us for use as commentators. As a matter of fact each one of us conducted critical and bibliographical research, according to specific themes or characters or quotations. Our bibliography ranges from books about English cuisine to books on heraldry! But our respective points of view and our reactions were meant to anticipate those of a hypothetical Italian 'common reader'.

Many editorial choices, such as the use of the Homeric titles for the episodes, were made on the basis of the practical consideration that a bilingual edition, by juxtaposing the original and one translation of it, points by its very making to the betrayal that translation implies, and in a sense authorizes further betrayal. Some of our notes may seem pedantic, some others may even sound extravagant, but we hope that none of them is superfluous if it enables the reader to pursue the line of interpretation by himself. Giorgio Melchiori once epitomized Mario Praz's contribution to literary studies in Italy; what the great critic had taught generations of Italian students was 'to connect works of art'. If 'to connect' means 'to think', we hope that our notes, even if they are copious, are not exhaustive: the reader still has a chance to add, to complete, to connect *Ulysses* with his experience. And that is why our notes and introductions are at the end of the book: this is a last attempt to set the reader free.

Let us now consider the English text we adopted for our edition. With great generosity, Hans Walter Gabler gave us access to his *Ulysses* text, at the time still unpublished, which had been established on the basis of the author's own manuscripts.

Mondadori's *Telemachia* reproduced almost integrally the Garland edition, but with substantial exceptions. In fact, we finally rejected some of Gabler's editorial choices. We did not object to the accuracy of Gabler's scientific method, but on the whole we preferred one version to another on the ground of logical or aesthetic internal evidence. In other words, we used our critical judgement when the textological reconstruction did not convince us.

The first example is taken from the Telemachus episode, and has already been mentioned by Clive Hart. Here is the passage given first in the version in which it was finally adopted by Gabler:

> He walked along the upwardcurving path.
>
> > *Liliata rutilantium.*
> > *Turma circumdet.*
> > *Iubilantium te virginum.*
>
> The priest's grey nimbus in a niche where he dressed discreetly. I will not sleep here tonight. Home also I cannot go. (1.735–40; *U* 23.15–20)

The fragmentary Latin quotation is taken from *Prayers for the Dying*, and in the text it reads: *Liliata rutilantium te confessorum turma circumdet jubilantium te virginum chorus excipiat*, which means: 'May the glittering throng of confessors, bright as lilies, gather about you. May the choir of rejoicing virgins receive you'. The complete quotation recurs during the dramatic monologue that ends with the final request to the mother's ghost or memory:

24

On Mondadori's Telemachia

No, mother! Let me be and let me live. (1.279; U 10.26)

Occurring as they do at the end of the very first episode, these mutilated Latin lines, may if printed in natural run-on sequence suggest a new meaning: 'May the throng of rejoicing virgins, bright as lilies, gather about you,' and, as Clive Hart has pointed out, their three-line arrangement echoes the refrain at the end of the Calypso episode. Doubts about Gabler's manner of visual display of text particularly arise when we take into account the fact that on subsequent proofs the end of the page occurred right after the first two 'stumps', and Joyce accepted the insertion of the third 'stump' *after* the subsequent sentence.

On the strength of rigid statistical principles, and on the basis of the copytext, Gabler decided to reject this proposal of graphic display. However, Giorgio Melchiori and myself thought that the new display form would improve the semantic pattern and aesthetic quality of the passage, as follows:

He walked along the upwardcurving path. *Liliata rutilantium*. *Turma circumdet*. The priest's grey nimbus in a niche where he dressed discreetly. *Jubilantium te virginum*. I will not sleep here tonight. Home also I cannot go. (1.735–40; U 23.15–20)

The lines obviously recall the *leitmotiv* of remorse, but at the same time, incomplete and interspersed in the narrative, they are musical and semantic stimuli. They enfold – *circumdet* – and explain the scene of the priest in the process of putting on his clothes, a priest who is portrayed as the statue of some saint in a niche, heavy with age and prudence, and therefore deprived of the triumphant, juvenile arrogance of faith. The brightness of the lilies counterbalances the greyness of the priest's nimbus. The gathering throng is opposed to the priest's chosen seclusion. Finally, the virgins' joy annihilates the priest's discreet gestures with a sudden musical link and semantic shift:

discreetly. *Jubilantium*

Let us now move to our second example of controversial use – one might perhaps call it 'abuse' – of the Garland edition. Gabler accepts the definition 'acatalectic tetrameter of

25

iambs marching' (3.23; *U* 37.26–27), given by Stephen at the beginning of the Proteus episode of the following two lines of a song:

> *Won't you come to Sandymount*
> *Madeline the mare?*　　　　　(3.21; *U* 37.24–25)

I do object to what Hans Walter Gabler has to say in the textual note:

Although the preceding lines are catalectic by whatever prosodic analysis one may apply to them, Joyce wrote and insisted on 'acatalectic' in the final working draft, in R, in proof and in the autograph errata list. . . . Joyce was either consistently in error himself or he imputes a shaky knowledge of the technical terms of prosody to Stephen. (G 1731)

This argument is shaky as it is most unlikely that Stephen should make such a patent mistake at the very beginning of an episode centred on his writing poetry.

Stephen Dedalus is in the process of saying the two lines aloud, and all of a sudden notices that the first line is trochaic, and even 'acatalectic' if one sounds the two vowels of the diphthong of *Sandymount* separately, whereas the second line is undoubtedly iambic and 'catalectic', i.e. without the fourth foot[8]. By his ambiguous use of the terms 'iamb' and 'catalectic' (and/or 'acatalectic'), Joyce was referring to a sort of 'sprung rhythm' characteristic of Mangan's poetry, of which he had spoken in his lecture on Mangan as early as 1902:

He might have written a treatise on the poetical art for he is more cunning in his use of the musical echo than is Poe, the high priest of most modern schools, and there is a mastery, which no school can teach, but which obeys an interior command, which we may trace in 'Kathaleen-Ny-Houlahan', where the refrain changes the trochaic scheme abruptly for a line of firm, marching iambs.[9]

It can in consequence be said that Stephen/Joyce has no 'shaky knowledge of the technical terms of prosody', as Gabler alleges, but rather 'a mastery which no school can teach', particularly when contrasting the written and the oral levels of prosody. That is the reason why we agreed on the expression 'a catalectic tetrameter of iambs marching', which is the accurate definition of the second line to which Stephen is

26

referring, as it is further rammed home by the two iambs he keeps repeating to himself:

Rhythm begins, you see. I hear. A catalectic tetrameter of iambs marching. No, agallop: *deline the mare.* (3.24; *U* 37.26–27)

To conclude my introduction to Mondadori's *Telemachia*, I would like to mention two instances in which the editorial work performed by Hans Walter Gabler and his team improved our appreciation and even our understanding of the text. I am quoting from the Proteus episode:

Unwholesome sandflats waited to suck his treading soles, breathing upward sewage breath, a pocket of seaweed smouldered in seafire under a midden of man's ashes. (3.150–53; *U* 41.2–3)

The last part of the sentence from 'a pocket' to 'man's ashes' has been restored to its place by Gabler in the Garland edition. Leaving aside the undeniable value of the newly inserted sequence, the consideration that the 'sewage breath' exhales from putrifying seaweed under human ashes, i.e. burned corpses, gives a deeper sense to Stephen's reaction to coast them, 'walking warily' (3.152; *U* 41.4) than the simple fear of being trapped in the sand. The new insertion also resumes the theme of 'Death by Water', which is one of the *leitmotivs* of the episode.

Gabler's edition finally clarifies the mystery of the French telegram, 'curiosity to show' that now reads:

– Nother dying come home father. (3.199; *U* 42.15)

Our Italian translation is based on a similar mistake:

– Mamma gratissima vieni subito babbo.

The so-called 'misprint' is really a 'curiosity to show' as *Nother* implies a negative form of *mother*, and besides, it sounds like an abridged form of *another*, suggesting an inner irrelevance of the death announced in the telegram.

With this introductory note, I hope I have made it clear that our *Telemachia* was not intended to be an 'authorized version' of Joyce's masterpiece, but to convey the multiple meanings of the text by emphasizing the process of interpretative readjustment, a process which is even more necessary now after the publication of the Garland edition.

A CRUX IN THE NEW EDITION

RICHARD ELLMANN

—Marina, Stephen said, a child of storm, Miranda, a wonder, Perdita, that which was lost. What was lost is given back to him: his daughter's child. *My dearest wife*, Pericles says, *was like this maid.* Will any man love the daughter if he has not loved the mother?

—The art of being a grandfather, Mr Best gan murmur. *L'art d'être grand* . . .

—His own image to a man with that queer thing genius is the standard of all experience, material and moral. Such an appeal will touch him. The images of other males of his blood will repel him. He will see in them grotesque attempts of nature to foretell or repeat himself. (*U* 195–96)

Typescript: as above except that *grand* is spelt *grandp* . . .

Rosenbach manuscript: as above except for the bracketed lines:

—The art of being a grandfather, Mr Best [murmured].

[—Will he not see reborn in her, with the memory of his own youth added, another image?

Do you know what you are talking about? Love, yes. Word known to all men. *Amor vero aliquid alicui bonum vult unde et ea quae concupiscimus.*]

—His own image to a man with that queer thing genius is the standard of all experience, . . .

Garland edition: as manuscript except for

—The art of being a grandfather, Mr Best gan murmur. *L'art d'être grandp* . . . . . (9.425–26)

Professor Gabler informed me well before his valuable edition appeared that he had recovered a lost passage in Scylla and Charybdis – the now famous one where Stephen defines love as the word known to all men. He thought I would be pleased and of course I was, since I had argued in *Ulysses on the Liffey* not only that this was the word Stephen waited in vain for his mother to utter in Circe but that love was central in the book as a whole. In spite of this gratifying confirmation, I felt grave doubts that Joyce would have welcomed the restoration of the

28

passage. It seemed to me that he might well have decided to expunge it. I so advised the editor, but to no avail. He has a textual note explaining why it is needed (G 1738).

Perhaps I could now state my objections to it more fully. In a book that in six hundred pages leads up to a good Samaritan situation between two men, and that ends with a wife fondly recalling days of her courtship by her husband, any dilation of the theme of love was bound to be perilous. But in addition, Joyce never uses the word 'love' without tension. No one knew better than he how quickly a mention of it could become sentimental. In his personal life, he was also chary of it. He wrote to Nora Barnacle during their courtship, 'You ask me why I don't *love* you, but surely you must believe I am very fond of you and if to desire to possess a person wholly, to admire and honour that person deeply, and to seek to secure that person's happiness in every way is to "love" then perhaps my affection for you is a kind of love.' Among the British Library notes for *Ulysses* is one that says that Bloom was 'loth to say he loved her,' and in the book itself Molly Bloom complains about Bloom's declaration of love, 'I had the devils own job to get it out of him.' When in the Cyclops episode Bloom remarks that 'it's the very opposite' of 'insult and hatred' 'that is really life,' he is forced to say what *it* is, and allows that it is 'love.' Then in embarrassment he modifies it by adding, 'I mean the opposite of hatred.' Bloom drops the subject and leaves. That simple statement of his is immediately mocked by those left behind. The citizen comments, 'A new apostle to the gentiles. . . Universal love.' John Wyse Power offers a weak defense: 'Well . . . Isn't that what we're told? Love your neighbour.' The citizen doesn't want to be caught in impiety, so he changes his tack from mocking love to mocking Bloom: 'That chap? . . . Beggar my neighbour is his motto. Love, moya! He's a nice pattern of a Romeo and Juliet' (12.1491–92). At this point the inflationary narrator takes up the love theme: 'Love loves to love love. . . You love a certain person. And this person loves that other person because everybody loves somebody but God loves everybody' (12.1493–1501). Does this twaddle invalidate Bloom's remark? Some have said so, but we may find the mockery less telling if we remember that it parodies not only

Bloom but Joyce's master, Dante, and Dante's master, Thomas Aquinas. (Aquinas says, in the *Summa theologica* I, q.20, 2.1, and a.2, that God is love and loves all things.) It is the kind of parody that protects seriousness by immediately going away from intensity. Love cannot be discussed without peril, but Bloom has for once nobly named it.

Given the importance of love in the book, Joyce obviously scrutinized any reference to it with great care. He allows Stephen to use the word chiefly in the quoted line from Yeats's poem, 'Who Goes with Fergus?', 'Love's bitter mystery.' In the Circe episode his mother's ghost reminds him, 'You sang that song to me. *Love's bitter mystery*' (15.4189–90). Stephen responds 'eagerly,' as the stage direction informs us, 'Tell me the word, mother, if you know now. The word known to all men' (15.4192–93). She doesn't. (He has asked the same question of an imaginary beloved in Proteus (3.435), also without an answer.) The Gabler emendation would have Stephen answer the question himself six episodes before Circe and a dozen hours earlier. His mother's ghost might then be well advised in not repeating what he already knows, and what anyway she has implied by her quotation from Yeats. But of course the peculiar effect of the question, which comes at the climax of Circe, itself the climax of *Ulysses*, is lost if we have been told the answer by Stephen. It has been argued that the Circe episode is full of echoes of earlier chapters, but this one would seem to be different in kind, involving as it does the propounding of a riddle already solved. In fact, the echoes in this chapter tend to be distortions rather than echoes, as with the Man in the Macintosh, Gerty MacDowell, the yews in the Bloom bedroom wallpaper, and the like. Even an apprentice novelist would hesitate to ask for the second time a question to which he has already given his readers the answer, and a novelist so reluctant as Joyce to use the word 'love' would scarcely tolerate this over-explicitness. The effect of leaving the question dangling is to magnify its importance. 'These are mysteries;' says Thornton Wilder in one of his novels, 'give them no names.'

In establishing principles of editing, we must bear in mind that Joyce is noted for discretion. He could see, for example, that there was no point in having Bloom in Ithaca ask for breakfast in bed when it would be more effective to have the subject mentioned only once, and that time by Molly. On every crucial question, such as the lengthily arranged convergence of Bloom and Stephen, Joyce is distinguished by what he withholds rather than by what he divulges.

What I want to urge is that Joyce omitted the passage from Scylla and Charybdis to improve his book. To do so I will examine the context in which it appears. Stephen is trying to explain both the tragic mood of Shakespeare, in which he wrote his fiercest plays, and the benign mood of the later romances. The first he attributes to infidelity and betrayal, the second to the birth of Shakespeare's granddaughter in 1608.

—Marina, Stephen said, a child of storm, Miranda, a wonder, Perdita, that which was lost. What was lost is given back to him: his daughter's child. *My dearest wife*, Pericles says, *was like this maid.* Will any man love the daughter if he has not loved the mother?

(9.421–24)

Stephen is deliberately obliterating the distinction between Shakespeare's daughter Susanna and his granddaughter, Elizabeth. Mr Best is brought in by Joyce to emphasize that a granddaughter has been born. 'The art of being a grandfather, Mr Best murmured.' Joyce improved this passage in the typescript by changing 'murmured' in the Rosenbach manuscript to 'gan murmur,' and by having Best preciously start to say the title of Victor Hugo's book in French, 'L'art d'être grandp . . .' when he is interrupted by Stephen. Gabler here inserts the passage from the Rosenbach manuscript. His textual note contends that Stephen's next question is necessary to further the argument. But is it?

The second question asked by Stephen is, 'Will he not see reborn in her, with the memory of his own youth added, another image?' This question augments the confusion of the first question, 'Will any man love the daughter if he has not loved the mother?' For it makes Elizabeth a blend of only two images, those of her grandfather and grandmother, when she must principally blend two different images, those of Susanna Shakespeare and her husband, the physician John Hall. (The births of Shakespeare's two daughters, Susanna and Judith, in the 1580s, do not suit Stephen's purposes at all.) Stephen is clumsily making Shakespeare the father of his granddaughter. Joyce, fastidiously scrutinizing these lines, could see that the arbitrary confusion of daughter and granddaughter – plausible if got over quickly – was implausible if drawn out.

It has been argued that the word 'image' contained in the second question is necessary because of what is said next:

– His own image to a man with that queer thing genius is the standard of all experience, material and moral. Such an appeal will touch him. The images of other males of his blood will repel him. He will see in them grotesque attempts of nature to foretell or to repeat himself. (9.432–35)

But *image* in the second question means the image of Shakespeare's once beloved wife plus his own ('with the memory of his own youth added'), while *image* in Stephen's next speech no longer refers to the composite of the two. It makes the granddaughter into Shakespeare's image alone, Anne being forgotten along with two other grandparents. In fact, since the word grandfather already implies a succession of images between the generations, the speech of Stephen is clearer without the second question, which establishes a composite when what is wanted is a reflection only of the artist.

Gabler's emendation continues with an aside by Stephen, also from the Rosenbach manuscript:

Do you know what you are talking about? Love, yes. Word known to all men. *Amor vero aliquid alicui bonum vult unde et ea quae concupiscimus* . . .

The Latin sentence collocates two clauses, 'Love wishes someone else's good' and 'whence we desire these things.' Together they do not make sense, though they seem to be in agreement. In the source from which they came they are in opposition. That source John T. Noonan Jr has located in Book I, chapter 91, of the *Summa contra gentiles*. Thomas Aquinas is distinguishing real love from the desire to please ourselves by means of another object:

Per hoc enim quod intelligimus vel gaudemus, ad aliquod obiectum aliqualiter nos habere oportet: amor vero aliquid alicui vult, hoc enim amare dicimur cui aliquod bonum volumus, secundum modum praedictum. Unde et ea quae concupiscimus, simpliciter quidem et proprie desiderare dicimur, non autem amare, sed potius nos ipsos,

*quibus ea concupiscimus; et ex hoc ipsa per accidens et improprie
dicuntur amari.* (Leonine text: Rome: Marietti, 1961. The Parma text,
1852–73, ends with *dicimur amare*, 'We are said to love'.)

By this, that we understand or in which we rejoice, we must have
in some way an object. But love wills something for someone. For we
are said to love that for which we will some good, as said above.
Hence, those things which we want, we are, properly and absolutely,
said to *desire*, but not love – rather to love ourselves for whom we
want these things. And for this reason – accidently and not properly
– these things are said to be loved.

Joyce must have wanted Stephen to bridge from
Shakespeare's genuine love for his wife to his pleasure in
seeing in his granddaughter his own image. The latter is self-
regarding only. But in looking at the passage again, he could
see that the Latin was (without further explanation)
unintelligible. He could see also that the emphasis on true love
was excessive when Stephen was about to dismiss it in favour
of artistic narcissism. By striking out the passage, he could
save Stephen's celebration of love for a more crucial point in
the book. With or without it, the transition from
Shakespeare's love for another to Shakespeare's engrossment
with his own image was abrupt. But with it, the weakness of
Stephen's argument was even more apparent.

In summary, then: any passage about love in this book
would have been carefully scrutinized by its author. It is most
uncharacteristic of Joyce, so reticent about love, to allow
Stephen to ask his dead mother a question to which he had
already given the answer. He could see, moreover, that the
second of Stephen's two rhetorical questions made for
unnecessary complications: one was that it confused daughter
and granddaughter so patently as to underline the
disingenuousness of Stephen's argument; another was that it
laboriously established the word *image* as a composite of male
and female based on love, when Stephen is about to banish the
female and keep only the male artist as the granddaughter's
progenitor. The definition of love which Stephen offers in
English as 'the word known to all men' insists upon love as
relationship. So does the first Latin phrase. Both are too
clamant when Stephen is about to propose that Shakespeare's
pleasure in his granddaughter is not that of wishing either her

or her grandmother well but of gloating over his own image in her. The second Latin phrase, if it had been extended and glossed, might have offered a transition, but as given it seems vaguely confirmatory of the first Latin phrase, or simply incomprehensible.

Professor Gabler speaks of the typist's eyeskip. It must be said that we do not have the typescript in which, if he is right, there were two ellipses. Since conjecture is in order, it seems reasonable to surmise that Joyce recognized what he had written as tortured and self-defeating and bethought himself that a desperate riddle about love would come in more appropriately when Stephen is under threat (as Bloom was to be in the Cyclops episode when he reluctantly named love) than when Stephen is offering his specious biography of Shakespeare. Professor Gabler would then be entitled to follow Joyce's example and give up love.

UNANSWERED QUESTIONS ABOUT A QUESTIONABLE ANSWER: THE RESTORED 'LOVE'-PASSAGE OF THE NEW *ULYSSES* IN THE LIGHT OF SPEECH-ACT THEORY

WILHELM FÜGER

None of the Garland edition's relatively few textual changes that may affect our basic understanding of *Ulysses* has attracted more attention than the restoring, in the Scylla and Charybdis episode, of that passage which, by all appearances, proves that the word known to all men is 'love'. At first sight, this insertion looks like an indisputable asset, because it provides a solution to a much-discussed problem. Richard Ellmann, who briefly summarizes this discussion in his review of the new edition, was thus enabled to expound why it is evident now that the theme of love pervades the book as a whole,[1] and in her well-documented contribution to the Philadelphia Joyce Conference (June 1985) Jean Kimball convincingly argued that the restored love-passage makes better sense of the book and even throws some new light on other parts of Joyce's *oeuvre*. Nevertheless, there are not a few critics, among them Ellmann himself, who, on second thoughts, feel somewhat uneasy about the restoring of this passage, less on editorial than on critical grounds.[2] For quite apart from certain inconsistencies (as to the Shakespeare parallels) that arise in connexion with the first two lines of the insertion – which I am not going to discuss here – , it would appear that the explicit solution of a riddle of the Macintosh type banalizes rather than enriches Joyce's text. In the pertinent discussions of the Monaco Joyce Seminar, at any rate, the general feeling prevailed that the unnecessary highlighting of this sentimentality-prone word somehow cheapens Joyce's artistic achievement; that the novel loses complexity by the disappearance of a puzzle that had hitherto been fascinating to many readers; in short that the insertion frustrates the post-structuralist critic's need for a certain degree of undecidability.

The editor, of course, need not worry about objections of this kind, for his task is to present us with what Joyce actually wrote and presumably intended to incorporate into his final text, not with what we would like him to have written. Even from a purely critical point of view, however, these objections can be shown to be less devastating than one might fear on first encountering them. For though we can hardly avoid conceding that the restoring of the passage somewhat decreases the text's 'obliquity necessary to preserve the novel from didacticism' (Ellmann), one can still maintain that, after all, the putative solution does not really solve anything, since the additional piece of text multiplies rather than simplifies the implications of the love theme. This can be made evident in particular by recourse to speech-act theory, and therefore I am first going to list a few basic linguistic insights into the latent rules governing the speech-acts of asking and answering,[3] whose relevance to our specific problem I will discuss subsequently:

(1) *Erotetic situations* (D. Wunderlich) result from the awareness of a deficit of information. This deficit can be overcome by efforts of one's own (e.g. trying out; looking up) or by appealing to other persons for practical help or relevant information.

(2) Appeals for information are made by verbal or non-verbal (e.g. gestural) *erotetic acts*.

(3) Erotetic speech-acts are preferably performed by *interrogative sentences*, but other types of grammatical structures (e.g. imperative sentences) can fulfil this function as well.

(4) Conversely, interrogative sentences need not necessarily aim at the increase of the speaker's information but may also serve *other purposes* (e.g. drawing the addressee's attention to something the speaker feels to be interesting or important).

(5) *Answers* to questions of information can be expected only if the questioner
　　(a) does not know the answer and sincerely wants to know it;
　　(b) has reasons for the assumption that the addressee of the question knows the answer.
Questions that fail to fulfil one (or both) of these conditions cannot claim to be regarded as *genuine* (e.g. rhetorical questions; examination questions).

(6) Except for the case of examination questions, *appropriate reactions to non-genuine questions* are:
– replies (which—in contrast to answers—can ignore the

36

propositional content of the question and instead problematize the act of asking itself; in short: shift to meta-communication);
– counter-questions (which may indirectly disclose the question's lack of justification or its absurdity);
– refusal to answer (silence; break-off of communication).

(7) *Adequate answers* to genuine questions must contain neither less nor more information than is expected by the questioner.

(8) In order to supply the expected kind of information, a *cooperative answerer* must take into account:

  (a) aspects of pragmatic significance;

  (b) possible implicatures of the dialogue.

Example of *pragmatic significance*: A tourist in Hyde Park whose question 'Where is Marble Arch?' is answered: 'In London', is given a true answer, but not an adequate one.

Implicatures are those assumptions that participants in a conversation – as long as they refuse to doubt the speaker's readiness to cooperate in principle – have to make in order to prevent a breakdown of communication, if one of them obviously offends against one (or several) of the general maxims that, according to P.H.Grice, have to be observed in any successful conversation. Unlike implications, implicatures do not depend on logical necessity, and unlike presuppositions, they are activated only on the part of the hearer (answerer).[4]

(9) By consciously *exploiting* such implicatures or infractions of pragmatic significance, literary artists can, from the outset, aim at conveying multifarious transverbal meanings, particularly in the case of questions and answers.

(10) Questions and answers are correlative constituents of an interactive schema, in which the role of the questioner and that of the answerer are, as a rule, attributed to different persons. *Questions to oneself* are either circumscriptions of statements such as 'I do not know / should like to know, if . . .', or else probings of one's mind or conscience; in the latter case, different levels of a person's consciousness are put in interaction.

In attempting to apply these general insights to the problems connected with the restored love-passage of the new *Ulysses*, one can and should first of all ask if and to what extent an erotetic situation can be said to exist for Stephen when, at the climax of the Circe episode, he 'eagerly' implores the ghost of his mother: 'Tell me the word, mother, if you know now. The word known to all men' (15.4192–93). Although this utterance is commonly understood as a question transformed into the imperative mood on account of Stephen's eagerness (impatience being one of the favourite motivations for such a procedure), it need not necessarily be regarded as a request for information, for it could as well express a demand for the pronouncing of a magic word, as it were, whose effect depends less, or not at all, on its content than on its being uttered by a specific person or in a specific situation. In the latter case, whether or not Stephen already knows the word would be irrelevant; whereas this difference would, of course, be decisive in the case of a request for information. If Stephen knows the word already, his question is not a genuine one and must consequently be supposed to serve other purposes than those suggested by the surface form of the sentence. But before speculating on these other possible purposes one is well advised in first considering the general consequences, for the mother's reaction, of the state of Stephen's knowledge and in trying to elucidate her specific surmises in this regard.

The mother does not comply with Stephen's request, at least not directly, and we are not told whether she is unable or unwilling to cooperate more effectively. Inability would imply that she either does not know the answer even now (a possibility that Stephen explicitly reckons with) or is not permitted to divulge the secrets of the dead to the living (shortly before, she is described as 'uttering a silent word'; 15.4161). Unwillingness to answer could mean that she, like the ghost of Hamlet's father, prefers to refrain from unfolding a tale too horrible for mortal ears; or else − because refusing to answer is one of the appropriate ways of reaction to non-genuine questions—her evading an adequate answer might also be interpreted as an attempt to intimate something like: 'I need/will not tell you the word, since you do or should at least know it already'. Since, however, her actual reaction is not silence but the posing of two counter-questions that recall acts of practised love, we had perhaps rather make allowance for a still more trenchant indirect reply in the sense of: 'Love is something that cannot and should not be talked about, but becomes manifest only in acts of love'. If this is the unspoken message of her reticence, its tenor would, incidentally, confirm what is clearly signalled by the example of Leopold Bloom, who, though unable to define love ('I mean the opposite of hatred', 12.1485), nevertheless practises it in its various forms.

Inferences of this kind are more or less inevitable as long as we take it for granted that Stephen knows the answer already. But can we really be sure that this is the case? In view of the restored love-passage one might feel inclined to answer in the affirmative, but if we do so we are at once confronted with a difficulty that Michael Groden pointed out: 'If Stephen already knows the word, why should he ask his mother "eagerly" to tell him what it is?'.[5] In order to get to grips with this problem we have to focus more sharply on the state of Stephen's knowledge about the word known to all men.

The last-mentioned phrase is part of a recurrent motif that first appears in the Proteus episode, where Stephen, within the context of an erotic fantasy, asks himself: 'What is that word known to all men?' (3.435). The question remains unanswered, and one wonders why. Is it because the answer is thought to be too obvious to deserve explicit mention – in other words, are we perhaps presented here with a rhetorical question, indicative of a cynical impulse of Stephen's, possibly even with a sort of examination question which, in his day-dreaming, he addresses to the imagined woman in order to test her reaction? Or shall we rather assume that he is really probing his mind for a word he once knew ('*that* word'; my italics) but by now has forgotten or repressed for some reason? Retrospectively, the latter view turns out to be the more plausible one, for when, in the context of the insertion under discussion, the motif reappears, we read: 'Do you know what you are talking about? Love, yes. Word known to all men' (9.429–30). Here Stephen seems to remember what three hours ago had escaped his consciousness, and the ensuing garbled quotation from Aquinas as well as the whole context clearly indicate that 'love' is meant to be the crucial word, not the immediately preceding 'yes'. Ten hours later, however, in Nighttown, Stephen talks to his mother as if he were ignorant of the word. Has he forgotten it again in the meantime, or does he doubt the validity of his former insight? Both these views would be acceptable in ordinary circumstances; but in the context of a situation where the innermost recesses of the subconscious are laid open neither of them can eventually conceal its lack of plausibility. Yet though we may therefore suspect that Stephen is less ignorant in this regard than would appear at first sight, his request to his mother's ghost need not be regarded as wholly unjustified. Since being familiar with a word and using it to talk about something is not tantamount to understanding its full meaning, Stephen's request might also be interpreted in the sense of: 'Tell me, mother, what the word known to all men really means'. In this case, too, the question would remain a genuine one as long as Stephen has sufficient reasons for the assumption that his mother will know the answer. As his restriction ('if you know now') makes clear, he is not at all sure about this, but neither can he exclude in principle the possibility of her knowing what he wishes to learn.

What still remains rather obscure in this connexion are the implications of the word 'now'. Ellmann offered the following explanation: 'Stephen is asking his mother to confirm from the vantage point of the dead . . . what from the vantage point of the living he has already surmised. Presumably the dead can fathom the "bitter mystery" '.[6] Confirmation of a supposition is, to be sure, a possible explication of Stephen's conditional supplement to his request, yet there are others as well. If we discard as too preposterous the idea of Stephen's suggesting that the word known to all men may not be known to all (or some) women, at least not in their life-time and possibly not even in the realm of the dead, there is still another intention that can be ascribed to his utterance. Since the Aquinas quotation following the solution of the love riddle contrasts unselfish with selfish love (true love versus desire), Stephen's 'now' may also intimate that, in his view, his mother's love for him had not been unselfish enough to pass for pure love.

Why a latent reproach of this tenor would not be wholly unjustified is illustrated by the scene in *Stephen Hero* where the mother urges Stephen to make his Easter duty. Though she maintains that going to confession would be 'better for you' (*SH* 136), her unconcealed embitterment about the loss of faith of 'a child of mine' (*SH* 138, 140) shows that she is primarily worried about her self-image, on which she is determined to model her children. She emphasizes her efforts 'to keep you in the right way' (*SH* 140), regrets that Stephen has been 'left too much liberty' (*SH* 139), even threatens to burn his books.

Understandably Stephen is 'much annoyed that his mother should try to wheedle him into conformity' (*SH* 137) by all sorts of questionable means, and it is at this moment at the latest that he starts to regard her love with scepticism, since true love would include respecting another individual's moral and intellectual autonomy, at least when this person is no longer a child. Seen in this perspective, Stephen's 'now' can be interpreted as an indirect criticism of his mother's former attitude towards him, connected with the hope that she may know better in her present state. It would even appear that the mother's reply proceeds from this very assumption, since her counter-questions sound very much like a self-defence. In her next reply (to Stephen's outburst of abuse) she continues to stress her good intentions, and in doing so she even obliquely and belatedly tells him the word he had asked her for: 'Years and years, I loved you, O, my son, . . .' (15.4203). Simultaneously, however, her insistent plea for repentance shows that she still blames him for suffering from 'the pride of the intellect' (*SH* 139), and this implicit counter-reproach indirectly reveals her conviction that Stephen, contrary to the hopes she had expressed at the end of *A Portrait of the Artist as a Young Man*, has not (yet) learned '*what the heart is and what it feels*' (*P* 252). Evidently her idea of love and Stephen's do not coincide, nor even converge, up to this very moment, and it remains undecided whether they ever can. To find out whose position, if either, is better grounded, thus continues to be a challenge to the reader's moral judgment, especially since any such endeavour would amount to nothing less than the demarcating of the legitimate claims of *amor matris* in its twofold sense of subjective and objective genitive. It may well be that, in Joyce's view, the recognition of the indissolubly mixed antagonistic tendencies inherent in what is perhaps 'the only true thing in life' (2.143) leads to the core of '*Love's bitter mystery*' (15.4190).

Thus, depending on what kinds and degrees of implicatures and/or aspects of pragmatic significance we are ready to admit or to postulate, there are various ways of making sense of the motif in its new shape and of avoiding the apparent inconsistency that Stephen wishes to be informed about something he already knows. Of course we can never be sure which one of these possible implicatures has to be regarded as the dominating, let alone the correct, one in any particular case; but there is no doubt that, in principle, we are supposed to reflect on possible implicatures of the characters' monologues and dialogues, because this is part and parcel of Joyce's game with the reader, not only within the context of the passages discussed here.[7]

Despite, or rather, precisely on account of, this ultimate undecidability, I feel that the final conclusion to be drawn from the preceding observations and reflections is nevertheless obvious enough: Whatever critical arguments against the restoring of the love-passage may eventually prove to be tenable, the objection that the insertion reduces the text's complexity will certainly not be among them. I am aware that in drawing attention to this bundle of additional ambiguities, crosscuttings, and dimensions of interpretation I have raised more questions than I have provided answers. But this is a practically inevitable consequence of probing into these intricately tangled matters, even a sort of indirect proof of my initial thesis. Should, however, these questions of mine be deemed to be more disconcerting than helpful after all, I can at least and in any case claim that they are genuine ones, since I do not know the answers, sincerely wish to know them, and have reasons for the assumption that among my readers there will be not a few who are more competent than I and who therefore might know (part of) the answers or at least be able to guide our search for them.

WHY DOES ONE RE-READ *ULYSSES*?

MICHAEL PATRICK GILLESPIE

The question has a certain disingenuous aura, calling to mind as it does a range of evanescent replies alternately banal and mystifying. The esoteric bromides that one might offer at a cocktail party to satisfy a mildly interested/antagonistic interlocutor hardly hold credence beyond the moment of utterance, and the more sophisticated explanations involving critical strategies and methods of analysis quickly lose the thread of the question in a maze of digressions. Aphorisms and jargon shed little light on the fascination that one feels for the work which Joyce himself sardonically styled 'his usylessly unreadable Blue Book of Eccles' (*FW* 179.26–27), but the compelling drive to justify one's aesthetic preferences does not allow easy dismissal of the question once raised. Certainly the answer can be related to efforts at exegesis or more precisely to the book's protean character which commands involvement while resisting the imposition of a single interpretation encompassing all its vagaries.

DIVINITY NOT DEITY THE UNCERTAINTY JUSTIFIED BY OUR
CERTITUDE (*FW* 282.R4)

Despite a plot revolving around the mundane existence of nondescript Dubliners on a fictional June day in 1904, the form of *Ulysses* exercises a sophisticated, seductive attraction over anyone seeking to impose meaning upon the work. Although it presents narrative details in a relatively straightforward manner and develops characterization in a clear and lucid style (once one overcomes the initial disorientation of the interior monologue), the sum of its parts never quite adds up to a completely coherent whole.'Thus the unfacts, did we possess them, are too imprecisely few to warrant our certitude' (*FW* 57.16–17). At the same time Joyce's method of composition invites, perhaps demands, the participation necessary to

43

resolve the confusion created by the 'significant silences' within the text. Time and again, by appropriating the creative impulse, by imposing a reading on material that does not offer self-evident explanation, one finds pleasure without exhausting possibility.

With premeditated care Joyce cultivates this aura of a work suggesting but not confirming the indeterminacy of its meaning. He has structured his novel around parallax perspectives which admit the cogency of a range of interpretations but which give none primacy. As a consequence an individual returns to *Ulysses* with mixed feelings: one's sense that experience, maturity, and serendipity will combine to bring forward new insights and new pleasures is balanced by the suspicion that any new understanding will prove no more permanent than previous comprehension. Until very recently, however, one could anchor efforts at interpretation on the linear certitude of the book's finite nature: Its fixed number of words would ultimately yield to 'that ideal reader suffering from an ideal insomnia' (*FW* 120.13–14) a set quantity of alternative meanings from which one could presumably choose the most preferable/pleasurable. The most obvious impediment to the realization of this supposition had been the corrupt state of all of the various editions of *Ulysses* that had appeared in print, but with the publication in 1984 of the Garland version, based on extensive research and sound editorial practice, one might have legitimately assumed that the textual ambiguities plaguing the work since its appearance had been resolved. Instead, through no fault of the editors, the new *Ulysses* calls attention to the apparent endless potential for interpretation because of the inevitable mutability of the text which resists efforts to submerge its variant readings in a definitive rendition.

IN THE BUGINNING IS THE WOID (*FW* 378.29)

Even before the Garland edition appeared, current critical theories, with their divergent views on the position of an author in relation to his work, combined to contribute a certain ambivalence to readings of *Ulysses*. At one extreme, consideration of a writer's function in a particular text goes no further than a dismissal of the idea that his role in composing the work might legitimately allow him to claim an influence on its interpretation. At the opposite pole, not only the writer's words but the entire social, intellectual, and psychological milieu in which he operated sets the standard for giving meaning to a text. Between the two a variety of attitudes assign varying degrees of significance to the artist's presence. No matter what specific position one assumes, however, authorial intentionality remains an important point of departure. G. Thomas Tanselle, in a careful survey of the history of the controversy over the importance of ascertaining authorial intention, makes a telling point regarding the implications of the debate generally overlooked by those most involved. 'Discussions of this kind, however, regularly take the text as given and focus on the activity of the critic as he faces that text; they do not raise the question of the authority of the text itself, apparently assuming that the text in each case is the text as the author wished it to be.'[1] Tanselle's study deals specifically with editing, and in it he goes on to reject the notion that editors should not be concerned with authorial intention, pointing out that if an editor is to present 'the text as the author wished it to be,' authorial intention, at least to that degree, necessarily obtains.

In his essay Tanselle touches upon the difficulty that one faces in determining, after the fact, precisely what an author intended to constitute the final form of his work. I believe that in Joyce's case, and I think that the efforts of Hans Walter Gabler and the team that edited the Garland *Ulysses* support this assumption, the issue becomes even more complex. The Gabler edition draws attention to the degree to which every printed version of *Ulysses* preceding it has only approximated the text which Joyce had envisioned, and tacitly in the description of its own composition it foregrounds its own provisional nature by openly acknowledging the subjective conditions informing the constitution of certain of its passages.

Most of the problems facing anyone wishing to create a printed version of the *Ulysses* that Joyce envisioned during the process of its constitution arise from Joyce's penchant for revision and from the often chaotic circumstances surrounding its composition. The work itself went through a number of drafts transcribed by a series of amanuenses before reaching the Dijon printinghouse of Maurice Darantière. Authorial emendations overlay the transmission of the text from its earliest stages of composition to its final proofs. Scribal errors and inconsistencies in Joyce's pattern of rewriting accrued by force of circumstances. And as a result contradictory changes often impinge upon the rendition of a particular segment of the text with no clear indication of Joyce's final intention. When the choice of a particular version rests upon critical judgement open to disputation by alternative renditions of equal or near equal validity, the notion of an ideal text, in terms of a precise reproduction of Joyce's concept of *Ulysses*, gives way to a range of potential renderings.

The inherent ambivalence produced by textual cruxes that remain irresolvable through objective methods should in no way undermine confidence in the integrity of Gabler's work. It does, however, suggest that any interpretive approach should begin with the admission of its own fallibility based on the provisory nature of any printed version of the work itself. Evidence within Joyce's canon suggests to me his own great awareness of this condition of ambiguity inherent in each of his works, and so, in acknowledging the uncertitude attached to any text as well as that attached to any interpretation, one embraces the form of the work as Joyce conceived it. Such a disposition expands rather than narrows the possible readings so that the physical artefact upon which one bases a reading embodies the same provisional qualities as the reading itself.

A COLOPHON OF NO FEWER THAN SEVEN HUNDRED AND
THIRTYTWO STROKES TAILED
BY A LEAPING LASSO (*FW* 123. 5–6)

My claim that Joyce accepted and even went on to manipulate the inevitable disparities between his image of a particular work and its typographical manifestation requires some support, so let me digress to outline the logic of my argument. By the time he began to write *Finnegans Wake* Joyce had obviously come to derive a great deal of pleasure from his sense of the mutability hidden in apparently fixed and immobile type. I believe, however, that this awareness came to him progessively, for from the beginning of his career he experienced a variety of impediments to his efforts to publish his work in a form conforming exactly to the fashion in which it was written. In 1906 he spent the better part of a year in epistolary haggling over the text of *Dubliners* trying to contain the blue pencil of his putative publisher Grant Richards, only to have Richards put an end to the matter by withdrawing his offer to bring out the stories. Between 1910 and 1912 he engaged in roughly the same debate with another potential publisher, George Roberts, which ended only when the Dublin printer, John Falconer, destroyed the sheets already prepared for publication. Three years later, episodes of the serial version of *A Portrait of the Artist as a Young Man* suffered abridgement when the printer for the *Egoist* unilaterally censored certain lines.[2]

Attempts to bring out *Ulysses* generated an even broader range of production problems. Incidents of public censorship began to accumulate almost as soon as the work became available. The printer for the *Little Review*, the American journal serializing the book, excised a number of segments of the early chapters, and the magazine itself was threatened when its editors, Margaret Anderson and Jane Heap, were prosecuted on obscenity charges by the state of New York.[3] Individual readers could be equally intolerant. Ellmann notes that Ezra Pound 'tried to persuade Joyce to abolish Bloom's flatulence and other questionable elements in the book' and that the husband of one of Joyce's typists after reading a portion of the manuscript for the Circe chapter threw it into the fire.[4] Joyce, or more precisely Sylvia Beach, finally did find a French printer, Maurice Darantière, who would bring out the text without subjecting it to the censorship of his own morality. Nonetheless, a number of factors combined to create significant disparities between Joyce's ideal of the final text and that created by Darantière: the different languages of writer and printer, the hectic production schedule, the idiosyncratic nature of Joyce's text, and Joyce's habit of adding material to each set of proofs or *placards* which he received made efforts to produce a precise rendition of Joyce's work seem impossible.[5] Although Joyce noticed many of the errors

47

and compiled an errata list for subsequent printings, he seemed dubious as to the possibility of ever completely clearing up the problem. (In his Foreword to the Garland edition, Gabler calls attention to this attitude by quoting a portion of a 6 November 1921 letter from Joyce to Harriet Shaw Weaver: 'I am extremely irritated by all those printer's errors. . . . Are these to be perpetuated in future editions? I hope not.')

These apparently inescapable variegations, introduced during the process of giving a text its physical form, naturally had an impact on Joyce's assumptions regarding the character of printed material, and this impression, in turn, shaped his perception of his own writing and influenced the structure he gave to his final work. Throughout *Finnegans Wake* formal organization and thematic development combine to produce the aura of ambiguity underpinning and undermining the work's carefully constructed prose. They affirm the malleability of meaning and testify to the fragmentation of intentionality by denying the primacy within words of a single signification. Joyce emphasizes not simply that the definition of specific words will vary greatly from individual to individual but that in its very transmission the integrity of the text undergoes radical change.

A prime example of the way these attitudes contributed to the formation of *Finnegans Wake* occurs in the segment describing the discovery of ALP's letter by the hen, Biddy Doran, amidst the filth of a midden heep (*FW* 110–12). The passage opens with a description of the text which immediately introduces the theme of indeterminacy. The organic nature of the repository has produced a chemical reaction in the ink of the article it has covered, and as a consequence, portions of the text have been obliterated, running together the narration and leaving its meaning open to speculation.

. . . originating by transhipt from Boston (Mass.) of the last of the first to Dear whom it proceded to mention Maggy well & allathome's health well only the hate turned the mild on *the van* Houtens and the general's elections with a *lovely* face of some born gentleman with a beautiful present of wedding cakes for dear thankyou Chriesty and with grand funferall of poor Father Michael don't forget unto life's & Muggy well how are you Maggy & hopes soon to hear well & must now close it with fondest to the twoinns with four crosskisses for holy paul holey corner holipoli whollyisland pee ess from (locust may eat all but this sign shall they never) affectionate largelooking tache of tch. (*FW* 111.09–20)

While the writing has not become completely devoid of meaning, its fractured structure alone cannot sustain the development of a coherent narration. The orthographically corrupt condition of the letter demands the imaginative intervention of the reader to impose some sense of coherence on it.

In the next paragraph, Joyce continues to develop the concepts (for him mutually dependent) of cooperative creation and provisional interpretation, moving from the particular to the general. He introduces the image of a distorted negative and implies that despite physical changes the essence of the horse, that by which we know it, remains. 'Well, almost any photoist worth his chemicots will tip anyone asking him the teaser that if a negative of a horse happens to melt enough while drying, well, what you do get is, well, a positively grotesquely distorted macromass of all sorts of horsehappy values and masses of meltwhile horse' (*FW* 111.26–30). The passage calls to mind Stephen Dedalus's Platonic thoughts in the National Library – 'Horseness is the whatness of allhorse' (9.84–85) – and it offers a form for recuperating the intentions of an author based on a combination of objective concepts and subjective impressions. In this suggestion, and in his championing on the next page of Biddy Doran as a literary critic, Joyce implies the responsibility of the reader to recover from the work its basic ideas and to develop them in the process of creating meaning. At the same time, this illustration of the impermanent quality of the physical artefact of transmission then becomes a presentation of the strategy for the comprehension of a necessarily fallible and protean artistic experience: the conjunction of an imperfect reproduction and an evolving imagination.

THE FIRST TILL LAST ALSHEMIST WROTE OVER EVERY SQUARE INCH OF THE ONLY FOOLSCAP AVAILABLE, HIS OWN BODY (*FW* 185.35–36)

Despite the elements fostering ambiguity which necessarily enter into the composition of the Garland *Ulysses*, once can still justifiably expect it to set down reliable limits (what postmodern critics have come to call paradigms) within which individuals can work to discover meaning. As noted above, many of the textual vagaries perpetrated through successive editions of *Ulysses* grew out of Joyce's idiosyncratic methods of composition. His accretive approach to writing can pose cruxes even in instances when all necessary documents of composition and transmission have survived. Consequently, the copy-text, the formal apparatus selected to guide the choices governing the production of the text, becomes a crucial factor in any projected edition,[6] and any discussion of the value of Gabler's work should begin with a consideration of this document.

Common practice has dictated the use of a single document as the copy-text, with scholarly debate centring on whether it should be an author's final fair copy manuscript (when available) or the first edition corrected by the author. Gabler has gone beyond either method by creating for *Ulysses* his own copy-text, i.e., forming one from what he considers the best elements of a variety of contemporary material. By normal standards of textual criticism, Gabler's composite copy-text stands as a daring innovation in a field generally characterized by the conservatism of its accepted procedures. He does not, however, so much introduce radically new methods as extend previous approaches to meet the demands of the particular problems confronting him. One can trace in his work echoes of the dominant ideas of the most eminent twentieth-century bibliographers, W.W. Greg and R.B. McKerrow, and in his use of a composite copy-text, he specifically develops techniques introduced by Fredson Bowers in editing Stephen Crane's newspaper pieces.[7]

Philip Gaskell, writing at a time when Gabler's edition was still in its planning stages, has produced a detailed examination of the methods which came to be applied to the Garland version, and his remarks both clarify the basic elements of a synoptic version and offer commentary on the central strengths and weaknesses of the approach.

A synoptic version would consist of a critical text (produced either by using [the 1922 Shakespeare & Co. edition], the first edition, as copy-text and emending it, or by building up an ideal text from the

pre-publication documents [the method which Gabler followed])
which would be marked to show which of its constituent parts came
from where. . . .

The advantages of producing a synoptic version are that the editor,
in considering all the evidence, can suppress inessentials (such
as errors of transmission) in order to concentrate on authorial variation and the textual and critical conclusions that can be drawn from
it. . . .

But this method also has disadvantages. Much of the evidence that
the pre-publication documents contain will necessarily be omitted,
but some of it may elucidate Joyce's text in ways that have not yet
been developed, and an editor would have to be able to see into the
future to include now all that might be useful then.[8]

While Gaskell's analysis does not offer a blanket approval, it
clearly outlines the basic features that one must accept in
order to see Gabler's apparatus for emendation as a legitimate
approach.

Since the Garland *Ulysses* is emphatically not a variorum,
editorial decisions will necessarily eliminate variant readings.
At the same time, it concerns itself with the evolution of the
text as Joyce intended it to develop, and so it reproduces
through the synoptic version of the work's various stages of
development the direct path of its artistic growth and of the
artist's aesthetic development. Finally, in the absence of a
single document suitable for use as a copy-text Gabler has
formed a hybrid from an amalgamation of sources to serve as
the foundation of his edition.[9]

Once one accepts Gabler's basic editorial procedures,
analysis of his specific efforts follows the same pattern as that
of any response to literary interpretation. The critical
junctures of evaluation come at points in the construction of
the copy-text when variant versions appear with equal
objective claims for inclusion. In those instances Gabler's
choices reflect his way of reading *Ulysses*, and the degree to
which others will accept his views will depend upon the
conviction of his argument and upon the perspective which
they bring to the work. Gaskell sums up this process in his
discussion of the editor's relation to the copy-text:

The copy-text is therefore converted into a critical text by means of a
technique of controlled eclecticism whereby the editor, in the light of

all the evidence, emends the copy-text by substituting readings from another text or by supplying new ones himself; he does this where he believes that the alterations represent the author's intended text more closely than the copy-text readings, because they correct errors, omissions, or unauthorized alterations.[10]

Although Gaskell is not as blunt about the process as I have been, one can see that it revolves around the critical judgement of the editor (the key word in the passage above being belief), and our response to the work as a whole will rest on an evaluation of that judgement.

Such a critique does not impute flaws to Gabler's system; rather it points out its necessary subjectivity. At the Frankfurt Joyce conference in 1984, Stephen Joyce went a bit further. In his speech accepting from Gabler the initial copy of the Garland edition, he chilled the festivities by mentioning that missing manuscripts belonging to Paul Léon and germane to the composition of *Ulysses* had not been consulted in the preparation of the edition. The cryptic tone of the comments of Joyce's grandson made the value of the material a moot point, but he took a plausible position in suggesting that some unconsulted documents may exist which would have been useful to consider while the edition was in preparation. Yet while such a contention underscores the provisional nature of Gabler's version, one should not presume that the possibility of its fallibility makes it a flawed work. Gabler himself at several points in his 'Afterword' acknowledges his edition as 'critically established,' i.e., a version formed in part at least by decisions based on the application of logic and available textual evidence. Accepted editorial procedures make this subjectivity a perfectly natural aspect of the text's make up, and one would expect that subsequent research will produce evidence for further refinement of the Garland edition. To equate this condition of mutability, however, with deficiencies in the version that Gabler has offered is to set unrealistic standards for the production of editions.

THE HOWTOSAYTO ITISWHATIS HEMUSTWHOMUST WORDEN SCHALL (*FW* 223.27)

The synoptic editorial approach adopted in the Garland

version foregrounds for readers of *Ulysses* the same requirement for participation in textual reconstruction that is presented so imperatively throughout *Finnegans Wake*. Yet, while this expanded sense of the potential for producing meaning in the text necessarily exerts a considerable impact on interpretive strategies applied to *Ulysses*, it is important to retain a clear sense of the limits of the new edition. Consequently, I would like to digress again to examine the basic concepts encompassed by the phrase critical edition, the label that has been generally applied to Gabler's work, because I wish to question certain assumptions which have accrued in relation to it.

In general, bibliographers use this term to identify a volume in which the editor has drawn upon his analytical skills to constitute a version of the text conforming as closely as possible to the final intentions of the author. While informed by intelligence and critical skill, such decisions remain subjective, and consequently such conclusions must stand as provisional and open to debate. Michael Groden, in an analysis of the structure of the Garland edition, presents a cogent and insightful overview of the text, but he makes statements regarding the nature of a critical edition that I believe place expectations upon the work that it was never intended to meet. Groden describes the nature of the text as follows:

Ulysses: A Critical and Synoptic Edition is not a corrected edition, one whose editor looks for places where the printed text is inaccurate and corrects them. Even though the new text does indeed expose some five thousand errors in all the previously published versions of Joyce's text, it corrects them only indirectly. Rather, by establishing and printing the text Joyce wanted – in other words, by producing a 'critical edition' – the new edition reveals that the first edition departs from Joyce's text about five thousand times, but not always in the same places.[11]

The crucial term to my mind is 'the text Joyce wanted,' for such a statement, made without qualifications, implies the objective ability to reconstruct a definitive version of *Ulysses*. Surely just the opposite condition obtains, for in a number of cases, highlighted by Gabler in his notes on emendation, critical, subjective judgement had to be exercised to arrive at a single reading.

Let me cite two examples used in Groden's essay to make my point. Commenting on the equivocal effect produced in certain cases by the introduction of material dropped during some stage of the process of composition, Groden points to the best known restoration of the new edition:

– Will he not see reborn in her, with the memory of his own youth added, another image?
Do you know what you are talking about? Love, yes. Word known to all men. *Amor vero aliquid alicui bonum vult unde et ea quae concupiscimus* . . . (9.427–31)

While acknowledging that the passage makes a similiar question asked by Stephen in the Circe episode superfluous (15.4192–93), Groden defends its inclusion: 'Given this editorial assumption of eyeskip – and therefore a rejection of the possibility that Joyce deleted the passage at the lost final-working-draft stage – both textual segments had to be restored to the text.' While the explanation is quite plausible it remains a subjective, critical response to the text and not, as Groden asserts earlier in the same paragraph, a bibliographical one.[12] Later in the essay, again referring to changes based on the Rosenbach manuscript, Groden comes to much the same conclusion.

Occasionally the Rosenbach Manuscript shows a clear deletion of the typescript reading in favor of a new one, but more often the extant manuscript shows only the variant reading. Here the editor's critical skills came into play as he had to decide which reading probably represents the more advanced of the two inscriptions.[13]

Once one acknowledges the requisite of applying critical skills, one can no longer assume the complete accuracy of the results. By this statement I most emphatically do not wish to question either Gabler's analytic abilities or Groden's assessment of the edition, but I do wish to call attention to the inevitable subjectivity surrounding such examination. Critical skills by force of circumstances rely on informed judgements to bring sense to material when facts are not present to make such speculation unnecessary. This opens them to the possibility of error, and one cannot ignore the potential fallibility of the work producing any critical edition without forcing it to bear a burden it was not meant to bear.

54

Why Does One Re-Read Ulysses?

(STOOP) IF YOU ARE ABCEDMINDED, TO THIS CLAYBOOK, WHAT CURIOS OF SIGNS (PLEASE STOOP), IN THIS ALLAPHBED! (*FW* 18.17–18)

The final test of any version of *Ulysses*, then, lies in its ability to offer a rendition of Joyce's compositional material in a manner which seems to follow the final form that he envisioned its taking while avoiding a prescriptive tone which leaves readers no room to exploit the ambiguities inherent in Joyce's work. Since, by the process of literary creation, an author sets the artistic parameters from which one derives any reading, the ultimate worth of the Garland edition will depend upon the precision with which it establishes the borders of those parameters. One can resolve the disparate demands of authority through acquiring a clear sense of the text itself. Because the physical artefact of *Ulysses* has been so corrupted and the transmission of documents of composition has been so blurred, the emendations necessary to restore authorial intentionality can be derived only from the analysis of a bulk of external material not available to the common reader. At the same time, insufficient evidence exists to remove subjectivity entirely from this process of restoration, for in many instances the circumstances surrounding the composition and revision of alternate renderings of a particular passage give any of several versions equal claim to primacy.

The constraints of space would seem to prohibit a complete delineation of the myriad of alternatives considered in the compilation of the final Garland version, but the synoptic pages offer within the text a plan tracing the origin of its constituent parts. In this fashion they furnish a conspectus of the work's textual development, allowing one to retrace most, though not all, of the stages of editing and to substitute alternative readings whenever they seem more logical. While many of an editor's decisions will derive from his own reading of the work, Gabler's willingness, through the synoptic text, to present the logic informing those decisions has the effect of opening the text of the modifications and to the reinterpretations of a range of readers.

For each reader the text exists not in the physical artefact of the book, or in an imaginative state separate from all else, but in a metaphysical condition allowing for the play of our

55

imagination with the work of author, editor, and other readers. This produces the paradoxical condition in which any response to the text has the potential for illuminating all other interpretations while at the same time no single reading stands as the final one. To make a final interpretive judgement is to kill the text, turning it into a monument. Even our own readings must be open to respond to the views of others and to shifts in our own perspectives. Critical editions and critical commentary are essential to maintain the paradigm created by the author and to push to the limit the ability of the text to give pleasure. Recognizing the presence of ambiguity in the text of *Ulysses* figures as an important step towards answering the question with which I opened this essay. When one gives up the aim of achieving perfect certitude in any reading of the book, one can accept and take pleasure in its continuing potentiality. This openness to the possibilities of the text, however, quickly slips into solipsistic reverie without some standard for measuring the efficacy of personal impressions, some credible guide for interpretation. Specifically one needs a text which admits ways of seeing the work not as a static artefact but as an organic operation. If as a consequence one must admit that cruxes will yield only to relative, temporary explanations, this assent recognizes Joyce's perception of the work's potential for continuing possibilities, for reforming one's response which 'age cannot whither . . . nor custom stale.' Adopting such a perspective, however, becomes extremely difficult without a version of the work offering the necessary alternatives for such a reading.

YOUR WILDESHAWESHOWE MOVES SWIFTLY STERNEWARD!
(*FW* 256.13–14)

The achievement of Gabler's edition of *Ulysses* does not come from a rendition of a definitive version of the work. Rather it satisfies the needs of an intelligent reader by confronting him with the complexity of Joyce's creative process in a (not the) recuperable form. In practical terms it clarifies the work that Joyce intended to present, alternately restoring or deleting according to Joyce's aims. Each change challenges the reader to accept or to reject, but not in a haphazard way because it foregrounds the cruxes and presents us with the choice of following or departing from its findings. Perhaps most important it causes us to reconsider the validity of previous interpretations. We must ask ourselves how valuable is any reading based on a corrupt text? If all readings are critical and in a sense provisional, what is the value of any interpretation? Authority, in terms of a static and inflexible artefact, becomes a false issue, for the impulse towards certitude is inimical to art. The ability of a text to evolve is its strength.

Like any good edition, the Garland *Ulysses* ultimately reflects the way its editor interprets the text, for one cannot (re)create from the complex and often contradictory materials of composition available without applying critical judgement to resolve certain cruxes. The decisions for forming the text, however, make up an overt reading that Gabler has adduced through carefully considered responses to ambiguous evidence. By offering the synoptic form, as he perceives it, of the text's evolution and by articulating in detail the principles and apparatus of his editorial methods, Gabler tacitly invites one to perform the same evaluations. He allows the reader the option of partial or complete acceptance or rejection, but more significantly, I believe, he reaffirms the necessarily provisional nature of any interpretation.

ART THOU REAL, MY IDEAL?

CLIVE HART

Plato himself might well feel confused, in the light of all this controversy, as to the essential characteristics of the real *Ulysses*. Although, as a member of the Academic Advisory Committee, I was implicated in the radical work leading to the construction of the left-hand page, I am temperamentally of the artistic right, a right-hand reader in search of that body of fleeting signs which will best lead to an understanding of the completed work. I find the history of the book, its process, encoded on the left, of great interest; but the finished product, recorded on the right, has much more power to engage my imagination. *Ulysses* leads us, I believe, towards integration rather than towards a trivialising dispersal of response in an 'endless play of possibilities of meaning.' In saying this I do not imply that I think *Ulysses*, or any part of it, means one thing only; indeed, I am not now focussing on meaning at all, but on pattern. I should therefore like to plead for right-hand reading, for deeming process to be the servant of organised product, for exercising the maximum of aesthetic sensibility in the apprehension of an artistic whole. The emergence of the Garland *Ulysses* has, however, called into question the nature of that whole.

In so far as I have reservations about the Garland edition they have to do less with the occasional errors and the several editorial choices which seem out of tune with the verbal music of the book than with the fundamental presuppositions about how a right-hand page comes into being and how it is to be understood. My worries can be expressed, as many other worries have been at this conference, in terms of the problematical nature of copy-text.

Editing a copy-text is an operation intended to result in the reconstruction of an ideal text. There is, however, no general agreement as to what constitutes an ideal text; the differences are both fundamental and irreconcilable. I discern four important ways in which one might understand the notion of

58

an ideal text of *Ulysses*. They imply different attitudes to the effects of the passage of time and to the nature of appropriate editorial action. The first imagines the text as an aggregation of Joyce's most originally creative and error-free moments of planning and conceptualising over a period of seven years, moments when the creative mind was most in command of fine points of detail and of the total design as then foreseen. The second is the text Joyce might have wished to see transmitted to us if a committee of assistants had been available, over the whole seven-year period, with the task of progressively realising a design based on a set of plans and general instructions undergoing continuous revision by the author. The third ideal offers the text freed from all mechanical error and presented in the state in which Joyce might have wished to leave it at the last stage of composition—if it were possible to discover what that state might be. This ideal imagines a super-alert Joyce going over his text word by word, with great care and full creative awareness, in February 1922, and telling an editor what he wants—wants then, in 1922. It is not altogether absurd to try to reconstruct that state of mind; it is certainly no more problematical than the reconstruction, for the first ideal, of the seven-year run of conceptual high-points. The fourth is a text freed from all forms of mechanical error over which Joyce had no control, however indirect, at the last stage of preparation of every discreet passage of the book. The Garland *Ulysses* tries to realise the first Platonic state by constant reference to the imaginary constructs of the second; although I willingly participated in its production, I should have been more comfortable with the third and in the long run choose the fourth. Like all the other ideals, it is unattainable in practice; we can never know what degradations of the text, if any, were wholly uninfluenced by the aura of Joyce's person and activities.

My reason for choosing the fourth ideal springs from an understanding of the nature of a work of art different from that of the editors. In discussions of the new edition the editorial difficulties generated by a long and complex book written over so long a period of time have frequently been explored. Less attention has been given to the aesthetic presuppositions underlying both the edition and the critical discussion of it. These presuppositions are raised in acute form by the editors' rationale of emendation. They are intimately related to questions of intention and the frustration of intention, but I believe that the discussions have not distinguished sufficiently clearly between the thwarting of intention by an outside agency and its thwarting by the writer himself. I wish to stress the need for such a distinction because I conceive of a work of art as having among its essential characteristics the quality of being the creation of an individual human consciousness making its own decisions (including, it may be, the decision to approach others for help) and making, in the process, its own errors of judgement, its own mistakes.

I could perhaps illustrate my point by reference to errors of fact incorporated into *Ulysses*. There are of course differing views about the nature of some of those errors. Among the most notorious, and most talked about in connexion with the Garland *Ulysses*, are Joyce's incorrect use of 'indication' for 'indiction' and the incorrect Roman dating for 1904 (17.98–99; *U* 669). As these occur in Ithaca, in which so much is meticulously documented but in which so much that poses as fact is erroneous, interesting arguments can be developed either for the retention of the errors or for their correction. I can imagine sympathising with both, but my trouble is that both arguments are, in my understanding of the nature of works of art, irrelevant. Before I proceed, let me say that I choose these two because – unlike other restorations and changes in the Garland *Ulysses* – these 'errors' do not, at least as far as can be ascertained, involve any transmissional inaccuracy. The Garland editors want to correct the errors, to right the wrong text. Now it may be that if some busy-body amanuensis had leaned over Joyce's shoulder while he was writing these passages – or correcting the proofs – and had said, 'Oh, by the way Jim, excuse my interfering, but I wonder if you have noticed that MXMIV is not actually correct as a Roman date for 1904,' he would have responded with an 'I am most grateful,' and have changed the date to MCMIV. But personally I don't care whether he would have done so or not. What seems to me to matter much more is that he made a mistake and let it stand. Whether the mistake is intentional is

beside the point. What seems to me to matter is that that is
what Joyce wrote. It matters because the work of art with
which I am concerned is precisely what Joyce wrote. Here I
need a fine distinction, one which is not always well made in
what I find advanced by commentators on copy-text and other
bibliographical matters: I need a fine distinction between what
Joyce committed to paper or authorised for commitment to
paper, and what emerged on paper without his blessing.
There's nothing new about that, one might complain: isn't
that what all editing is about? Perhaps it ought to be, but it is
not quite what I find to be the case. Where I should like to be
able to work is in the gap between what Joyce wrote in the
sense of manipulating his pen, and what he wrote in the sense
of consciously wishing to say. Somewhere in that gap is where
the generative activity occurs, transmuting the creative
potential of the imagination into created, observable reality.
Such activity is inescapably subject to the most fundamental
pressures of artistic temperament. It is not the editor's job to
compensate for the consequences of that temperament. In this
connexion I would echo William Broome's remarks in the
preface to his *Poems on Several Occasions* (1727):

The question is not what the author might have said, but what he has
actually said; it is not whether a different word will agree with the
sense, and turn of the period, but whether it was used by the author;
If it was, it has a good title still to maintain its post, and the authority
of the manuscript ought to be followed rather than the fancy of the
editor. (6–7)

What the artist actually does will often contain elements
which do not conform with what he says he wishes to do or
might reasonably be presumed likely to say he wishes to do. Any
'correction' of such material causes the work to cease to be the
expression of one integrated consciousness, turns it into a work
of art by a committee – and therefore in my sense no longer a
work of art at all. I hazard an analogy: in one of Vermeer's most
familiar paintings, a girl reading a letter, there is a reflection of
her head in the window. It is well known that the reflection is
slightly too large to be realistic. There is no doubt that Vermeer
wished to give an accurate rendering of reality, with as fine
grained a texture as possible. If someone had watched him in the
act and had pointed out to him the undue size of the reflection he

would doubtless have repainted it. Would anyone seriously wish to repaint that picture now? I see little difference between doing that and correcting Joyce's 'errors' in Ithaca – except of course that, in contrast with Vermeer's case, there is some likelihood that in *Ulysses* the departures from realism may in any case be intentional. But I do not want to be sidetracked by intention: the important thing for me is that in both cases the works of art contain a tension between a striving towards accuracy and a departure from it – a tension on the surface of the work which is an inherent part of its nature. The true Platonic *Ulysses* is a *Ulysses* with many flaws – flaws which accurately represent Joyce's many shortcomings: his oversights, his misconceptions, his muddle, his arrogance, his impracticality. Now the 1922 first edition does not, with any degree of accuracy, reflect that congeries of personal and artistic failings. Nor does the Garland text. What I should like to see, as the manifestation of the Platonic ideal, is an edition which fully reflects the seven-year period of creative work on the book, but reflects it in a finished product taking into account all that happened to wear down the fine edges of some originally well honed ideas, that allowed some bright perceptions to fade, that introduced contradictions and incompatibilities into what was once a consistently conceived pattern. Joyce must be allowed to have forgotten some material, to have mishandled much, to have fallen short of his own ideals, to have lost, at forty, some of the inspirations of his mid-thirties. It is in the nature of the artist's work that a splendid phrase, conceived of today, will be forgotten and irretrievable tomorrow, that it will be replaced by a flabbier substitute. And we must allow that substitute to stand. The alternative procedure – I find it depressing that the Garland edition adopts it – is to construct an *Überkünstler*, an artist who never existed, a Joyce made out of the best moments of Joycean consciousness, a Joyce who never forgot, who never lost his place, never mislaid his proofs, a Joyce who constructed a work of art as if he were a computer. One of Joyce's salient characteristics was a desire for order coupled with a personality and a choice of life-style that made the achievement of orderliness difficult. Or perhaps one should put it more pointedly and say that he both wanted order and emotionally, temperamentally repudiated it. Order, accuracy, in the production of most of *Ulysses* would not have been difficult to ensure. Card files could have been used in place of slips of paper and notebooks; careful keying of proof corrections and additions to manuscript could have rendered reproduction by typists and compositors if not faultless then certainly much less prone to error; greater care with the family finances would probably have left sufficient money for trained secretarial assistance at crucial moments in the book's progress; duplicate sets of proof could have been carefully checked against one another. But none of this, surely, sounds like James Joyce. If *Ulysses* were being written today, can we imagine Joyce using a word-processor, checking the addition of Bloom's accounts on a calculator, using a concordance to ensure consistency in the italicising of the City Arms Hotel? I think not. He was not that sort of man. Conventional wisdom, reflected in the Garland edition, attributes much of the disorder to an important personal matter which was in itself beyond Joyce's control: if he had not been purblind, it is asserted, his work on the text would have been much more accurate. That is no doubt true; but if he had had normal sight he would have had a very different sense of language and of his own personal relationship to the world – and would have written another book. Physical disability is not an external, mechanical matter; it has profound aesthetic consequences.

Since he did not exercise total control over his text, it is necessary to distinguish between those blemishes in the finished product which emerge from the inherent fallibilities of the artist's temperament and physique and those which can in no sense be attributed to him. My one important criticism of the new edition is that this discrimination is not, in my view, well made. To do so is not, however, an easy task.The extremes present, of course, no difficulty: if Joyce makes a brilliant change today, forgets it, and tomorrow makes an alternative and much less brilliant change, there is no question, in my view, but that the second version must be accepted because it is the truly Joycean version – the version which incorporates the Joycean self-destructive forgetfulness. Nor is there any inherent difficulty in the case of last-minute printing errors: they have no connexion with the creating consciousness. There is nevertheless an indistinct middle

63

ground, concerned most particularly with the possibility or otherwise of passive authorisation. If Fritz Senn is right (and I believe he may be), Joyce never saw the inclusion of the redundant 'Agenbite of inwit' in Telemachus (1.515; *U* 17). If Joyce assumed in good faith that the relevant passage had not been tampered with, he can hardly be said to have authorised a manipulation of his text entirely unconnected with his own thought processes – though perhaps an author of more obsessive-compulsive habits might have checked to make sure. On the other hand he several times read and made corrections on the heavily punctuated Eumeus. In such a case, his passivity, his non-interference, seems to me to have constituted an inexpungeable element in the creation of the finished product. No doubt the chapter is more effective in its original, lightly punctuated form – but I want Joyce's text, not a super-text which results from the making of a cockatrice: Joycean creativity stitched to Gablerian accuracy. We must not, I believe, try to rescue Joyce from his own inadequacies – or alleged inadequacies. (One might recall the sad case of Anton Bruckner.) It is impossible to make a clear separation, as the Garland edition attempts to do, between, on the one hand, such personal failings as inattentive proof-reading, and, on the other, the primary creative spirit. Joyce could have taken care to get his text accurately printed only if he had been a wholly different man – the kind of man who could not have written this book; I don't know whether what that writer might have written would have been better or worse, but I am confident that it would have been radically different.

I am if anything still more worried by another version of the Garland cockatrice: the incoherent amalgam of so many different Joyces in the clear-reading text. In the main I have no problem with the left-hand page, which, despite its rebarbative appearance, is genuinely synoptic. The right-hand page, however, turns synopsis into conflation, generating, in many places, an impossible work of art. It is quite common in the Garland text to find words and phrases restored as if they had no potential effect on their surroundings. In contrast with my earlier arguments I do not now refer to the simple restoration of lost passages the absence of which Joyce might well never have noticed, but to the editorial choice of earlier and allegedly more inspired readings which came to be replaced by weaker substitutes. The Garland edition takes far too little notice, in my view, of the reflexive nature of *Ulysses*. If I may stress the obvious, words constantly intermesh, echo each other, produce resonances at great distances across the pages. It is the later versions, the ones Joyce actually adopted, embedded in the developing text, which generate the echoes, not the lost earlier ones, however much more satisfying these may seem to be on their own terms. This failure of coherence is most acute where the Garland text adopts readings from branching documents which never rejoined the main line of textual descent. Not present in the subsequent versions of the relevant passages which Joyce repeatedly revised for further enrichment of his material, they did not influence the tightly integrated network of his prose. Although the proportion of the book so affected is relatively small, I am surprised and troubled by the adoption here of a conflational procedure long since in disrepute with mediaeval and Renaissance editors. I seek a more truly Joycean restitution of *Ulysses* and should stress that I do so not because I want an accurate expression of Joyce's personality and intentions, but because I seek a book which is fundamentally consistent with itself rather than consistent in the superficial sense which I believe to be (almost) true of the Garland edition.

Personally I confess to being greatly attracted by that other Platonic ideal – the perfect *Ulysses*, totally harmonious, entirely error-free, the *Ulysses* that has never existed, can never exist. Such a work would not be a work of human art; it would be a supernatural work, a heavenly work, a work of God. And however much Joyce might have wished to be able to write a book that seemed as if it were created by a god, he did not manage it, and knew he could not manage it. Perhaps it would in any case have been blasphemous: Gabler wants a pure, sleek *Ulysses* with no freewheeling part; I prefer Joyce's *Ulysses*, creaking and squeaking here and there.

BALANCING THE BOOK, OR PRO AND CONTRA THE GABLER *ULYSSES*

DAVID HAYMAN

It isn't often that Joycean or any other serious scholarship attracts the sort of media attention lavished on the Garland edition. Even the uninitiated seem to have been waiting with bated breath for the disclosures contained in the 'definitive' edition that would enable readers, critics, and scholars alike to see finally what Joyce meant to write rather than what printers and others have created for us in the whispering game of transmission. The goal of Hans Gabler and his team was to produce with computer assistance a text free of human error, one which takes into account not only the editions produced during Joyce's lifetime but also the manuscripts and typescripts that led up to them. Not unexpectedly, the new edition, with its carefully elaborated procedures, its meticulous attention to even the smallest detail, its handsome format and its elevated price, was greeted as a triumph by early reviewers.

Though some were mildly uncomfortable with certain procedures, some details of presentation, and changes that altered accepted readings, the edition's initial success was both understandable and right. It did indeed remove an accumulation of errors. It added material 'inadvertently' dropped at various stages of production and reproduction. It righted errors of omission and commission resulting from Joyce's own carelessness, fatigue, poor health, and the haste with which the closing chapters were readied for the press. Equally important, it attended, as did Joyce himself, to details of punctuation, a major source of the book's verbal rhythms as well as its coherence.

As a by-product of the effort to establish a reliable reading text, the editor has generated something approaching a textual

66

history, producing a diachronic 'synoptic' version printed on the left-hand pages opposite the 'reading' text. There, with the aid of a sophisticated (some say too sophisticated) code we can follow the vicissitudes of the novel through the years. Together with the 'Historical Collation', this system helps those of us bent on incorporating the changes in our corrupt working editions to rethink a remarkable number of details. This may in fact be the major accomplishment of the new edition which has certainly sharpened our glosses.

Still, a closer reading suggests that we do not yet have the promised definitive version, that we may never have it. To a book notoriously full of undecidabilities, Gabler has added a few new ones with perhaps too much assurance. We may wonder that Joyce allowed *Ulysses* to go through so many versions without noting that Eumaeus is riddled with errors because an overzealous and meddling typist added a great deal of unauthorised punctuation. We are assured, aurally if not in print, that, by permitting Stephen to answer the question, what is the 'word known to all men,' Joyce provided something like the solution to the book.[1] Or again, we learn that Joyce wanted to punctuate his stage directions differently, beginning most of them with a lower case letter and placing no period at the end. The new edition goes further in altering the book's format, printing dialogue flush with the left-hand margin and occasionally redistributing dialogue elements as well as other sentences and phrases. Such changes are all, we are told, consistent with the author's wishes as evidenced by the last direct 'authorial intervention' which Gabler sees as the most authoritative.

We should be grateful for those changes that clarify our reading and bring us closer to Joyce's intentions; but what about those that may add fresh errors and obscure those intentions? As others in this volume have shown, and despite the injunction, 'Thou shalt not look a gift horse in the mouth,' the problems with this edition begin precisely with its most obvious contributions. We are finally obliged to ask how well we understand the rationale behind Hans Gabler's decisions; how many of them are to some degree subjective; and what is the precise nature of the computer programme with the help of which this version of *Ulysses* was realised? Others have dealt with these questions on a higher level. Since I see myself as a close reader of the text, my approach has been and remains more pragmatic and direct. It grows directly out of the experience of annotating a 'gorescarred' copy of Random House 1961 with the aid of Gabler's 'Historical Collation' and is based upon my attempt to systematise my responses:

1. Positive changes can be indicated by a hierarchial sequence of Ⓧ x Ⓧ
2. Negative changes by ? (?) (?)
3. Items that make no appreciable difference in my reading by a simple x.

Not unexpectedly, three quarters of Gabler's ameliorations fall within the third category; the question marks and x's vary considerably in size in accordance with the perceived importance of the change. On occasion a second reading has obliged me to reevaluate a ?, replacing it with a barred question mark and ratifying Gabler's decision. There are very few double-circled x's and ?'s though there are at least twice as many of the former as of the latter. And then there is a final category, one which has been only randomly established in my book: the O's. These items, of which there may eventually be a considerable number, constitute a major positive and negative commentary on Gabler's method and results. They denote those details which have fallen through the net established by a computer programme capable of dealing only with errors signalled by alterations in the text. Since they are not supported by manuscript witnesses, they constitute the most subjective aspect of my annotation, but they reflect my sense, as an experienced reader of *Ulysses*, of Joyce's methods of writing, revising, and meaning as well as of the consistency of Gabler's corrections. As we shall see, they also raise important procedural questions.

We may begin by sampling what I consider to be minor but significant and positive alterations. I stress this order of change because others have attended to the more obvious ones. My first example is a barred ? from the Bloom segment of Nausicaa, a sentence that for years has read, 'Handed down from father to mother to daughter, I mean' (*U* 372). Gabler has discovered that Joyce meant to add a comma after the first 'to', clarifying the line of descent and the rhetorical flow of Bloom's thought (13.917). In Oxen of the Sun, we read the following from Mulligan's speech: '. . . he had resolved to purchase in fee simple for ever the freehold of Lambay island from its holder, lord Talbot de Malahide, a Tory gentleman of not much in favour with our ascendancy party' (*U* 402). This confusing passage is greatly improved when it is altered to read '. . . gentleman of note . . .' (14.683).[2] Finally, at *U* 424, in the conclusion to Oxen, there is an indication of how effective Gabler can be at clearing up confusion. There, the word '(attitudes)' misrepresents the allusion to beatitudes contained in Gabler's restored version: '(atitudes)' (14.1459).

Having recognised a portion of Gabler's contribution which we must be careful not to over- or underestimate, we may now consider a sampling of the items I would question.

In his effort to make the text of *Ulysses* consistent with Joyce's stylistic quirks, Gabler has joined a great number of words printed separately or hyphenated in earlier editions. Still, all too frequently we find likely candidates that remain unjoined, have become unstuck, have acquired hyphens or kept them. Bloom's ruminations on death and fertility in Hades yield the following conjectural advertisement: 'Well preserved fat corpse gentleman, epicure, invaluable for fruit garden' (*U* 108). Gabler inserts a comma after 'corpse' but fails to write 'wellpreserved' (6.772). My colleagues in Monaco suggested that there is an amusing ambiguity in the current version, a pun on pickling or some other mode of preservation; but I would say the pun remains when the words are joined in accordance with Joyce's practice (which of course should not be mechanically followed). On the other hand, it seems strange that the street names 'Saint-André-des-Arts' (*U* 200) and 'Cours-la-Reine' (*U* 201) lose their hyphens (9.577 and 9.641) but 'Penelope stayathome' (*U* 201) becomes 'Penelope stay-at-home' (9.620).

Gabler's emendations occasionally highlight the need for further changes. Thus, in Oxen, we read, 'Whereat Crotthers of Alba Longa sang young Malachi's praise of that beast the unicorn how once in the millennium he cometh by his horn (,) the other all this while (,) pricked forward with their jibes . . .' (14.234–35; *U* 389).[3] In the midst of this underpunctuated sentence Gabler inserts two commas, one quite rightly after 'horn,' the other far less plausibly after 'while'. In this instance, the second comma succeeds in separating 'other' from its verb, thus violating English usage. There should either be no comma here or else another comma after 'other.' But the real problem is in the status of 'other' and its agreement with 'their': the fact that, as subject of the sentence, 'other' refers not to any individual but to the whole group of roisterers, the 'others'.

Two pages further on, Gabler unwittingly discloses another inconsistency. By capitalising one reference to the BVM, he points up the need to do the same for the others (and perhaps for two references to 'mother'): 'No question but her name is puissant who aventried the dear corse of our Agenbuyer, Healer and Herd, our mighty mother and mother most venerable and Bernardus saith aptly that (S)he hath an *omnipotentiam deiparae supplicem*, that is to wit, an almightiness of petition because she is the second Eve and she won us . . .' (14.294–99; *U* 391). In fact, the new capital S, which may be an error made by Joyce or Gabler, calls into question the status of a string of pronouns in the sentences that follow.

There are a number of problems with Gabler's version of a sentence describing the young Bloom in the manner of Lamb: 'Or it is the same figure, a year or so gone over, in his first hard hat (ah, that was a day!), already on the road, a fullfledged traveller for the family firm, equipped with an orderbook, a scented handkerchief (not for show only), his case of bright trinketware (alas! a thing now of the past!)(,) and a quiverful of compliant smiles for this or that halfwon housewife reckoning it out upon her fingertips or for a budding virgin(,) shyly acknowledging (but the heart? tell me!) his studied baisemoins' (14.1048–55; *U* 413). Gabler has added a '!' after 'alas' and deleted a comma after 'past!).' We may wonder why there is no '!' after 'ah' and why the clause qualifying 'virgin' was set off by commas but the one qualifying 'housewife' was not. We may also question the spelling 'baisemoins' for 'baisemains.' There is nothing like this corruption in the *OED*, which lists both 'baisemain' and 'baisement,' and Joyce certainly knew better (though Lamb possibly did not). Apparently Gabler's witnesses provided him with no evidence that such changes were needed and his computer programme failed to alert him to inconsistencies in his text.

There are a great number of other passages into which a

textual change has introduced fresh errors and revealed the need for further changes. Thus, in the following instance, a comma added after 'breakfasts' has created the need for another, that was not added after 'which'. I cite only the offending members as they appear in the new edition: '. . . which added to the quantity subtracted for Mr Bloom's and Mrs Flemming's breakfasts, made one imperial pint . . .' (17.314–15; *U* 675). There can be no question that, by failing to separate 'which' from 'added', the new version makes nonsense of this passage. But the passage is otherwise corrupt. Joyce meant to write 'Mrs' rather than 'Mr Bloom' in conjunction with 'Mrs Flemming.' For support we need only turn to *U* 677, where we read that 'the viscous cream [was] ordinarily reserved for the breakfast of his wife Marion (Molly).' In Calypso special mention is made of 'her cream' on the tray Bloom takes to Molly (*U* 63). Thus, once again, an alteration in the text has brought to light a hitherto unnoticed error in the published text. One wonders why Joyce failed to note the discrepancy and if a different approach to the editing procedure would have altered this, admittedly minor (if anything is minor in this novel), detail in the new edition? Would another editor have been more sensitive to the niceties of English punctuation, to say nothing of the logic of the book? Would he have thought to indicate the problem in his notes?

As Gabler's practice confirms, Joyce did not like hyphenated words. It is no surprise therefore that many of the new readings do no more than suppress hyphens mistakenly added or retained. On occasion, however, for reasons that are less than clear, the Gabler edition adds fresh ones. No wonder then that a number of these objectionable marks remain unaltered in the new text. An egregious instance is 'dog-gone' in the following sentence from the revivalist harangue at the end of Oxen: 'Come on, you dog-gone, bullnecked, beetlebrowed, hogjowled, peanutbrained, weaseleyed fourflushers, false alarms and excess baggage!' (14.1581–83; *U* 428). It should be noted that not only is doggone usually written as a single word but four flushers is usually two words. It would be consistent with Joyce's practice to write doggone and quite likely that the hyphen was acquired when the word fell at the end of a line.

There is a more problematic, but far more interesting, item in Circe, where Bloom's father appears as an anti-Semitic stereotype *'garbed in the long caftan of an elder in Zion'* (15.248–49; *U* 437). Not only is the more usual and meaningful locution elder of Zion, since the 'in' suggests a location rather than a role, but the most obvious reference in this context is to the infamous pamphlet: *The Protocols of the Elders of Zion,* which was current at the time of the composition of this chapter and to which Stephen refers obliquely in Ithaca. The apparent error is important because it shows how thoroughly Bloom's self-image is clouded by anti-Semitic clichés. It would have been nice had the editor's investigations turned up evidence that the 'in' was an error.

Since the treatment of street names is of relatively little moment, the failure of the new edition to correct the mishandling of the place-name 'Harold's cross bridge' in Circe (15.700; *U* 454) need not excite us. There can be no question, however, that Joyce would have capitalised the C in 'cross,' which, rather than referring to a crossroads, constitutes an integral part of the place name.

A bit subtler, but also fairly obvious, is the case of the word 'shoot' which is found in a comic sentence from Ithaca and retained by Gabler. That Joyce meant to write 'shot' is clear from the deliberately forced rhyme scheme in this account of the advantages of shaving at night and the risks of shaving in the morning: '. . . a paper read, reread while lathering, relathering the same spot, a shock, a shoot, with thought of aught he sought though fraught with nought might cause a faster rate of shaving and a nick . . .' (17.283–86; *U* 674). Here, if we take into account the nature of the verbal play, it is unlikely that the word 'shoot,' whose sense in this context is at best ambiguous, satisfies the demands of the context in which words are generated largely by sounds.

I shall return later to the implications of all this and to the problem of the editor's responsibility to Joyce and his text. For now, let me note that, while the details pointed to here do not reflect editorial carelessness or inaccuracy, and though they do not significantly weaken the edition, they do suggest that the job is not quite finished and that more could have been done even without textual and manuscript evidence (and computers).

Other, more serious problems are underscored by my various '?' categories, questions that make me uneasy about the edition in its present state and about the prospect of its publication in a trade edition that would fix the reading of *Ulysses* for many years to come. I advance these items knowing full well that some of them will be judged acceptable by others and that many will have manuscript or other support.

In some instances, Gabler has been very rigorous about details of presentation and punctuation. As noted earlier, he has found reasons to alter conventions of French printing that have pertained since 1922 and printed dialogue flush with the margin. The result is both ugly and confusing, but we are told that Joyce wanted it that way. We are also told that Joyce had other ideas about the punctuation of the stage directions. The explanation given for this alteration in the 'Textual Notes' (G 1747) is to my mind less than satisfactory. We read that the 'division [between narrative and speech directions], *though not invariably and faultlessly observed in Joyce's autograph*, is yet sufficiently recognisable [*sic*] to be adopted and regularised [*sic*] in the critical text' (my italics). We are asked to accept as permanent what Joyce may have seen as a tentative rather than a final format. Gabler's regularisation seems, to say the least, unnecessary. The same may be said of his handling of those words (in Latin or Greek) which earlier editions customarily printed with joined vowels (e.g. 'Aegospotami' at 7.568; *U* 133). Here they are intentionally printed without the ligature.

Concerning the stage directions, I would suggest that even though Joyce did at one point make an effort to use Gabler's punctuation for Circe, we should be able to assume his passive acceptance of the printed version and perhaps posit the existence of a draft utilising that punctuation. After all, Joyce had every opportunity to correct the current punctuation in proof and in later editions. The case of the ligatures is different. Obviously, neither Joyce nor his typists could use them, but it is equally obvious that the printing convention is just that and that Joyce did not object. None of these alterations (and there are others that should be applauded) makes much difference to our reading, but all affect, adversely at times, the appearance of the text.

In other instances, we find Gabler introducing or retaining inconsistencies which are doubtless in part justified by Joyce's practice. The new edition adopts the convention 'U.p: up' for the famous postcard message but retains for the initial appearance the version 'U.P.' (8.257; *U* 158). In Sirens Bloom thinks 'Poor Mrs Purefoy,' and adds, in the Random House *Ulysses*, 'U.p.: up' (*U* 280). This Gabler corrects to read 'U.P: up' (11.903). Somewhat irrationally, in Molly's unpunctuated and virtually uncapitalised monologue, we find the Random House reading 'up up' changed to 'U p up' (18.229; *U* 744), a spelling that can only be explained if the first 'U' is seen as beginning an utterance. It is therefore inappropriate in Penelope. Or again, the edition deletes the periods after initials in proper names (e.g., 'John F. Taylor' at *U* 141 and *passim*) but retains 'J.J. O'Molloy' and 'Hugh C. Love,' and a cluster of punctuated initials from a bicycle race poster (*U* 144 and *passim*; *U* 245; *U* 237). More serious, perhaps, is the decision to write 'pisser Burke' in Cyclops[4] while retaining Nosey Flynn, Corny Kelleher, Red Murray, Bantom Lyons, Buck Mulligan, etc. But see 'long John Fanning' (10.995, 997, 1017, 1021, 1026, 1027; *U* 247) in Wandering Rocks. We note a number of inconsistencies in the use of capitalisation and italic. The translation of the Irish name for Dublin, 'Ford of Hurdles' in the Random House version of Wandering Rocks (*U* 245), becomes 'ford of hurdles' in Gabler (10.930); the fabric 'lisle' (*U* 670) becomes 'Lisle' (17.154); a 'panama' hat (*U* 248) becomes a 'Panama' (10.1044); 'Grogan's the tobacconist' (*U* 221) becomes 'Grogan's the Tobacconist' (10.89). Significantly, the evocative capital 'Word' (*U* 422), suggestive of the thundering divine presence, becomes simply 'word' in Gabler's version of the transitional sentence from Oxen of the Sun: '. . . with the reverberation of the thunder the cloudburst pours its torrent, so and not otherwise was the transformation, violent and instantaneous, upon the utterance of the word' (14.1388–90). It is true that the utterer of this word is not God but the artist-god, Stephen, but we may wonder if Joyce would really have wished to destroy the comic ambiguity. Finally, there is the puzzling case of the word Miss, which is not consistently treated in any edition, not even Gabler's. Joyce, who objected to the period after Mr and Mrs, insisted on their capitalisation. Gabler finds that it should be 'miss' throughout 'Sirens' but retains Mr and Mrs in that chapter and keeps 'Miss Kate Collins' (*U* 145) in Aeolus and 'Miss Mitchell' in Scylla (*U* 192).

There are also a few inconsistencies in the emendation of italic. Though Joyce tends to italicise foreign words, Marie Kendall is now a 'charming soubrette' (10.1220; *U* 253). We have a viceregal 'cortège' (10.1250; *U* 254) though it is still 'Henry, *dernier cri* James' (10.1216; *U* 253) and the '*élite* of Erin [that] hung upon his lips' (*U* 263); and, in Circe, Stephen speaks of himself as 'The [*sic*] distrait' (15.3594; *U* 558) though that title is still clearly italicised in Scylla. Since, perhaps for good reasons, most of the italics have vanished from Penelope, one is hard put to explain why the 'Irish Times' (*U* 745) is now written '*Irish* times' (18.255).

The new edition attempts to standardise Joyce's punctuation, but here there are many problems. For example, there is usually a colon preceding dialogue elements without internal attribution. But all too often we find the colon deleted as when Bloom thinks 'Pass a common remark.' before saying '—The rain kept off' (8.1093; *U* 181). When 'he said' is followed by a participle, Joyce generally uses a comma. But it is not unusual for the new edition to delete such marks in places where they clearly belong: '—Good day, sir, Stephen answered(,) blushing.' (7.530; *U* 132); '—Antithesis, the professor said(,) nodding twice'; '—Will you tell him he can kiss my arse? Myles Crawford said(,) throwing out his arm for emphasis' (7.952 and 981; *U* 146). Yet, on the same pages we still find sentences like '—What is it? Myles Crawford said, falling back a pace' or 'Come along, the professor cried, waving his arm' (*U* 146). Question marks are frequently deleted where they seem necessary. It is one thing to write, '*Why I left the church of Rome*' with a period rather than '?', but one may ask why the '?' was removed from 'Wonder would he feel it if something was removed' (8.1110; *U* 181). As he leaves the library toward the end of Scylla, Stephen thinks he sees E.C. and muses disconnectedly: 'Is that? . . . Blueribboned hat . . . Idly writing . . . What? Looked? . . .' (*U* 215). In the new edition this passage is both improved and complicated: 'Is that . . .? Blueribboned hat . . .? Idly writing . . .? What? . . . . Looked . . .?' (9.1123).

The Random House version is easy enough to understand. Stephen first wonders if he is seeing her, then notes that she is wearing a blueribboned hat and writing and then questions her gesture and possible glance. It makes sense to place the '?' after the ellipses, but the mimesis and poignancy are weakened by the added question marks and the consistency by the punctation after 'What.' Bloom's question in Cyclops, '. . . isn't discipline the same everywhere?' (*U* 329) becomes a flat statement in Gabler's version (12.1360) as does John Wyse's question '(I)sn't that what we're told?' (12.1490; *U* 333). (See also *inter alia* Gabler's handling of questions on *U* 151.22 and 154.16).

Equally disturbing and more frequent are the irrational deletions and additions of commas. This is, of course, particularly true of the many changes resulting from Gabler's decision to reject as 'non-authoritative' those marks he says were added by the 'new typist, who typed only "Eumaeus" ' and 'restyled the episode extensively by overriding the paragraphing, using quotation marks and, more seriously, introducing hundreds of commas as well as frequent dashes and ellipses to elucidate the syntax . . . As edited, the episode returns radically to the fair-copy styling, which is also extended to later additions in a few unavoidable instances' (G 1749). We may wonder why Joyce himself followed the new punctuation when making additions rather than correcting it. We may also wonder why so many of the commas added (rather than deleted) by Gabler strike us as odd or wrong. But it would require another essay to study the problems raised by his handling of that chapter. More immediately, we can point to the comma added in Hades after 'thought' in the sentence, '—Yes, Mr Bloom said, and another thing I often thought (,) is to have . . .' (6.405; *U* 98). Surely, Joyce did not intend to separate the noun 'thing' from its verb, though this would be standard German punctuation. Again, did Joyce really mean to delete the comma after 'out' in this sentence from Aeolus: 'Passing out, he whispered to J.J. O'Molloy:' (7.365; *U* 127)?

Sirens introduces some particularly knotty problems, most of which relate to a single typescript (tC) from which very few nonsuspect or essential readings were taken. The problematic nature of the Sirens syntax exacerbates the difficulty of assessing the merit of Gabler's alterations. Still, we may learn something from a comparison of two versions of the following sentence:

Great voice, Richie Goulding said, a flush struggling in his pale, to Bloom, soon old but when was young. (*U* 285)

Great voice Richie Goulding said, a flush struggling in his pale, to Bloom soon old. But when was young? (11.1070–71)

Gabler's version adds ambiguity to an already ambiguous locution. But is it the right sort of ambiguity? Sirens is notoriously free with syntax, grammar, and even, at times, punctuation. So we may try to rationalise this new version inspired mainly by tC, but we could do the same with the earlier version and might even do better. The comma deleted after 'great voice' tends to give the voice rather than the words to Richie. This sort of deception is not rare in Sirens, though it adds nothing but confusion to the grammatical structure. Still, one may wonder if Joyce intended that effect. The deletion of the comma after Bloom is even less productive since it cuts the initial statement off from its qualification: Dollard's voice was much better when he was young. Further, it loses the ambiguity which, by joining Bloom aging and regretting his lost youth to Dollard, did double duty. The terminal question mark is not helpfully ambiguous. Clearly, it does not square with the initial assertion. I submit that we were better off before even though the difference is not immediately available.

Other dubious changes affect rhythm, consistency, and/or sense somewhat less ambiguously. In Cyclops, Joyce consistently separates dialogue from attribution by a comma. Why then does Gabler accept the deletion of commas in the following simple unit: 'Hoho begob, says I to myself, says I' (12.996; *U* 319)? If it is to distinguish quoted thought from quoted dialogue (see an analogous change at *U* 320.22), it seems a superfluous gesture, especially since it is not consistent with Joyce's rhetoric in this chapter. Perhaps one could read this Dublinism the same way with or without the commas, but that it not true of the following sentence, which is altered by the pause after 'stones', a pause that, even if it serves a mimetic purpose, violates the rhetorical practice of

77

this chapter: '—Ay, says Alf. Reuben J was bloody lucky he didn't clap him in the dock the other day for suing poor little Gumley that's minding stones(,) for the corporation . . .' (12.1100–02; *U* 322). Sometimes the altered punctuation is simply ridiculous, as when, in two separate instances, a comma is inserted before a parenthesis that is already followed by a comma (see 17.232 and 238; *U* 673).

Less strange, but certainly unhelpful, is the deletion of a comma after 'tie' in the crucial description of Mulligan dressing from Telemachus: 'And putting on his stiff collar and rebellious tie(,) he spoke to them . . .' (1.513; *U* 16). The omission of a necessary pause does not improve the rhythm of this subtly balanced locution. In another context, we may wonder why the editor chose to separate a subject from its verb by inserting a comma after 'him' but none after 'man' in 'A young man clinging to a spur of rock near him(,) moved slowly frogwise his green legs in the deep jelly of the water' (1.680–81; *U* 21)? Surely, the unnecessary comma spoils the shape of this sentence while introducing something like German punctuation procedures. Equally strange is the removal of two commas from a sequence of three rational ones in the mimetic passage, 'I am surrounded by difficulties, by .... intrigues(,) by ..... backstairs influence(,) by .....' (2.343–44; *U* 33). In this case it should be all or none. Finally, a perfect evacuation is spoiled by the deletion of a comma after 'patiently.' The effect in the following sentence is to suggest that Bloom is reading about his own constipation: 'Midway, his last resistance yielding, he allowed his bowels to ease themselves quietly as he read, reading still patiently(,) that slight constipation of yesterday quite gone' (4.507–09; *U* 69).

The new edition occasionally corrects spelling errors that have crept into the text of *Ulysses*. But it also adds fresh errors and makes questionable changes, not without support, but not necessarily to the advantage of the text. Most of the alterations listed below relate to changes that were made in the 1932 resetting on which Stuart Gilbert collaborated and on which Gabler throws doubt. However, even without evident support in Joyce's hand, the Random House version is in each of these instances preferable to an unmotivated misspelling. There is no reason, for example, to change 'barbicans' (*U* 11) to 'barbacans' (1.316). Gabler advances a plausible-sounding but unsatisfactory reason for accepting the spelling 'metamspychosis' (4.351), seeing it as a half-way position between Molly's 'met him pike hoses' and 'metempsychosis' (G 1732). No explanation is given for accepting the palpable French misspelling 'brillantined' (4.489) over the English 'brilliantined' (U 68). Nor do we have an explanation for the substitution of the incorrect 'vailed' (5.111) for 'veiled' in the description of Mr Bloom's lustfed 'eyelids' (U 74). More damaging is the substitution of an utterly fictive 'Monsieur de la Palice' (9.16) for Stephen's correct and historical 'Monsieur de la Palisse' (U 184), a change that unjustly turns the young man's 'sneer' back on him.

Perhaps we may skip over emendations of correct spelling dating from 1932 like 'spilikins' (17.661) for 'spillikins' (U 686); 'entituled' (17.734 and 2259) for 'entitled' (U 688 and 735). And may even give the editor the benefit of the doubt when he accepts 'moaning' (18.814) for 'morning' (U 760) in Molly's description of Mulvey's behaviour: 'he was shy all the same I liked him like that morning (moaning) I made him blush a little when I got over him that way . . .'. But surely 'theyre' (U 755) is preferable to an incomprehensible homonym 'there' (18.619) in this passage from Hester's letter concerning fragile shawls: 'amusing things but tear for the least thing still theyre lovely I think dont you.' And something fishy is certainly lost when the 'plaice' (U 764) that the Blooms' cat stole becomes a 'lovely fresh place' (18.938–39).

Once we have systematised the above, we are left with a miscellany of questionable items, each of which, like the items at the bottom of our spelling list, makes a real difference and should at the very least be rethought. Though Gabler obviously has a case when he says that the phrase 'Agenbite of inwit' (U 17) was a misplaced insertion meant for page 16, where it was later placed, there are reasons to think that Joyce found the error a fortunate one. At its first appearance, this most significant of expressions was associated with Mulligan and cleanliness, as well as with Lady MacBeth: 'They wash and tub and scrub. Agenbite of inwit. Conscience. Yet here's a spot' (U 16). It seems obvious that its placement on page 17, after Mulligan's alleged call for a 'clean handkerchief,' chimes with the cleanliness/conscience reference. The phrase contributes not only to the rhythm of the passage describing Mulligan's frantic activity but also to the sense of the accompanying commentary, where the words may well be Stephen's projections of Mulliganish discourse and motivation. In addition, the removal of the phrase does not clarify a paragraph that is a powerfully undecidable moment in Telemachus, one that seems to join Stephen and Buck by word and recorded gesture. Finally, the repetition helps anchor the phrase in our memories and prepares us for its reappearance elsewhere. These are, of course, arguments for restoring the phrase. (I wish I could make as strong a circumstantial case for the deletion of the 'love' passage added to Scylla.)

After admitting that, in a description of young Sargent's hair, 'tangled' (*U* 27) 'may seem more attractive' than 'thick' (2.139), Gabler argues that the latter's appearance in the *Little Review* (+ the *Egoist*) versions validates it (G 1730). But it seems far safer to accept the stronger reading over the frequently corrupt periodical version. Sargent, a reflection of Stephen's own youth, could and should have hair that brings to mind our view of Stephen in the cracked mirror of Telemachus ('Hair on end'; 1.136).

In Lestrygonians, when reflecting on the name 'Dubedat,' Bloom performs a (comic) etymological exercise on its first syllable: 'Du, de la, French' (*U* 175). The point is missed[5] when the phrase is printed without commas as '*Du de la* French' (8.890) which has the effect of suggesting that Bloom is playing a mimetic game with the syllables rather than comically deriving 'du' from 'of the'. Like a number of other changes made at *U* 175–80, this one falsifies the rhythm of the phrase.

Even before Gabler mistakenly capitalised 'Tobacconist' (10.89), it would have been hard to imagine the precise situation described by the sentence beginning, 'He passed Grogan's the tobacconist against which newsboards leaned . . .' (*U* 221). Were it not for the apostrophe in Grogans, the new version of the phrase 'Grogan's the Tobacconist' could be interpreted as the full name of a shop against which boards could lean. My own suspicions, that 'the tobacconist' should be enclosed by commas and the 't' should be lower case, are both supported by a structurally similar sentence a few lines down, one which also contains a doubtful change: 'In Youkstetter's, the porkbutcher's, Father Conmee observed pig's puddings, white and black and red, lie (lying) neatly curled in tubes' (10.99–100; *U* 221). There is no question in my mind that 'the tobacconist' qualifies and does not continue Grogan's shop's name. That is, it performs the same function as 'the porkbutcher's' does for 'Youkstetter's.' Furthermore, I would suggest that changing the participle, 'lying' (*U* 221) to the verb form 'lie' (10.100) introduces a serious grammatical error.

If the problems discussed above are fairly straightforward, the two problematic changes in Wandering Rocks are not. The powerful but normal word 'Crushed' in Bloom's kinetic response to his reading of *Fair Tyrants*, 'Feel! Press! Crushed! Sulphur dung of lions!' (*U* 236) is changed by Gabler to 'Chrished!' (10.623) and explained with reference to a misreading of a Joycean revision to the proofs of the first edition and a corrective reading, probably by Stuart Gilbert, in 1932. Since Joyce may well have approved of this change, despite initial doubts, I find reasons to support the Gabler version with its pun on, or euphemistic allusion to, Christ. In a similar case, though Gabler takes pains to defend his substitution of 'puked' (10.634) for 'spat' (*U* 236) and though my colleagues at Monaco did their best to find a rationale for the new word, I believe that Gabler has weakened one of Joyce's more effective kinetic passages. To make my point, I shall have to quote the entire paragraph:

Phlegmy coughs shook the air of the bookshop, bulging out the dingy curtains. The shopman's uncombed grey head came out and his unshaven reddened face, coughing. He raked his throat rudely, spat (puked) phlegm on the floor. He put his boot on what he had spat, wiping his sole along it(,) and bent, showing a rawskinned crown, scantily haired. (10.632–36)

Both of Gabler's emendations come from the same source (tB); both were either overlooked by the typist who transcribed these pages or, as Gabler suggests, the revision postdates the typing; or, as I would suggest, the changes may at some point have been rejected. The comma is clearly appropriate, completing the surround of 'wiping . . . it,' but 'puked' seems inappropriate. The immediate response at Monaco was shock, not at the strength of the word but at the idea that one could think of puking phlegmy spit. The image of anyone deliberately rubbing his shoe in vomit, which, unlike phlegm, stinks, is out of keeping both with the carefully modulated but powerfully affective language of this passage and with Bloom's 'troubled' reaction. Gabler clearly has the facts on his side, however, and only taste can overrule his decision.

There may be some reenforcement for an anti-puke position, again on grounds of taste, but this time in relation to rhythm and consistency, in another unfortunate decision justified by the same set of revisions. A description of Stephen's 'Two old women fresh from their whiff of the briny' (see the 'midwives' from Proteus and the heroines of 'The Parable of the Plums') contains a reference to 'one with a sanded (tired) umbrella' (10.819; *U* 242). It is not unusual for the narrator to attribute to an object the feelings of a character (who could well be 'tired'), but here I submit that the conjunction of 'sanded' and 'tired' spoils the flow of the phrase and adds nothing that is not already available in the word 'trudged' describing the women's walk. I suggest that, if Joyce had been really serious about this addition, he would have added a comma after 'sanded.' It seems likely that he weighed a choice of two words and came down on the side of 'sanded' which reenforces the Proteus reference, and that he discarded the unnecessary qualifier. In this instance, the absence of witnesses does not speak for the inclusion of a dubious term.

Among the sensual highpoints of Sirens is the image of a music-mesmerised Lydia massaging (masturbating) the 'smooth jutting beerpull.' The older version reads, '. . over the polished knob . . . her thumb and finger passed in pity: passed, repassed and, gently touching, then slid so smoothly, slowly down, a cool firm white enamel baton protruding through their sliding ring' (*U* 286). The mimesis to which sound and sense contribute is complete. From tC, Gabler picks up and accepts the change 'reposed' (11.1115) for 'repassed.' Arguments can be made for either version, but I would suggest that the effect of reposing is captured by 'gently touching,' but the effect of repeated erotic movement is lost with 'reposed'.

Less controversial is the substitution of 'Hand (12.612) for

'Hard' (*U* 309) in the description of the executioner in 'Cyclops': 'Hard (Hand) by the block stood the grim figure . . .' Joyce at his most exotic would be unlikely to speak of someone standing *hand by* anything. It is relatively easy to be deceived by the similarity between the Joycean r and n. One may wonder, however, why the editor also thought it right to separate rather than join the usually hyphenated 'terra' and 'cotta' on the same page (12.621; *U* 309) or why he chose to add an apostrophe to the name 'O'Molloys' in the sentence beginning 'And lo, there entered one of the clan of the O'Molloy(')s . . .' (12.1008; *U* 319). The effect of that apostrophe is to make the name twice possessive. An equal but opposite error occurs when an ' 's' is deleted from 'what's' in the sentence, ' – A dishonoured wife, says the citizen, that's what's (what) the cause of all our misfortunes' (12.1163–64; *U* 324). Once again the 1932 edition is right; Joyce and the citizen meant 'that is what is the cause.'

The new edition frequently succeeds in reordering passages, but it also, on occasion, fails in the attempt. Thus, we have the following sequence which I reproduce in its old and new versions:

—Is he a jew or a gentile or a holy Roman or a swaddler or what the hell is he? says Ned. Or who is he? No offence, Crofton.
    —We don't want him, says Crofter the Orangeman or presbyterian.
    —Who is Junius? says J.J.
    —He's a perverted jew, says Martin . . . (*U* 337)

—Is he a jew or a gentile or a holy Roman or a swaddler or what the hell is he? says Ned. Or who is he? No offence, Crofton.
—Who is Junius? says J.J.
—We don't want him, says Crofter the Orangeman or presbyterian.
—He's a perverted jew, says Martin . . . (12.1631–35)

Clearly, the 'restored' order violates the logic of the conversation by separating question from response twice. Granting that this could occur in a conversation, I would suggest that, at this point in this one, it need not.

Having completed this *sampler* from my annotations, I can only reiterate my sense that, while it is a genuine and even a major contribution to Joyce scholarship, the Gabler edition in its present form should not serve as the trade edition. Instead, it should serve as a working document from which a better (if not a perfect or definitive) trade edition can be produced. Since so many of Gabler's decisions have, of necessity, been subjective and critical, we should not accept his text without serious question as the *word* of Joyce. After all, the author would under no circumstances have seen and cannot be said to have produced the postulated edition derived as it is from sources which he may even have rejected as well as forgotten or overlooked. An improved reading should provide readers with a text that contains as few inconsistencies and absurdities as possible, that violates Joyce's apparent principles as little as possible, that clears up as many confusions as possible, and that does not introduce new errors. To use the editor's own words, the new reading text should be 'offered to all lovers of Joyce for their enhanced enjoyment of *Ulysses*' (G viii).

In producing (generating?) his current reading text (and even his 'Synoptic' text), Hans Gabler has done at once too much and too little. By pushing our awareness of Joyce's procedures back beyond the admittedly corrupt printed versions to the typescripts and even at times the manuscripts, he has found reasons to introduce a great many fresh readings. But he has also introduced a quantity of fresh uncertainties and some errors. It seems obvious that the 1922 edition is not and should not be the standard, but when we go back to the available manuscripts, we have the problem of knowing where to stop and what to honour. What, finally, is the nature of authority? Must we accept the last available notation in Joyce's hand and reject the strong possibility that further changes were made in lost revisions or even by means other than Joyce's hand? Should an 'Historical Collation' list only changes in late drafts and selected editions? When, if ever, should awkward and unsatisfactory readings be accepted and how far must we go to protect the author from himself? Should we not be made privy to the reasoning behind so many subjectively-motivated alterations? Finally and most controversially, should we make an effort to correct obvious slips and inconsistencies? Should they not, at the very least, be footnoted or listed in an appendix? I suggest that this is the moment when these and other responsibilities must be faced especially since the Gabler edition has already gone so far in second-guessing the master.

The proposed trade edition will be suspect if it does not acknowledge the possibility that some of its prized witnesses, to use bibliographical language, could be unreliable, that there are real authority problems in the sources used in the editing of important chapters like Wandering Rocks, Sirens, Eumaeus, and even in the source of the new format of Circe. That is, it should accept its own fallibility or minimise the risk of fallibility. It should also reflect an awareness of the value of internal evidence and a critical sensibility measured against other critical sensibilities. Unfortunately, in its present form the 'new' *Ulysses* is flawed, the victim perhaps of its editor's natural (given the complex, frustrating, and frequently unrewarding nature of his task) zeal and even perhaps of his competence as a bibliographer and the temptation to become a textual legislator.[6]

RECONSTRUCTING *ULYSSES* IN A DECONSTRUCTIVE MODE

SUZETTE HENKE

Thanks to Hans Walter Gabler, we now have a 'definitive' version of the text of *Ulysses*. With the help of a computer and modern technology, Gabler has ostensibly 'righted' the multiple errors that have plagued Joyce scholars for more than sixty years. At last, the text of *Ulysses* is centred, pure and definitive. We can cast off the shackles of historical error, thumb our noses at that careless Dijon printer who never had the grace to learn the language he was printing, and take pleasure in knowing that we now know, at last, what Joyce always intended for us, as readers of *Ulysses*, to know through our confrontation with the text.

But what if we should decide, in a fit of pique, to cling tenaciously to the old version indelibly inscribed on our consciousnesses by the editors of Random House and Bodley Head? The question is playful, sceptical, and admittedly carnivalesque. While the world glories in textual epiphany and the computerised gift of a truth worthy of the Ithacan narrator, one can imagine a single reactionary reader closeting himself in the bowels of the Irish National Library and burning corrupt texts of *Ulysses*, along with himself, in a bibliophiliac *auto da fe*. Could this happen, in fact or in our imaginations? Is there, perhaps, a bit of this hind-sighted and self-blinded buffoon in every one of us who has taken the current text as 'truth' and must now revise his perceptions? Is it possible that some of us may feel like all those pious Catholics who revered the hagiographies of Saints Christopher and Philomena before they were so precipitously dethroned by the Vatican? The sainted and canonised text of *Ulysses* having reigned for half a century, has now been de-texted and dethroned.

Rather than answer these boldly rhetorical questions, I would like to cite, instead, an interview given by Kay Boyle in the 15 July 1984 issue of the *New York Times Book Review*.

86

Reconstructing Ulysses *in a Deconstructive Mode*

Describing her first meeting with James Joyce, Boyle reminisces: 'It must have been in 1927, and *Transition* was printing Joyce's "Work in Progress . . ." Joyce was at this party, and as usual the party was divided into two factions – Sylvia Beach and Joyce and Nora Joyce on one side of the room and Gertrude Stein and her cohorts and admirers on the other side of the room. They were not on speaking terms. And what I think is so amazing about it – their difference of opinion which caused them to be mortal enemies was a disagreement on the manner of the revolution of the word. Now, in one edition of "Being Geniuses," it said that they disagreed on the manner of the revolution of the "world" – they put an "l" in there. And I crossed it out in all the copies that I've been able to, but I can't imagine either Joyce or Gertrude Stein being interested in a revolution of the world' (32).

Kay Boyle was infuriated by an editorial error so like that made by the bleary-eyed Martha Clifford in *Ulysses*. Composing a flirtatious epistle to her 'naughty boy' and would-be lover Henry Flower, Martha piquantly declares: 'I called you naughty boy because I do not like that other world. Please tell me what is the real meaning of that word' (*U* 77). Was Kay Boyle aware of the delicious Joycean irony of the misprint she had found in *Being Geniuses Together*, the memoir that she and Robert McAlmon had 'co-authored'? Or was she simply irate that the 'manifesto' of *transition* was corrupted by careless typography?

And what about those fortunate enough to be reading one of the copies of the book already corrected by its author? They would certainly have the benefit of an almost Dadaist 'double vision,' as the automatic writing of faulty typography altered a text in such a way as to reproduce an error similar to the one purposefully and meaningfully inscribed in the pseudo-text of an epistolary discourse 'framed' by a larger, fabulated text and addressed to a fictitious character, Henry Flower, fabricated as a *dramatis persona* by a fictional character, Leopold Bloom, in order to give a fictitious dimension to a clandestine epistolary flirtation by translating the Hungarian name Virag literally and offering a metonymic surrogate for the 'real' self emerging as Judaic epic hero in the mimetic drama of Joyce's novel. Like her fictional predecessor Martha Clifford, Kay Boyle can insist that 'I do not like that other world.' And in so doing, she offers her reader a 'double text' centred on the world of words that Joyce himself revolutionised. Jung would identify a kind of unconscious, ironic synchronicity in the inverted slippage of the printerly error denounced by Boyle.

What I am trying to suggest is that the new, corrected and centred version of *Ulysses* gives contemporary readers a kind of deconstructed version of a palimpsest that re-creates all the errors and synchronicities introduced into the text by various 'careless' printers, editors, and copy-readers. Like children playing an infantile game of 'gossip,' we can enjoy all the inept transitions that corrupted Joyce's world of words and introduced gaps, slippages, and errors into the 'authorised' manuscript originally composed.

Some twentieth-century readers will, indeed, be loath to part with the *Ulysses* on which they have teethed their postmodern sensibilities. And so, the new version poses a deconstructive dilemma. By proposing a centred text, along with its historical variants, it allows us to reconstruct Joyce's work as a bricolage of 'correct' readings, along with historical and marginal emendations. The errors give us a supplementary pseudo-text, a discourse creeping into margins of memory and reader-response so long as the 'working' version of *Ulysses* continues to resonate in the memory of the pre-1984 Joycean. Demanding to be erased from memory, the corrupt text calls attention to itself by its very prominence in the history of critical interpretation. We will be forced to read *Ulysses* as we now confront Derrida's *Glas* – as a deconstructive, many-layered textual game of dialectical components. *Ulysses* becomes a lexical play field with infinite possibilities for joyous dissemination of the *sèmes* that compose its textual variants.

One thinks, for instance, of that 'word known to all men,' the name of 'love,' not definitively identified by Joyce scholars prior to the release of the 1984 canonical edition of *Ulysses*. Until that time, the unknown term constituted a perplexing textual aporia, a riddle that posed endless questions and wove its mysteries throughout the fabric of Joyce's epic. Must we now unweave the mystery and, like Homer's Penelope, begin our labours of love afresh, knowing that *ars amoris* announces itself at the centre of human consciousness? Not exactly.

Because solving the riddle, unwinding the skein of this tangled mystery, puts into play still further mysteries of textual interpretation.

Richard Ellmann was correct when, in *Ulysses on the Liffey*, he identified the 'word known to all men' as 'love'. It is a vocable that proves ineffable both for the ghost of May Dedalus and for Leopold Bloom, who can define the term only by a process of denegation, as 'the opposite of hatred.' Stephen Dedalus, confronting the ghost of his dead mother, begs: 'Tell me the word . . . The word known to all men' (*U* 581). But the emaciated corpse of May Dedalus cannot mouth the utterance that Stephen desires and she counsels, instead, piety and penitence: 'Prayer is all powerful. Prayer for the suffering souls in the Ursuline manual, and forty days' indulgence. Repent, Stephen' (*U* 581). 'Shite!' screams the outraged son, uttering another monosyllable more commonly known to contemporary truth-seekers frustrated by the enigmas of metaphysical obscurity. Perhaps May Dedalus does not know the 'word' in her current spectral reincarnation; or maybe '*Amor matris*, subjective and objective genitive, . . . the only true thing in life' (*U* 207) has faded from her ghostly consciousness. Or perhaps the 'word known to all men' has never, in fact, been known to women.

On the other hand, it is entirely possible that Stephen's earlier reminiscence, 'love, the word known to all men', was incorrect. The identification might simply have been the projection of male erotic need, or an articulation of desire for mother, muse, or lover – all the women Stephen would like to approach for solace and for inspiration.

Cheryl T. Herr, for instance, in an article entitled 'Theosophy, Guilt, and "That Word Known to All Men" in Joyce's *Ulysses*,' reminds us that Madame Helena Blavatsky identified the word known to all men as 'an unknown word equivalent to the true name of God . . . which identifies the "Unknowable Cause" of the universe' (*JJQ* 18.1 (Fall 1980) 49). Was Stephen acquainted with this particular aspect of theosophical tradition, which he satirises in Scylla and Charybdis by imagining necromancy and fraudulence in the 'Yogibogeybox in Dawson chambers. *Isis Unveiled* . . . The faithful hermetists await the light, ripe for chelaship' (*U* 191)?

Joyce might be suggesting, as well, that 'love' may simply be a 'word' and not a reality to the young, inexperienced and misogynist artist who 'knows' this ubiquitous monosyllable as a textual surface, a sign on the white field of a desiring consciousness, but not as a palpable and concrete experience. Stephen has 'known' women in the biblical sense, but love remains a word with which he is still unacquainted. He has not yet tested the joy of true 'knowledge' promised by the female figure that might interrupt his narcissistic reveries – just as Nora Barnacle stepped in to fill that gap in amorous knowledge for Jimmy Joyce on 16 June 1904. On the fateful date memorialised in *Ulysses*, Stephen Dedalus will meet Leopold Bloom and establish, through him, a different bond of filial love – one that might, eventually, inaugurate another kind of personal and artistic knowledge.

And so the answer to our speculations about the meaning of that word known to all men, provided by the 1984 corrected edition, only gives birth to other, more perplexing queries that riddle the text with multiple meanings and instigate further textual and lexical disseminations. In foregrounding the concept of love as the mysterious symbolic term known innately by all men, the new edition both solves the half-century riddle and opens up a free play of signifiers in this highly elusive and enigmatic novel.

'Love,' of course, in English and in most European languages, can have multiple, even contradictory, significations. The term can denote concepts of Eros or of Agape, *amor matris* or filial devotion; it may refer to a wide spectrum of meanings, from human copulation to that divine emanation with which the Son (Logos) perceives and loves God the Father and, in so doing, begets from all eternity the sacred, trinitarian figure of the Holy Spirit.

And, we might ask, does Stephen himself 'get it right'? Perhaps the 'word' is actually the Tetragrammaton, the sacred and ineffable name of YAHWEH, the unspeakable Hebrew signature that is 'known' to all men but never, in fact, uttered by the lips of the devout Jew. This identification would be closer to the Jewish and Kabbalistic lore that informs the text of both *Ulysses* and *Finnegans Wake* and forms a substructure of mythic 'knowledge' throughout the later canon.

The word known to all men remains, finally, veiled in mystery, as obscurely 'unknown' as it was before the revelations made possible by the 1984 text. Thus the new edition of *Ulysses* functions as a device for lexical dissemination and doubling, a source of endless delight to the quizzical reader who never loses sight of Joyce the pierrot artist laughing in carnivalesque mode and taking pleasure in the explosive heterogeneity initiated by the release of a definitive version of his multi-layered novel. One can appreciate the new edition as a landmark in Joyce studies, inaugurating a new era in the 'Nova Hibernia' of Joycean scriptural exegesis. But at some level, perhaps, one cannot help being 'of twosome twiminds' about the rich, epiphanic possibilities opened up by the new, computerised version of Joyce's blue book of Eccles.

DUBLIN 1904*

RICHARD M. KAIN

There's one day that all of us know – better than any day in our lives. In fact, few of us were alive then, more than eighty years ago. It was the middle of June – the 16th, to be exact. A warm day, with a thunderstorm in the evening. In Arnold Bennett's words, it was 'the dailiest day possible'. For this audience there's no need to describe 16 June 1904. It's the year that interests me. It was one of the most eventful in the Irish Revival. I'll explain. I confess that I'm an incurable romantic when it comes to talking about the Dublin of 1904. If the city is indeed 'Dear Dirty Dublin', I shall emphasize the Dear – and what better place to be romantic in than here in Monaco. I think of Wordsworth's lines about the French Revolution in *The Prelude*:

> Bliss it was in that dawn to be alive
> But to be young was very heaven!

To be young. In 1904 Joyce was twenty-two, and others were still in their thirties – Synge, A.E., and Yeats.

When I visited Ireland in 1948 – I too was in my thirties then – it was the lively Constantine Curran who first made me aware of the Dublin of 1904 – not only 16 June: Curran, vivacious and versatile, an art and drama critic, an expert on eighteenth-century architecture, and Registrar of the Supreme Court. In his eighties he published three books – the authoritative and beautiful *Dublin Decorative Plasterwork* (1967), *James Joyce Remembered* (1968), and his reminiscences, *Under the Receding Wave* (1970). He had been a lifelong friend of James Joyce, and one evening kept us until early morning as he read his file of Joyce letters, now at University College Dublin. Trams had long since stopped: he walked with us to the Shelbourne Hotel, conversing all the way, from Rathgar, several miles away.

* Professor Kain's talk was the first *formal* event in the programme: its main purpose was, in consequence, to set the scene of *Ulysses* in its original cultural context.

92

Dublin 1904

In 1948 Dublin was still an eighteenth-century city. Its lovely squares had not yet been disfigured by broken façades and the steel and glass structures that Dubliners appropriately call office blocks. The trams celebrated in *Ulysses* still held sway over traffic of drays, cycles, cabs, and occasional automobiles.

Curran pointed out that University College was not the 'day school of terrorised boys,' as Joyce described it in *Stephen Hero* (*SH* 232) but had among its students those who were to become leaders in the emerging nation.

I have never experienced such entertaining conversation as that at Curran's. Padraic Colum was there, gentle and musing, and his wife Mary, whose reminiscences (*Life and the Dream*, 1947) catch the spirit of the time.

Wilde once said to Yeats, 'We Irish are too poetical to be poets; we are a nation of brilliant failures, but we are the greatest talkers since the Greeks'. Oliver St John Gogarty attributed this to the climate:

We inhale the Atlantic vapours and they turn us into mystics, poets, politicians and unemployables with school-girl complexions.

He adds that by the time they reach England 'these vapours have lost their enervating and transforming powers'.[1]

Douglas Goldring describes a literary evening in 1916 in his anonymous *Dublin Explorations and Reflections by an Englishman* (1917), a book rather hard to find now. 'The atmosphere is at once novel and charming', he writes, with the faces 'all astonishingly expressive'. 'And what talk! It is not chatter, it is not gossip; it is Conversation' (166–67). Of George Russell, the poet-philosopher-economist, he exclaimed: 'Never have I encountered any great man so verbally dextrous with gigantic questions, so easily profound' (168). Yeats 'has always said memorable things, and on a diversity of subjects' (169–70). Goldring does observe that 'Depreciation, however – and depreciation of a particularly brilliant kind – has often struck me as being one of the characteristics of Dublin' (178). I have heard it said that an Irishman never wants to leave a party early, as he is sure he will become the next topic of conversation.

Dubliners have sharp memories for epigrams, and I recall discussions as to whether the conversational blue ribbon be bestowed on the Greek scholar Dodds, expert on Plotinus, or on Sarah Purser, the artist responsible for Sir Hugh Lane's gifts to the Municipal Art Gallery, and, who, at the age of 82, had persuaded the government to turn over to the gallery the fine mansion, Charlemont House.

My Irish friends had great respect for scholars – especially if they could claim Irish blood. They talked about Helen Waddell's translations of mediaeval lyrics (*The Wandering Scholars*, 1927), and about Robin Flower's work on early Irish verse (*The Irish Tradition*, 1947). There seemed to be little interest in the sagas that Yeats adapted to the stage in his seldom performed plays. Anecdotes were told – and retold. Yeats at the theatre, peering from the edge of the curtain to estimate the size of the audience, or A.E.'s picking up a book of his poems and rapidly sketching an Irish scene on the title page. George Moore was a master of gossip – and, appropriately enough, was the subject of gossip. When he changed the title of his reminiscences from *Ave Atque Vale* it was said that he might have thought '*Atque*' was the name of a Roman centurion. And that when he discovered the subjunctive he was so delighted that he determined to use it in everything he wrote. But he could give as well as receive. In *Hail and Farewell* he recalls a visit from Martyn and Yeats to discuss the Irish theatre: 'Edward great in girth as an owl . . . . blinking behind his glasses, and Yeats lank as a rook, a-dream in black silhouette' (*Ave*, 91). Henceforth the owl and the rook play their roles. Moore observes that the rook 'likes parlour magic', and the owl 'cathedral magic' (68). At a performance in the dingy Antient Concert Rooms Moore reflects that 'There is something melancholy in the spectacle of human beings enjoying themselves', and with Yeats 'listening reverentially to the sound of his verses', his black cloak and hair added 'to the melancholy of the entertainment' (99).

Moore had few good words for anyone. Exceptions were A. E., who was almost alarmed at his canonization, and Gogarty, then only a bit over thirty. Gogarty was hailed as 'the arch mocker, the author of all the jokes that enable us to live in Dublin' (*Salve*, 178). But even this arch mocker could be sentimental – at times. Though he detested de Valera's Ireland, and moved to America, he exclaimed: 'How I love the old town where every man is a potential idler, poet or friend!'[2] (He might have added: 'or enemy'.)

Joyce, another mocker, who thought Dublin a centre of paralysis, wrote to his brother:

It seems to me that I have been unnecessarily harsh. I have reproduced none of the attraction of the city . . . its ingenuous insularity and its hospitality . . . I have not been just to its beauty . . . (Ellmann 231.)

Shaw and Wilde are the best known wits, but at the time of my early visits to Dublin Gogarty led the pack. His talk was enriched by allusions to the classics and spiced with wit and malice. It reflected his versatile talents, as athlete, poet, surgeon, and raconteur. I remember his striding across a Connemara meadow, the shore far below gleaming in the sunlight, and the ocean in varying colours of green and amethyst. He marched on, in the face of Atlantic breezes, while I, about half his age, trotted alongside, trying to catch his words. All the while he was discoursing, and the tempo of his discourse matched his pace. We heard of the wreck of the Armada on the rugged coast, and of the half-legendary Grace O'Malley. Tags of Irish and Greek, of Swinburne and Yeats, salted his speech. A virile Oscar Wilde, he was incapable of saying anything dull. Something of his style is preserved in his books, and, though he now despised Joyce, in the character of Buck Mulligan.

Here are a few gems from his best book, *As I Was Going Down Sackville Street*:

Of contemporary Dublin:

This town will soon be another modern Athens, dirty and full of lawyers. (57)

Of a speech by Augustine Birrell:

He looked like an old headmaster come out of retirement . . . We had to wait on his words. So had he. (128)

I must get back to 1904. A comprehensive – and tedious – diary is that of Joseph Holloway. This master of the obvious attended everything that was going on in town, and then returned to his lodgings, so littered that one could hardly walk across a room. There he sat down to compile and index his never-ending manuscript diary, about two thousand words every day, some 25,000,000 words altogether. The editors Robert Hogan and Michael J. O'Neill have sifted through Holloway's 221 volumes. These 'Impressions of a Dublin Playgoer' remind me of a description of Gertrude Stein as 'a monument sitting on patience.' O'Casey called it 'an impossible pile of rubbish,' and thought its accession by the National Library 'another example of Eire's love of triviality.'[3] Padraic Colum was less severe, but did remark that Holloway had 'no real literary judgment.'[4] He had no style either, and yet is a valuable chronicler of the Irish scene for the first forty years of this century.

Something of interest occurred almost every month. During January Yeats was lecturing in the United States and Canada. Joseph Hone has described his public speaking:

His voice was musical, touched with melancholy, the tones rising and falling in a continuous flow of sound . . . His myopic gaze as he spoke was turned within, looking into the darkness . . . He seemed indeed to be discoursing with himself rather than to be persuading others, as his Miltonic periods flowed in unbroken rhythm.[5]

Many have remarked on this self-absorption and absent-mindedness. I once heard a college professor recall how he had taken Yeats for an afternoon drive through the New England countryside, pointing out the hills and lakes, only to discover the poet gazing into his lap.

In January Joyce wrote in his sister Mabel's school copybook an essay entitled 'A Portrait of the Artist.' He submitted it to John Eglinton, who was about to publish a journal, *Dana.* Eglinton later recalled:

The little magazine laboured through a year . . . It might have had a rare value now in the book market if I had been better advised one evening in the National Library, when Joyce came in with the manuscript . . . He observed me silently as I read, and when I handed it back to him with the timid observation that I did not care to publish what was to myself incomprehensible, he replaced it silently in his pocket.[6]

As for *Dana,* we'll get to that later. It does have something of the rare value that Eglinton suggested; I found a file only after a search of twenty years, and in the gilt-stamped pull-off box there is a receipt from Hodges-Figgis for fifty-three pounds, at,

I believe, a $2.80 pound, or $148. The shop has recently listed it for £160 (3 August 1985).

The Joyce essay is, of course, the germ of the novel, though most of the material was rejected after having been incorporated into *Stephen Hero*. The opening paragraph is an arresting manifesto for a new form of fiction which would convey the fluidity of consciousness. The prose is a bit heavy-going, or, in brother Stanislaus's dry remark in his diary, 'a little sententious and congested,' because 'He locks words of too great weight together constantly and they make the rhythm heavy' (entry of 31 August 1904).[7] Joyce begins:

The features of infancy are not commonly reproduced in the adolescent portrait for, so capricious are we, that we cannot or will not conceive the past in any other than its iron memorial aspect. Yet the past assuredly implies a fluid succession of presents . . . [8]

These words suggest a concept of Henri Bergson, then a lecturer at the Collège de France. Whether or not Joyce knew of Bergson, such concerns were in the air, or in Carl Becker's fine phrase, they were part of the climate of opinion. In fact, Stanislaus Joyce's diary expresses a similar idea a few months later, perhaps derived from discussions with his brother. Stanislaus speculates on 'thought succeeding thought without utterance, like harmonies in music' (172; 18 July 1904).

To return to the 'Portrait' essay. The first paragraph concludes with a description of ideal writers 'who seek through some art, by some process of the mind as yet untabulated, to liberate from the personalised lumps of matter that which is their individuating rhythm, the first or formal relation of their parts.' The resulting portrait will be 'not an identificative paper but rather the curve of an emotion.'[9]

Just twenty-two years old, Joyce had already become something of a celebrity in Dublin. Swaggering disdainfully he wore his threadbare clothes with élan, and was noteworthy alike for his high-flown ideals of art and his bohemian behaviour. He had had an article on Ibsen published in the distinguished *Fortnightly Review*, and had earned an item in the *Freeman's Journal* for his quite grandiloquent paper on the Irish poet Mangan, given at a session of the college Literary and Historical Society. The newspaper had commented that it 'was generally agreed to have been the best paper ever read before the society' (Ellmann 96).

I have two stories about the *Fortnightly Review* essay. I was told by an elderly librarian that he recalled Joyce's coming into the National Library almost every day to ask whether the April issue had arrived. Then too, a somewhat unscrupulous book dealer once told me he had bought a file of the *Review*, about forty volumes as I recall, in order to get the Joyce item. I was amazed at such an extensive purchase, but he reassured me that it was no problem. He had sold the nineteenth-century run in one sale, and the twentieth-century run in another, conveniently keeping out the 1900 volume, in which appeared 'Ibsen's New Drama,' by James A. Joyce. James A. Joyce was then eighteen.

A volume could be compiled of reminiscences about this artist as a young man. My favourite is told by Oliver St John Gogarty:

Early one day we wandered off in the direction of the city. We were certainly at a loss, a loss for fares or for the subsequent entertainment . . .

By which, of course, Gogarty means drinks at the 'Ship' in Abbey Street. The tale continues:

Joyce saw him first, a tall figure coming rapidly in our direction. I looked and recognized 'old Yeats,' the father of the bard. He was out for his morning constitutional. As he came nearer he appeared an uninviting figure, old, lean and very tall. His dark eyes burned brightly under shaggy eyebrows. 'It is your turn,' Joyce whispered. 'For what?' I asked. 'To touch.' Reluctantly, and with trepidation, I spoke to the old man, whom I hardly knew. 'Good morning, Mr. Yeats, would you be so good as to lend us two shillings?' Savagely the old man eyed me and my companion. He looked from one to the other. At last he broke out: 'Certainly not,' he said. 'In the first place I have no money; and if I had it and lent it to you, you and your friend would spend it on drink.' He snorted. Joyce advanced and spoke gravely. 'We cannot speak about that which is not.' But old Yeats had gone off rapidly. 'You see,' said Joyce, still in a philosophical mood, 'the razor of Occam forbids the introduction of superfluous arguments. When he said that he had no money that was enough. He had no right to discuss the possible use of the nonexistent.'[10]

The year 1904 was an *annus mirabilis* for Joyce. Six of his lyrics were printed – in *Dana*, and the English *Saturday*

Review, *Speaker*, and *The Venture*, the last his first appearance in a book. Three of the *Dubliners* stories were published in the *Irish Homestead*. And, of course, 16 June, the elopement with Nora Barnacle, and their departure from Ireland, marked by the vituperative doggerel verse, 'The Holy Office.'

On 25 February the most widely known of all Irish plays was produced – Synge's *Riders to the Sea*. Holloway recorded his impressions:

Mr. Synge has given us an intensely sad . . . picture of the lives of the humble dwellers on an isle of the West . . . and, as it was interpreted with rare naturalness and sincerity, it held the interest of the audience in a marvellous way. This was a triumph of art, for the players as well as for the dramatist . . . and a profound impression was created . . .

Miss Honor Lavelle as the half-demented, wholly-distracted old 'Maurya' gave an uncanny rendering of the part . . . and was most impressive in the scene with her dead son . . . The author was called at the end and very heartily applauded.

Holloway saw a second performance the next day, and reported that 'The audience was so deeply moved by the tragic gloom of the terrible scene on which the curtains close in, that it could not applaud' (35). The play retains its power, as I experienced this winter at a performance of the Vaughan Williams opera, with its evocative music.

The Synge of Holloway's diary is quite different from Yeats's characterization of him as a solitary, completely self-absorbed person. Despite Holloway's distaste for most of the plays, which reflected public opinion of the time, Holloway found him 'a gentle and lovable man' (125) and wrote of his 'chats' – a favourite word – with him, and of Synge's 'friendly chat' with W. J. Lawrence, who also had objected to the author's disregard of popular taste. Another glimpse: during a rehearsal, 'Mr. J. B. Yeats sketched J. M. Synge in the dressing room. He sketched on the corner of a table, and Synge rested against the back of a chair' (50). This is undoubtedly the often printed drawing. The elder Yeats had been doing portraits and sketches of prominent Dubliners – always intermittently, as he was a perfectionist; and an incorrigible conversationalist.

Important exhibitions were held. In May, Hugh Lane,

Markievicz, later one of the 1916 patriots, and George Russell. Holloway was fascinated by 'the strange, misty, almost uncanny quality' of Russell, remarks that could apply equally to his verse.

Most ambitious – and later controversial – was the showing of about 300 works of art, planned by Lane to form the nucleus of a municipal gallery. Suspicions arose, of expense, and of Lane's commission, but twenty-five works were donated, though many of the best – by Corot, Courbet, Manet, Monet, and above all, Renoir – remained in Lane's hands until his death on the *Lusitania* in 1915. His unwitnessed bequest to Dublin was disputed by the Tate Gallery, which kept thirty-nine paintings until a compromise was reached in 1959, when an alternating loan programme was established. In 1904 J. B. Yeats, Russell, and George Moore lectured on the exhibits. Holloway thought Moore interesting, but his delivery 'distinctly monotonous,' as 'he plumped for French art, "in contrast with which the English Academy has fallen to the level of Madame Tussaud's" ' (48).

In March Yeats returned from his American tour, which, it is to be hoped, will be documented by some enterprising scholar. Holloway is most amusing in his annoyance at Yeats as a play director. 'The great Yeats, by his interruptions every minute, proved himself an impossible man to rehearse before,' he notes once (39). At another time:

A more irritating play producer never directed a rehearsal. He's ever flitting about and interrupting the players . . . showing them by illustrating how he wishes it done, droningly reading the passage and that in monotonous preachy sing-song, or climbing up a ladder on to the stage and pacing the boards as he would have the players do.

(45; 31 October)

There was also a long argument with the patron, Annie Horniman, who had designed fire-engine red costumes for the kings in one play. Yeats thought they looked like 'extinguishers,' or 'Father Christmas,' but Miss Horniman was adamant. However, 'After much putting on and taking off, and an abundance of plain speaking . . . a compromise was arrived at . . . and the red-clad kings were allowed to carry their cloaks on their arms, though Miss Horniman was of opinion that the red unrelieved, somewhat marred the colour scheme she had intended' (49–50).

More serious than colour schemes were personality conflicts in the theatre group, and attacks by those who felt the plays unflattering to the Irish people. Arthur Griffith's periodical, *The United Irishman*, and one Frank Hugh O'Donnell led the offensive. O'Donnell had circulated a diatribe, *Souls for Gold*, against the opening programme of 1899, and in 1904 he followed with the pamphlet, *The Stage Irishman of the Pseudo-Celtic Revival*. Another quarrel arose when some actors left to perform at the Louisiana Purchase Exposition in St Louis. But the second English tour in March had been a success.

In the spring there appeared a small grey bound volume, with a labelled title:

NEW SONGS. A LYRIC SELECTION MADE BY A.E. FROM POEMS BY PADRAIC COLUM, EVA GORE-BOOTH, THOMAS KEOHLER, ALICE MILLIGAN, SUSAN MITCHELL, SEUMAS O'SULLIVAN, GEORGE ROBERTS, AND ELLA YOUNG.

There is a woodcut frontispiece, 'THE PLOUGHER DRAWN BY JACK B. YEATS,' and the first poem, 'A Portrait (*A Poor scholar in the Forties*)' by Padraic Colum concludes with the classical hedge-master's defence that the Latin and Greek he teaches might leave

> Years hence in rustic speech, a phrase,
> As in wild earth a Grecian vase.

Note that Joyce is not represented. The book is mentioned in *Ulysses* as forthcoming only. Is this a case of wishful thinking? One bit of evidence, revealed in the new Synoptic Edition of *Ulysses*: Joyce's original wording had been that A.E. 'has gathered' the verses; this was changed, in the *Little Review* printing and the first edition, to 'is gathering' (9.290), as though the book had not yet been published.

New Songs was reviewed by Gogarty in the first issue of *Dana*, which, you remember, rejected Joyce's 'Portrait of the Artist'. With the exception of Colum's 'A Drover' and Seumas O'Sullivan's 'The Twilight People' Gogarty found in the volume 'a perfection which belongs to the conservatory, an

101

artificial perfection.'[11] *Dana* was subtitled '*An Irish Magazine of Independent Thought*' and the contributions of the two editors, Eglinton and Frederick Ryan, stress the importance of Irish independence from political and religious pressures. The twelve issues printed poems by A.E., O'Sullivan, Gogarty, and Joyce.

It was Russell's edition of *New Songs* that evoked the often-quoted words of Yeats: 'Let us have no emotions, however abstract, in which there is not an athletic joy'. Yeats wrote to A.E., apologising for some slighting remark he had apparently quoted from Lady Gregory. He explained that 'Some of the poems I will probably underrate . . . because the dominant mood in many of them is one I have fought in myself', that is, 'sentiment and sentimental beauty.'[12]

I have a theory about *Ulysses*. Unusual that, isn't it? This is no earth-shaking interpretation of the whole book, but a comment on one of my favourite episodes, the discussion of Shakespeare in that little librarian's office adjoining the reading room. It is simply this. Since Dedalus was not invited to George Moore's that evening, as were the others, Joyce may have intended to top Moore's celebrated monologues. Stephen is very conscious that he is putting on a show. 'Unsheathe your dagger definitions' (9.84) he reflects, at the time when Plato and Aristotle are mentioned. And, as he recreates that June day when *Hamlet* was first presented, he congratulates himself to himself on his own performance: 'Local colour. Work in all you know. Make them accomplices' (9.158). Then, a moment later: 'Composition of place. Ignatius Loyola, make haste to help me!' (9.163). Or, more clearly: 'I think you're getting on quite nicely. Just mix up a mixture of theolologicophilolological' (9.761–62). He coaches himself in Latin rhetorical terms: '*Amplius. Adhuc. Iterum. Postea*' (9.848). (In English: Furthermore. Heretofore. Again. Hereafter.) There's no doubt that Stephen admires his work. He urges himself to 'See this. Remember' (9.294). And, as they leave: 'One day in the national library we had a discussion' (9.1108).

I must emphasize. Stephen is putting on a show. And he knows it. He admits that he doesn't believe his own theory. After all, conversation is an art not to be taken seriously. At least, not in the Dublin of 1904. The Synoptic Edition affords some insights into the passages just quoted. After Stephen's 'dagger definitions' observation, Joyce added to the Rosenbach manuscript the witty definition, 'Horseness is the whatness of allhorse,' long a favourite of mine. And he also improved on the Rosenbach 'theololigal philolol,' two words, with the jawbreaking *Finnegans Wake* word – here I need a blackboard – 'theolo' 'logico' 'philo' 'lo' 'logical,' which adds the sense of 'logical' to both theology and philology. In the list of rhetorical terms, *'Iterum'* replaces *'Rursus.'*

A personal note. My own first taste of editorial collation – task and tedium – make me deeply respectful of the effort involved in the Synoptic Edition. In 1947 I read a paper at the Modern Language Association annual meeting, in which I compared the texts of *Ulysses* in *The Little Review* and in the first edition. The Rosenbach text and Joyce manuscripts were then not available. In fact my copy of Sylvia Beach's

CATALOGUE

OF A

COLLECTION CONTAINING

MANUSCRIPTS & RARE EDITIONS OF JAMES JOYCE . . .

lists as item 6:

A selection of typescript pages with autograph corrections by the Author, from 5 to 15 lines per page.

A note follows:

These pages may be acquired separately by those who might like to enrich their copy of 'Ulysses' with a little manuscript of Joyce.

How many odd pages might have been sold, and how many might sometime turn up in old copies of *Ulysses*?

Joyce could share Stephen's pride in the discourse. In my opinion, it is one of the richest episodes. Within the framework of Shakespeare interpretation it presents Stephen's psychological tensions, and widens to speculations on the artist as creator and on Christological theories.

Shakespeare was the object of considerable discussion at the time.[13] The comprehensive biographies of Brandes and Lee had appeared in 1898, and Frank Harris was publishing articles in the *Saturday Review.* In 1899 Oscar Wilde wrote that 'Harris is upstairs thinking about Shakespeare at the top of his voice.'

Wilde himself was but one of many Irishmen concerned with Shakespeare. Others, mentioned in *Ulysses*, were Dowden, Madden, Barton, Shaw, and 'your dean of studies,' that is, Father Darlington, who had published in *The New Ireland Review*,[14] and who may have mentioned the then recently discovered diary of Thomas Platter, which refers to the actors' costumes.[15]

Extant are four Joyce manuscripts on the subject of Elizabethan drama: 'Shakespeare,' 'The English Drama,' 'Shakespeare's Dates,' and about sixty untitled sheets, undoubtedly materials for the lectures of 1912 and 1913 in Trieste.[16] As late as 1918 Joyce sent a list of questions to Karl Bleibtreu, advocate of the Earl of Rutland's authorship.[17]

Back in 1904 Joyce had undoubtedly held forth on *Hamlet*, for, as John Eglinton remarks in *Irish Literary Portraits*, 'the present writer experiences a twinge of recollection of things actually said.' At another point he questions, 'Dost thou remember these things, O Joyce, thou man of meticulous remembrance?'[18]

Eglinton is somewhat ridiculed in the chapter, largely because his name, William K. Magee, and his pen name, John Eglinton, gave scope to Joyce's love of word play. Just as Buck Mulligan becomes Monk (9.773), Cuck (9.1025), or Puck (9.1125), so Eglinton is transposed to littlejohn, and in his various roles to *Eglintonus Chronolologus* (9.811), Judge (9.1017), or, in view of his advocacy of Continental writers, John Eclecticon (9.1070). In *Finnegans Wake* style he is the Chinese 'Chin Chon Eg Lin Ton' (9.1129). But most elaborate of all are the successive renderings of his name, as found in the Synoptic Edition. First, in upper and lower case letters, then in capitals run together – JOHNEGLINTON – thirdly, using part of his last name elided – MAGEEGLINTON, and finally, MAGEEGLINJOHN (9.900)

Joyce not only bettered Moore's evening, but by virtue of writing and rewriting he bettered himself. Might he not be termed one of the greatest rewriters? The Synoptic Edition shows that in addition to the celebrated omission of the lines about love, he made significant revisions after *The Little Review* version.

To *The Little Review* text Joyce added a few more Elizabethanisms – among them 'bloodboltered' (9.133, from *Macbeth*), '*limbo patrum*' (9.150, from *Henry VIII*), 'meacock' (9.938, from *The Taming of the Shrew*), 'How now, sirrah' (9.192), 'Go to' (9.195), and 'Marry' (9.193). A more extended insert is self congratulation. Stephen speaks of Saint Thomas, 'whose gorebellied works I enjoy reading in the original' (9.778–79). Another point of pride is Stephen's studying at the old Marsh's Library, near St Patrick's Cathedral. In *Stephen Hero* Joyce refers to Stephen's going there 'a few times in the week' (*SH* 176) which in Proteus becomes a meditation on 'the stagnant bay of Marsh's library where you read the fading prophecies of Joachim Abbas' (3.107–08). A librarian there once delighted in showing me that Joyce had signed the readers' book only twice!

During the summer, Holloway saw Joyce, and described him with more perception than usual. At the home of the newly-married Cousins family, on 8 June, he writes:

Mr. Joyce – a mysterious kind of youth with weird penetrating eyes (which he frequently shades with his hands) and a half-bashful, far-away, wistful expression on his face – sang some dainty ballads most artistically and pleasingly, some to his own accompaniment. As he sings, he sways his head from side to side to add to the soulfulness of his rendering. He is a strange boy; I cannot fathom him. (40)

Another glimpse of Joyce is given by Margaret Cousins in the unusual dual autobiography of herself and her husband James, *We Two Together* (1950), a scarce book published in India. She writes:

James Joyce was a favourite of mine though he was reputed to be a 'bad boy.' I delighted in his lovely tenor voice especially when I accompanied some of his Irish songs with nobody but ourselves to hear in our little drawing room. Padraic Colum came, and others.
(106)

In late August Joyce sang on a programme of the Irish Revival Industries Show. Holloway remarked that John McCormack, then at the outset of his career, was not so impressive as Joyce. Of the famous singer, Holloway says, 'This young vocalist is gifted by nature with a remarkably strong, pleasing tenor voice, but he has no idea how to use it, nor a scrap of emotionalism in his rendering.' In contrast, 'Mr. James A. Joyce possesses a light tenor voice which he is inclined to force on the high notes, and he sang with artistic emotionalism' (43). According to Richard Ellmann, *The Freeman's Journal* wrote that Joyce 'sang charmingly.' However, 'Mr. J. F. McCormack (*sic*) was the hero of the evening' (Ellmann 168n).

Despite the charming tenor voice, and the prospective elopement with Nora Barnacle, Joyce revealed his deep-seated paranoia in a pasquinade, the doggerel verse of 'The Holy Office.' The lampoon was apparently first printed in Dublin, but the printer was not paid, and only a second Continental printing survives. Joyce casts himself as the defiant artist hero; his enemies the Irish contemporaries, Yeats, Russell, Lady Gregory, Gogarty, Moore, Synge, and others.

The 'motley crew' that Joyce affected to despise was not doing too badly in 1904. Douglas Hyde's translations of *The Love Songs of Connacht* were published by the Dun Emer Press, later the Cuala Press, presided over by Yeats's sister Elizabeth. Mulligan in *Ulysses* refers to a 1903 volume as 'printed by the weird sisters' (1.367), undoubtedly alluding not only to the witches in *Macbeth* but also to the fact that the Irish Industries which the Yeats sisters initiated was in the locality of Dundrum, the site of the Central Lunatic Asylum.

Lady Gregory's *Gods and Fighting Men* was published, and Arthur Griffith's articles on 'The Resurrection of Hungary' were issued in a booklet. Griffith recounted the establishment of the Austro-Hungarian dual monarchy in 1867, a possible solution for Ireland. There was also an Irish dictionary by Father Patrick Dineen.

Leopold Bloom reportedly gave Griffith the idea for Sinn Fein (12.1574 and 12.1624–27), and Father Dineen appears in the National Library (9.967). Joyce didn't miss much, even if it involved anachronism, as in Mulligan's reference to the Abbey Theatre (9.1131).[19] A.E. published *The Divine Vision and Other Poems*, and it may not be amiss to observe that most of the entries in Stanislaus Joyce's Dublin diary are dated in 1904.

Yeats was busy as usual, with various articles, an issue of the theatre magazine *Samhain*, and, most interestingly, a reprint of his 1897 limited edition of esoteric tales, *The Tables*

of the Law/The Adoration of the Magi. Joyce's 1904 'Portrait
of the Artist' essay describes Joachim Abbas, mentioned by
Yeats, as one of the 'hierarchs of initiation'[20] that infatuated
the young writer. Stephen Hero finds a copy of the Yeats book
on a bookcart, 'every word of which he remembered' (*SH* 177),
and recited to Lynch. Yeats prefaced this 1904 reprint with a
note:

I do not think I should have reprinted them had I not met a young man
in Ireland the other day, who liked them very much and nothing else
that I have written.

We can all guess the identity of that young man, so adept at
insults.

On 27 December the Abbey Theatre opened, to enjoy almost
a half century as one of the best known theatres in the world.
It caught fire in 1951, and was subsequently replaced by a
larger, modern structure. Some Dubliners claim that it could
have been restored; others elaborate tales of the fire. In any
case, a notable landmark was lost. As architect, the diarist
Joseph Holloway had done a good job of converting two old
buildings into an intimate theatre. Richard Fallis has written
the best description I have read:

The theater-goer entered through a small vestibule which with its
paneling and stained-glass windows looked more like the anteroom to
a Presbyterian church than a theater.[21]

Fallis does not mention the narrow, dimly lighted lobby with
its portraits, which, I believe, were all rescued. To continue
with the description:

In the theater itself were, downstairs, rows of plain wooden theater-
seats, pit and stalls, and upstairs, a rather narrow horseshoe-shaped
balcony. Altogether, the room would hold about 500 patrons. The
stage was about forty feet wide and about sixteen feet deep.

A good picture of the interior is in the *Short History of Anglo-
Irish Literature* (1982), by Roger McHugh and Maurice
Harmon.

For Holloway 'The night was a memorable one, and the
house was thronged and genuinely enthusiastic.' The first play
was Yeats's *On Baile's Strand*, which Holloway thought
'excellently played,' with special mention of Frank J. Fay, 'the

music of whose speech and the beauty of whose diction, together with the natural dramatic effectiveness of his acting, excited all to admiration.' As for *Cathleen ni Houlihan*, Maire nic Shiubhlaigh's presentation was superb:

Of all the 'Cathleens' I have seen, this was the truest embodiment. The sorrows of centuries were on her brow and in her eye, and her words pierced the heart . . .

'A merry, homely, little farce by Lady Gregory, *Spreading the News*, caught on at once.'

Though the small second-night audience was alarming, Holloway concluded that

The opening of the Abbey Theatre was the most momentous event of the year in Dublin to my mind. History may come of it! Who can tell! (51)

When I remember Gogarty and Colum and O'Sullivan, and Curran, and recall Curran's accounts of Arthur Clery, Thomas Kettle, and others of that college generation, I endorse Eglinton's opinion that 'Dublin was certainly at this moment a centre of vigorous potentialities.' He mentions the language movement, the theatre, and 'numerous young writers, and even more numerous talkers, of incalculable individuality.' University College undergraduates, he remarks, with 'their ribalt wit and reckless manner of life, their interest in everything new in literature and philosophy . . . far surpassed the students of Trinity College.'[22]

Even Joyce, in the persona of Stephen Hero, admits that

It must not be supposed that the popular University of Ireland lacked an intelligent centre. Outside the compact body of national revivalists there were here and there students who had certain ideas of their own and were more or less tolerated by their fellows. (*SH* 38–39)

Joyce's more typical stance as 'Unfellowed, friendless, and alone' reminds me of my father's favourite gibe about Theodore Roosevelt. Roosevelt had made such political capital of his leading the Rough Riders against the Spanish in Cuba that he was caricatured as storming the enemy single-handed. As I recall the phrase, it was 'Alone on San Juan Hill,' but my memory, or my father's, may be faulty. I have found only a variant, Mr Dooley's 'Alone in Cubia.' Roosevelt and Finley Peter Dunne later became friends.

Would Joyce, master of allusion, be embarrassed by a reference to Mr Dooley? And what would he think if he knew that 'Unfellowed, friendless, and alone' almost echoes 'unfriended, unprotected, and alone,' the lament of the 'modern major general' in *The Pirates of Penzance*?

I would like to share with you a passage by James Stephens. Though published a bit later than 1904, it catches the spirit of the city, and anticipates Joyce's description of Dublin streets. Stephens describes Nassau Street corner, where Bloom, in *Ulysses*, after seeing 'beard and bicycle' (8.523–24), that is, the poet A.E., 'stood before the window of Yeates and Son, pricing the field glasses.' Yeates and Son were still in business there in 1948. Here, in *The Charwoman's Daughter* (1912), is Stephens, who loved the cityscape as much as did Joyce:

Perhaps this point is the most interesting place in Dublin. Up one vista Grafton Street with its glittering shops stretches, or rather winds, to the St. Stephen's Green Park . . . On the left Nassau Street, broad and clean . . . runs away to Merrion Square, and on with a broad ease to Blackrock and Kingstown and the sea. On the right hand Suffolk Street, reserved and shy, twists on to St. Andrew's Church . . . At the back of the crossing Grafton Street continues again for a little distance down to Trinity College . . . skirting the Bank of Ireland, and on to the River Liffey . . .

To the point where these places meet, and where the policeman stands, all the traffic of Dublin converges in a constant stream. The trams hurrying to Terenure, or Donnybrook, or Dalkey flash around this corner; the doctors who, in these degenerate days, concentrate in Merrion Square, fly up here in carriages and motor cars, the vans of the great firms in Grafton and O'Connell Streets . . . never cease their exuberant progress . . . and from all sides the vehicles and pedestrians, the bicycles and motor bicycles, the trams and the outside cars rush to the solitary policeman, who directs them all with his severe but tolerant eye.[23]

A great year, 1904. But the promise of those days was not entirely fulfilled. John Eglinton, looking back from the thirties, speculated that Ireland had once seemed 'on the point of some decisive transformation.' He asked:

What then, was wanting to this movement? for it has passed away, leaving Ireland more intensely what it has always been . . .[24]

His bitter answer was:

It was not in the interest of the constituted spiritual authorities that such a dream should ever be realised: a new movement of the human mind in Ireland was precisely what was feared.[25]

Eglinton, moving to England after the formation of the Free State, was neither first nor last of Irish exiles. In his generation, Joyce led the way, then Moore, later Stephens and O'Casey and Gogarty. In the end, even A.E. And Yeats was a bird of passage – London, Coole Park, Dublin . . .

With the exceptions of Yeats and Joyce and O'Casey, the major works of the Revival had appeared before 1916. In fact, few literary movements continue for more than a generation. Eglinton himself admits that 'The great literary period of Greece, England, Spain, did not last much longer' than 'about a quarter of a century.'[26]

Dublin in 1904 was a time of high hopes, lively controversy, and genuine achievement.

ITALICS IN *ULYSSES*

CARLA MARENGO VAGLIO

> On his pinksir's postern . . . had been nailed an inkedup name and
> title, inscribed in the national cursives, accelerated, regressive,
> filiform, turreted and envenomoloped in piggotry . . .
>
> *(FW* 099.16–19)

The existence and use of italics have their origin, even
etymologically, in the types used by Aldus Manutius for his
edition of Virgil in Venice in 1501. Their particular graphic
form, 'adapted for the cursive writing of the 15th Century',
sends us back though, to handwriting. The story of writing and
calligraphy and that of printing seem to be indissolubly yoked
together in the practice and use of italics. The connexion with
the more general term *cursive* is always in the background.

Being a case of fragmentariness 'frankly' exhibited, italics
ideally lend themselves to an assessment of the literary word
as modified and conditioned by the historical situation and
conventions along which it operates. On the one hand, James
Joyce is quite conscious of the fact that each and every sign has
been fully exploited and somehow fixed in a given role, and is
therefore in no need of a writer:

So why, pray, sign anything as long as every word, letter, penstroke,
paperspace is a perfect signature of its own?

(FW 115.06–08)

On the other hand, he tries to impress his own signature
despite the many codifications, and to build the space for his
own work in a tradition where every form has already been
fully exploited. What is 'orthodox' and codified is
diametrically opposed to what is self-made. Carried on at
length and with consistency, the device corresponds in every
sense to the creation of an internal double order of discourse
that can both disrupt and integrate the main stream of
meaning. Joyce is well aware of the differential that opposes
roman type to italic type, and of the possibilities that are
offered to the writer in order to shape the modes of fruition and

111

reading of his text. Within this system, what is upright is opposed to what is slanted, what is massive and rocky is contrasted with what is fluid and fragile, what is spaced and highly formalized clashes with what is cursory and seems to have a precarious existence. For Joyce, the freedom of speech becomes one with the freedom of speed of discourse – 'I am all of me for freedom of speed' (*FW* 448.16–17). The different speeds in writing – 'Write me your essayes, my vocational scholars, but corsorily, dipping your nose in it' (*FW* 447.06–08) – qualitatively determine different speeds in reading.

Joyce is also aware of the symbolical implications of the two graphic shapes: to the area of italics belongs all that is arbitrary, idiosyncratic and original, all that does not ask for formal recognition, but springs directly from the author's private knowledge and culture, from *his* jottings down, from *his* set of quotations, originating in unruly passions and fits of enthusiasm. It is *cursive* in that it allows for curses – 'the innocent exhibitionism of those frank yet capricious underlinings' (*FW* 121.19–20). To the area of roman type belongs all that assumes a public voice, all that has an air of unquestionable solidity, in a word, all that is 'textual'.

But Joyce is always bent on the problem of the inner dialogism of language as one of the more stimulating and fruitful subjects of reflection. Thus, the act of appropriation, which the quotation in italics betrays, is always shown to be an act of distortion and misappropriation. Therefore, the two modes that are so neatly separated in the graphic medium are continuously blurred and blended in the actual practice of writing. No distance, no spaces, no formally binding characters are allowed to nest within the work that interrogates itself endlessly. That is the reason why inverted commas, as a way of distancing, of expressing a reserve, as a presumption of quoting the 'actual' words, are not used. 'Being tantamount to inferring from the nonpresence of inverted commas (sometimes called quotation marks) on any page that its author was always constitutionally incapable of mis-appropriating the spoken words of others' (*FW* 108.33–36), italics have absorbed and fully exploited the various techniques of the quotation process. If Joyce has to make a choice between quotation and transposition, he will always

112

choose transposition, in other words, misquotation, corruption, dislocation, or mimetic rendering. From his own point of view, it is the nature of language itself, with its inner stratifications and various directionalities, that authorizes this faith in transposition as opposed to quotation.

The Joycean text is one in which its surface, its outward aspect, should not be taken for granted and accepted at face value: the meaning of words too is not to be assumed literally and at first sight, or not only so. Concurrently, such a text makes a clear appeal for trustworthiness in its graphic, visual, and pictorial shape and dimension. Given the plurilingualism of Joyce's text in which the word emerges as semantically boosted by various clashing implications, italics are a borderline case: they cannot be dismissed as 'accidence', such as punctuation, spelling, capitalization, hyphenation, all of which are deeply rooted in typographical conventions. They are, on the contrary, signals, or demarcation signs, having a high meaning potential, and revealing a lot about authorial stance, perspective, and degree of intentionality in stylistic rendering. While showing the text to be heterogeneous and fragmentary, stopping linear sequels, continuously activating a *trompe l'oeil* effect, italics tend to erect a system of signification materialized in a continuous string, which is fully actuated through their interaction and ideal conglomeration despite the distance at which they occur in the text. No better definition of italics can be attempted than 'changeably meaning vocable scriptsigns' (*FW* 118.27–28). They are a graphic shape that has to be spelled out, and in which ear and eye are totally engaged: 'what can't be coded can be decorded if an ear aye sieze what no eye ere grieved for' (*FW* 482.34–36). They convey a shift in voice, an intonation, a possible inflection that makes itself silently heard to the reader. Just like accidence, italics belong to the very last phase of the work. They give it the final touch, setting its materials in correct hierarchical order, foregrounding what has been appropriated by the text, but is still signalled as external to it, or in a special relation to it, grafted on to it, and made recognizable, much as they are intended to be fully integrated and lost into it. The manuscript underlining, which italics virtually 'translate' and render, presupposes an act of deciphering, which in its turn determines a re-writing loaded with stage directions, and instructions for 'performing', and faithfully reproducing rhythms, pauses, punctuations, inflections, etc. They are voices that emerge from the text as characters in their own right.

Italics are the emphasizing device by means of which Joyce foregrounds quotations, allusions as well as borrowed words and phrases. Conventions are thus reinforced, and traces, signatures, and arcane words emerge and redistribute themselves in the text. In its turn, the formal principle they derive from generates a network of forces capable of building up constellations of words and meanings. The reader is given orientation clues in the process of extrapolating and reconstructing the 'original' sources from which the text borrows. There is a radical modification of the sources themselves not only along the formal line – the italics themselves – but also along the substantive line of deviation from source: this is achieved by deliberate misquotation, incomplete quotation as well as by hybrids, dislocutions, etc. Italics represent in Joyce's work the area of quotational flexibility, and the infinite and indefinite renewal of language. This primary activity is shown to originate in the interplay of the elements of a binary opposition centred upon the feature of [FOREIGNNESS], defined alternatively as 'foreign, or alien, to the main enunciative voice' or 'proceeding from the main enunciative voice', and to a certain extent rooted in the system of typographic conventions. Joyce operates efficiently within this system of limitations, showing the continuous recirculation of the word by means of which what is familiar and 'cliché' can appear in an exotic posture. On the other hand, what is firmly anchored in the idiolect of the enunciator, and is therefore unique and unrepeatable, can through repetition become a password and trigger a new series of other passwords. Intratextuality, inner self-plagiarism as well as intertextuality are also at work in the Joyce text.

This double configuration lies on the one hand in the fact that italics signal a certain degree of alienation of the word within the text, often achieving expressionistic effects of the kind postulated by the Sklovskian 'device of making strange'. On the other hand, however, italics reveal in their concatenation a line of discourse that runs parallel to the 'main' one, set in roman type. There is a definite strategy of integration and combination of the two: what is presented as a side issue, as an irrelevant and unnecessary prop, as an arbitrary whim of the artist introduced in order ultimately to achieve effects, clogging the rhythm and the pace of the prose, is instead the very centre of aggregation for all the various materials of the work.

The perspective within which italics are resorted to and endowed with their full value and specific weight is that of the writing in its final stage of completion, that of the printed whole that adopts unifying strategies in typographical matters which represent the last possible *mise à point* of the registers and of the tonalities by analogy with the principles of harmony in music. The Joyce principle of 'postreintroducing' (*FW* 246.26), and of 'retrogressive metamorphosis' that binds together in an indissoluble knot the initial and the final stages of the work is here exploited in all its possible potentialities.

A telling instance in this respect is Tom Kernan's catch phrase, which is now reproduced in italics in the Garland edition, as it refers back to the moment in which it was originally uttered:

Trenchant, Mr Power said laughing. He's dead nuts on that. And the *retrospective arrangement*. (6.149–50)

The 'retrospective arrangement', which reappears six more times in the novel, and never again in italics, remains in our conscience a marked phrase, a sequence of words which, though it is freely adopted and circulated, never loses its own initial tagged character.

The very first occurrence of italics in the text of the novel tells us a great deal about the strategies of their use in *Ulysses*. If our analysis is correct, this instance precedes and foreshadows the first major disruption of the text occasioned by the appearance of the word 'Chrysostomos' (1.26), which had apparently not at all been justified by the formal progress of the narrative up to that particular moment.

Stately, plump Buck Mulligan came from the stairhead, bearing a bowl of lather on which a mirror and a razor lay crossed. A yellow

dressinggown, ungirdled, was sustained gently behind him on the mild morning air. He held the bowl aloft and intoned:
– *Introibo ad altare Dei.*   (1.1–5)

Italics appear here as an instance of formal arrangement of the text, as one of the many formal devices that control it. Their intrinsically visual nature, opposed and contrasted to that of the roman type which introduces them, and which they are set against, is not at first sight disorienting or disconcerting, for it seems to belong to a perfectly well-justified and customary typographical choice. Upon closer scrutiny, however, one detects an unexpected twist: the thoroughly uninventive and unimaginative use of italics in this passage conceals a repetition on a microscopic scale of the strategic moves of the text as a whole. We realize that the words, taken from the *Introit*, represent the ritual formula that marks the *incipit* of the text, starting it afresh, and signalling a new opening. The initial 43 words are thus assigned the clearly subordinate role of preparing the new beginning, whereas the reader, divided between the two successive openings, may be at a loss as to which of the two he is going to give the dominant function. Exhibiting clear binarity, the roman/italics contrast achieves effects of retardation and false start, blurring the contours of the fictional world that is being created by giving the reader an ample amount of ambiguous and even contradictory information.

Set side by side, these two successive openings enhance the theatrical atmosphere of the first episode of the novel. They also impose and foreground language on stage, performing in a manner which is as lively and as colourful as that of any of the other characters. If one cares to look at the very first page with an eye bent on visual language, it is not difficult to find out that what is said in roman type, with its impressive massive weight – coextensive with the characters portrayed – is repeated in the slanted profile of italics, which are fluid, moody, and fragile. The rock and the river, the solidity of stone and the fluidity of flux are symbolically there from the very beginning. The flow is turned on and off by Buck Mulligan, and the tautological nature of the relationship between the two sets of elements expresses in itself the barrenness of their interrelation and defines the text as endless deletion and unweaving, quite in line with the slogan 'In the buginning is the woid' (*FW* 378.29). In *Ulysses*, the ideal voyage of language sets off from the very beginning of the text.

The floating status of the text and its resemanticizing power are pregnantly illustrated by certain emendations concerning italics in the Garland edition. One of the most telling, in connexion with the identification of suprasegmental traits in the use of italics, is the new form given to the famous 'Sounds solid: made by the mallet of Los *demiurgos*' (3.17–18). What was ascribed to a foreign language by the previous reading '*Los Demiurgos*' and made into a phrase that carried a vague but powerful Spanish echo, is now distinguished first into a 'Los', a cryptical allusion but belonging to the English tradition, and then into the *glose* proper, '*demiurgos*' which gives the Greek with no possible overtones.

The anxiety for putting the text right, for normalising it, which is in the previous example fully supported by textual evidence, is, in certain cases, carried too far in that it deprives the text of its necessary frame of reference and set of conventions, which are a constitutive part of its existence; this is the case, for instance, with the diphthongs *ae* and *oe* in Latin words which consistently substitute for the more antiquated *æ* and *œ* previously used; or *ü* which is used instead of *ue* in German words (as in *Übermensch*); or *I* instead of *J* (as in *Iubilantium*) and so on. In the case of

Five, six: the *Nacheinander*. Exactly: and that is the ineluctable modality of the audible. Open your eyes. No. Jesus! If I fell over a cliff that beetles o'er his base, fell through the *Nebeneinander* ineluctably! (3.12–15)

where capital letters are assumed for the German substantives, an inferior degree of integration into the text is given to the words themselves by the capitalisation, an integration and a blending postulated by the stylistic mode of the chapter: the 'ineluctable modalities' of the visible and of the audible. I am not too sure either that correctness should be the sole justification for the introduction of the accent in

> *Là ci darem la mano*
> *La la lala la la.* (5.227–28)

The song is only 'hummed' and if there is an attempt at a mimetic rendering '*là*' should not be accentuated, but rather left underlined as a sort of redundant item.

A perfect adherence to rhythm and to the mechanisms producing nonsense, as is often the case with the singing of songs in a foreign language, is reached with the emendation:

Lacaus esant . . . Taree tara.   (8.623)

The string of sounds establishes and implants itself irrespective of word boundaries and of meanings, as in:

> Acatalectic tetrameter of iambs marching. No, agallop:
> *deline the mare*   (3.23–24)

'*Deline the mare*', a chunk of quotation, acquires, through its being singled out in italics in an incomplete form, a kind of autonomy open to new signification.

The stentoreous voice of Buck Mulligan intoning the high and elevated words of the *Introit* is impotent and unable to revive the full meaning of the religious rite whose formulae have become through the ages empty mumblings, indistinct and mechanical repetition. Writing originates in this absence of sense, in the effort to decipher what is in continuous movement and escapes us, defying all linguistic limitation, in the effort to read what deletes itself, endlessly baffling all interpretation. The passages in italics are self-effacing signatures on the one hand, and powerful idiosyncratic bundles of sense on the other. They send us back to their sources and origins just to let us discover that what seems to be original is a replica, what seems to be a source is an echo, what seems to derive in a straight line is deflected, what seems to be a matrix is a by-product.

'*Lui, c'est moi*' (3.182–83): the ideal quotation, memorable and short, that exists in everybody's conscience so that it is echoed and repeated at ease represents the perfect example of the twisted quotation, of the phrase that, because it is so well-known, only exists to be twisted and ultimately made untraceable.

A perfect example of twisted Latin quotation is taken from the Vaticinia Pontificum: '*Descende, calve, ut ne nimium decalveris*' (*U* 40). In the original this reads '*Ascende, calve ut ne amplius decalveris, qui non vereris decalvere sponsam, ut conam ursae nutrias.*' In the Random House text it seems to be inverted in its key terms; in the Garland text *Descende* and

118

amplius are restored: *'Descende, calve, ut ne amplius decalveris'* (3.113–14). But the suspicion remains that this could be a wilful error. There are no naive readers, no primitive values, no original texts. There are no texts that are repositories of science or of wisdom, especially not those belonging to the Catholic tradition. The intoning of a liturgical passage does not send us back to origins, but rather confirms a transmissional value (and therefore a falsifying one) of tradition, a standard way of reading and accepting. High and traditional do not in this text identify; we are led, instead, to an identification of tradition and the layering of elements, of tradition and falsification, and of ultimate imposture. The transmission is never a direct one, the relationship of text to text is never one-to-one. The text finds coherence in its own discontinuity, in its own corruption and endless decomposition, in laying bare its qualities of literary artefact.

The words voiced by Buck Mulligan at the beginning are revealed as a merely literary device, generated in a whirling vortex that, rebounding on the initial words, actually sets them into being with a leap backward. This retroactive bounce and bustrophedic move from the triviality and idiosyncrasy of the quotation (in italics) to the roots and permanence of language (in roman) represents and illustrates the work of language in *Ulysses*: from the transient rubbish that quotations embody, from the emptiness of metalinguistic terms that intersperse the text (as seen in Eumeus) in their full range: from *contretemps*, to *dénouement*, to *entrée*, to *séance*, to *ad hoc*, to *de rigueur* they stem the main discourse. Conversely, setting the word high means to ensure its corruptibility, its vulnerability. To read in the original, as Buck Mulligan suggests ('You must read them in the original. *Thalatta! Thalatta!*', 1.79–80) is a delusion. It does not mean to aim at a philological reconstruction or at literal adoption of forms and sounds but rather to let the forms and the sounds freely interfere and interplay in a text that defines itself as ubiquitous, as more absent than present on the page, as disarticulated and at the same time rearticulating, as continuous mediation, as slanted language, as 'slanguage' (*FW* 421.17).

If there has to be an authority, it is that of the spoken word

set against that of the written; italics are precisely the device
by which the word is reembodied, made capable of assuming
and carrying its own intonation and inflexion, giving
imperious stage-directions, stopping the flow of narrative,
accelerating it, imposing a rhythm on the reader even before
and almost irrespective of any semantic analysis of the word
itself. The disappearance of italics in the second mention of
the misquoted 'L. Boom', (*U* 647) as opposed to the quotation
of the entire passage from the *Telegraph* in which it first
occurred (in italics) opens up possibilities for the recirculation
of the word to the point that L. Boom becomes an 'alias' of
Bloom, the character misquoted becomes a character in its
own right:

Boom (to give him for the nonce his new misnomer) whiled away a
few odd leisure moments in fits and starts with the account of the
third event at Ascot on page three. (16.1274–76)

By the time we reach Circe we know that a plurality of orders
is at work, we know that we cannot accept at face value the
highly systematized use of italics there (stage directions given
in parenthesis, therefore with another graphic delimitation,
direct speech in roman type) at least without expecting a
contamination of that order. First of all it is worth noticing
that the new order is an inversion of the order in which italics
were used at their first occurrence and in the following pages:
there, italics stood for the actually spoken words framed and
surrounded by the narrative context in roman type; here they
represent the stage directions firmly limited and almost
imprisoned by the parenthesis. This rigid order is infringed as
soon as the necessity for a quotation in a foreign language
presents itself: '*Vidi aquam egredientem de templo a latere
dextro. Alleluia.*' (15.77) and, later, even more evidently:
'(*Altius aliquantulum.*) *Et omnes ad quos pervenit aqua ista*'
(15.84; *U* 431). It is almost as if italics were trickling down
from the closed world delimited by the parenthesis and were
invading the roman type field, contaminating it and in this
way subtly undermining the theatrical structure of the
chapter. If there is no formal order that delimits and separates
stage directions from speeches proper, then everything is on
stage exactly as it was the case in the opening of the book,

fighting for survival, striving to assume a role, an identity, a voice, an intonation, a vibration. If italics are a way of emphasising, then the changes and alterations that affect them are, if possible, of even greater importance and consequence to the interpretation of the text.

TEXTUAL CRITICISM, LITERARY THEORY AND THE NEW *ULYSSES*

IRA B. NADEL

> – Bosh! Stephen said rudely. A man of genius makes no mistakes. His errors are volitional and are the portals of discovery. (9.228–29)

In his 1983 study, *A Critique of Modern Textual Criticism*, Jerome J. McGann declares that 'textual criticism is in the process of reconceiving its discipline.' He supports this claim by identifying three central issues under review: the idea of copy-text, the concept of authorial intention, the determination of textual authority. For copy-text McGann favours the notion of an eclectic text, departing from the strict definitions outlined by W. W. Greg and Fredson Bowers. McGann rejects the principle of authorial intention exposing the contradiction inherent in an 'ideology of final intentions,' but in matters of textual authority he supports the validity of the printed text over any other source because it comes closest to what the author wanted the public to read. For McGann the social dynamic between the individual author and the means of literary production always fashions the printed text. McGann furthermore emphasizes that an author's intentions toward his manuscript may differ from that of his intentions toward his published text – as in, for example, Joyce's conscious production of a typescript of *Ulysses* with three carbons for prospective sale to the New York dealer, John Quinn – a departure from his usual compositional practice.

The job of the textual critic is that of recovery and the creation of a critical text may actually be hindered, or at least complicated, by the interferences of the author in the transmission as well as composition of his work. McGann broadens the notion of authorial intention, however, by showing how an author necessarily cooperates with the institution publishing his work. Furthermore, the production of the work is as much a part of its audience as its author, thereby enlarging the issue of 'final intention' beyond the sphere of the individual author. Collaboration in the transmission of texts is unavoidable, just as the notion of 'final authorial intention' remains fundamentally problematic. Aligned with these issues for McGann is the difficulty of establishing literary authority, an often contradictory condition which inverts the historical assumption that an early version is the more correct or pure example of a text. Reconstituting an original work may be a process involving the present, not the past. A textual critic, McGann suggests, is a kind of archaeologist who recreates the past from clues in which a single object or text can be read as containing the entire history of that work as it emerged into the present.[1]

McGann's study focuses on methodology and theory, and poses challenging questions to anyone concerned with the matter of text and the quality of what we read. Joyceans – as Joyce himself demonstrated in his own list of errata to the second and third impressions of *Ulysses* – are especially conscious of such matters and the Garland *Ulysses* is the *summa* of that preoccupation. My interest, however, relates to how the edition responds to the issues McGann outlines and how it might be understood as altering certain procedures of textual criticism. In short, how new is the new *Ulysses*?

Like McGann, who presents a history of textual criticism, I, too, shall begin with the past. A history of the textual scholarship of *Ulysses* might properly begin with Joyce himself who, in recognizing the plethora of errors in the first edition, altered in page proof the original publisher's notes to read 'the publisher asks the reader's indulgence for typographical errors unavoidable in the exceptional circumstances.' Those 'exceptional circumstances' are now well-known and have often been described.[2] The publication of the second and third impressions of the first edition included a list of errata noted by Joyce and subsequently worked into the plates of the fourth impression (1924), to which a second list of four pages of errata was added. The eighth printing of *Ulysses* in 1926, what we know as the second edition, absorbed the corrections in the reset text, although it introduced a series of new errors as various scholars have recorded.[3]

The next major revision was in 1932 when the text was 'specially revised, at the author's request, by Stuart Gilbert' for the Odyssey Press edition. Gilbert apparently did little more, however, than glance at the proofs.[4] In 1934 the first authorized American edition appeared, hastily and mistakenly set from Samuel Roth's pirated and corrupt text of 1929 (with its incorrectly printed date of 1927) including the famous misprinting of Buck Mulligan who 'went over the parapet laughing to himself' instead of the correct 'over to the parapet.' Such errors were occasionally corrected in subsequent Random House editions until the work was entirely reset in 1961, creating a new host of errors as Jack Dalton was quick to register.[5] In 1936 the first English edition of the novel was published by Bodley Head with Joyce again providing some corrections based on a cursory review of proof with failing eyesight while in Copenhagen. An important fact in this history of the transmission of the text is that the only edition of which Joyce himself thoroughly corrected proof was the first edition of 1922; and with the incorporation of the errata lists of the second and third impressions it remains the least corrupt of the printed editions before the appearance of the Garland *Ulysses*.

Bibliographers and scholars lost no time in extending Joyce's emendations, beginning in 1936 with an article by R. F. Roberts in *Colophon*. Focus on revisions, textual development and errors proliferated with important contributions by Joseph Prescott (1944), A. Walton Litz (1961), Jack P. Dalton (1966), Norman Silverstein (1969), Phillip F. Herring (1972), and Michael Groden (1977). The opening sentence of Dalton's 1966 essay pointedly summarizes the principles that guided these and other critics: 'The more one values a book, the more one should value an authentic text of that book.' Dalton's early collation of the 1961 Random House edition revealed some 4000 errors. This was actually the 5th resetting since the first edition, with some 1700 errors accumulating over thirty-five years from resettings with almost 2000 corruptions going back to manuscript items which had never been properly printed. The source of many of the transmission errors was the 1936 edition, the first set in England.[6]

In all of the textual studies of *Ulysses* preceding the Garland edition certain topics remained constant: the impossibility of recovering an uncorrupted text, an analysis of Joyce's compositional method, the divergence between pre-existent manuscripts and published sources, the overall difficulties in editing Joyce. The work in process took precedence over the work as product, with the analysis of textual development rather than the establishment of an authorized text the focus. The latter was a difficulty more often commented than acted upon until Hans Walter Gabler and his associates undertook the complex task of editing *Ulysses*.

The physical process of producing the text of the Garland *Ulysses* is outlined in my stemma, to which I shall return, and by various articles by Michael Groden, Gabler, and others.[7] I am more interested, however, in the assumptions that have led to the creation of the Garland *Ulysses* and its implications for future editions of Joyce's work. Two sentences from Gabler's 'Afterword' concentrate the issues: 'The first edition [of *Ulysses*] comes closest to what Joyce aimed for as the public text of *Ulysses*. Yet it does not present the text of the work as he wrote it' (G 1891). This is a radical statement for several reasons. First, Gabler posits a dichotomy between what we have assumed to be the rationale for a work's composition, its appearance in print, and the nature of its critical authority, its reception; he furthermore implicitly argues that the printed, public version of the work substantially differs not only from its actual text but from the author's intention, presumably the public appearance of his work. Gabler's statement also suggests that a phantom text may exist which supersedes the published form of the work. By extension, this implies that the personal or authorial control of the author over his text has become sabotaged by its publication, that the socialization of the production of texts that McGann described is in many ways opposite to the intentions of the author.

Gabler partially recognizes the theoretical and critical implications of his statement by emphasizing that transmission and composition force distinctions between corrections and authorial matters of revision and expansion (G 1892). This leads to a critical paragraph summarizing the editorial principles and textual practice of the edition:

This edition's whole rationale is based on the assumption that the legal act of first publication did not validate the actual text thereby made public to the extent of lending authority to its high incidence of corruption. Instead, the act of publication is conceived of as an ideal act, to which the edition correlates an ideal text freed of the errors with which *Ulysses* was first published. Thus, it is taken to be the main business of the critical edition to uncover and to undo the first edition's textual corruption. Thereby, the edition endeavours to recover the ideal state of development as it was achieved through the traceable processes of composition and revision at the time of the book's publication on 2 February 1922. (G 1892)

The paragraph should give us pause, for in it Gabler comes closest to expressing the theory of his edition and its method which essentially focuses on pre-publication transmission and documents of composition. Again, a dichotomy exists: in documents of composition Gabler holds that the text possesses full authority; in documents of transmission, the text is 'potentially faulty' unless proven to possess authority (G 1892).

Gabler's statement, embedded in the final pages of the three volume edition, is important theoretically as well as descriptively for in it he establishes an intersection between textual criticism and literary theory. At the nexus of his dialectic between the printed form and the actual text is the question posed by Roland Barthes, Julia Kristeva and Stanley Fish: What is a text? Gabler's positing of a text other than the printed version of *Ulysses* is the effort to reconstruct what Barthes calls 'that incontrovertible and indelible trace, supposedly of the meaning which the author has intentionally placed in his work.' 'It is the written in so far as the written participates in the social contract,' Barthes continues, and it 'marks language with an inestimable attribute which it does not possess in its essence: security.' The text for Barthes becomes 'the very theatre of a production where the producer and the reader of the text meet.' But the text remains what it means etymologically, a tissue; the job of the textual critic, which Gabler acknowledges, is to reconstruct the tissues or inter-connexions of tissues/texts that comprise *Ulysses*. In Barthes' words, the goal is to secure 'the guarantee of the written object' since the text is 'a weapon against time' and 'authenticates writing.'[8]

The effort of Gabler to recover the actual text of *Ulysses* differs little from our own efforts to theorize about texts; his physical quest to reconstitute what he calls the ideal text in its ideal published state, freed from error, is no different from the goal of critics to obtain an ideal reading of a work. Through the creation of what Gabler will call 'the continuous manuscript text' (G 1895), the generation of a manuscript that has never before existed because Joyce never composed a unified, error-free fair copy of the entire novel, he establishes in Barthes' words 'a methodological field' where a variety of approaches, judgements, decisions and methods are at work (39). One might actually argue that the task Gabler sets for himself is literally and theoretically 'to expose the grammatological structure of the text,' to identify its origin and end, precisely the desire of the deconstructive critic who, in the unmaking of a text, also implies the possibility of its rebuilding.[9] In seeking and recording the vestigial elements of Joyce's text, the ineffable 'traces' and erasures Derrida describes, Gabler turns *Ulysses* into a palimpsest pursuing the 'ideal act of publication' from 'an ideal text . . . freed of errors' (G 1892). By the textual acts of recension and recovery, Gabler hopes to reclaim a work Joyce never totally wrote in a state of publication which the novel never achieved. This parallels the idea of text established by Derrida – 'a differential network, a fabric of traces referring endlessly to something other than itself, to other differential traces'.[10]

Gabler's procedure is involved, and the accompanying stemma may guide us. Distinguishing between an 'Early-Version Text' and an 'Edition Text,' Gabler began by inputting a series of holograph, autograph, and compositional documents including the Rosenbach manuscript (actually fifteen chapters of *Ulysses* in fair copy and three in final working draft), chapter typescripts, and serial publication of the work. The addition of emendations, autograph notations, and revisions to proof soon established a multi-layered overlay that collectively established the 'Early-Version Text,' in essence a corrected and emended version of the Rosenbach manuscript. This in turn was collated with the 'Edition Text,' a collation of the 1922 first edition and the 1926 second edition, a corrected eighth printing of the first edition. Computer-generated difference lists between the 'Early-

Version' and 'Edition Text' were then compared. List 1 contained the record of all Joyce did to the 'Early-Version Text,' list 2, every discrepancy between that version and the 'Edition Text.' The two were not identical because of authorial changes the compositors missed and compositors' changes the author never intended. Each discrepancy required judgement and decision, complicated by changes that might have been authorial but if so were made on sets of proof no longer extant. Other errors included emendations by the author to compositors' changes but without remembering what he originally intended.

It is at this juncture in the development of the text that the greatest care in determining which reading has authority for the text is necessary. Knowledge of Joyce's stylistic habits, preferences, and understanding of the compositional process are paramount. Fundamental is the question of authorial intention. Once these decisions had been taken and the corrections made, a 'continuous manuscript text' was created by grafting choices and a coding system on to the 'Edition Text' which became the copy-text for the Garland edition. This in turn assumed two forms, the 'Synoptic Text', printed on the verso of the new edition and so called because it is a synopsis of the textual development of the novel, and, on the recto page, the 'Critical Reading Text,' a clean, uncoded but corrected text eliminating Joyce's deletions.

In its procedure, the edition appears accurate, complete and, in our custom of computer-generated texts, uncommon. But in methodology, it is innovative if not radical in its approach, beginning with its new idea of copy text. Much ink has been spilt over the definition and re-definition of copy text, essentially the difference between the Greg–Bowers school which argues for the earliest manuscript as the copy-text or the Thorpe-Gaskell school which argues for the first printed edition corrected by the author as the copy-text. The emergence of an eclectic copy-text whereby authority may vary from the first edition to manuscript, depending on the establishment of authority, is a compromise position. Philip Gaskell states that in most cases, however, copy-text should be 'an early printed edition, not the manuscript . . . since for many authors the actual writing of the manuscript . . . is a means of composition, not an end.' But G. Thomas Tanselle expresses the compromise position concisely: '[a] copy-text is simply the text most likely to provide an authorial reading. . . at points of variation where one cannot otherwise reach a decision.'[11] Gabler follows this method, reconstructing a text that he believes satisfies his goal, the establishment of the corrected text of the novel and the analysis of the process of its composition. The fragmented state of Joyce's manuscript materials forces Gabler to construct his ideal text which becomes, in a departure from the traditional practice of using either an autograph manuscript or a corrected first edition, his copy-text. The 'Continuous Manuscript Text,' newly constructed and without precedent, stands as an innovative copy-text based on accumulation rather than single evidence to establish a complete manuscript. This principle is also one of narrative, as though Gabler were reconstructing a story in the process of dismantling a pre-existent tale.

But it is the very establishment of the 'Continuous Manuscript Text' that causes problems because, although accuracy of text has been largely achieved based on the formalized collations, the decision-making process of selecting authorized readings remains a discrete activity. Explicit on the procedure, programmes, and process for establishing textual variants, Gabler is less clear on why certain readings are chosen over others. Since documents of transmission become those of composition when Joyce begins to revise them, it is difficult to maintain their distinction and integrity despite Gabler's desire to do so. For example, the now well-known restoration of the word 'love' in Scylla and Charybdis, that appeared in an early fair copy but not in a later typescript, in Gabler's view because of an eyeskip, was also not restored by Joyce in either typescript or proof. His dislike of proofreading, poor eyesight or fallible memory may not have caught the omission. Or he may have decided its absence would not be missed. But Gabler includes it, setting aside the principle of printing the latest text corrected by the author.

Two further examples include a disputable section in Hades when, at Dignam's funeral, Bloom, thinking about bad air that gathers in sealed coffins and sometimes requires holes to be drilled, thinks 'out it rushes: blue. One whiff of that and you're a doner' (6.611–12; *U* 213). The Rosenbach typescripts, early proofs and serial versions have 'doner'. However, Joyce changed it to 'goner' in the last set of proofs he corrected and it appears in the reset Random House edition of 1961 (*U* 104). But Gabler rejects it. This inconsistency of practice, here neglecting to accept the holograph revision, is buttressed by readings based on suggestive rather than documentary proof.

Another case in point occurs in Circe when Moses Dlugacz appears to Bloom during a vision of the Israeli landscape and hoarsely says 'Bleibtreustrasse, Berlin W.13' (15.991; *U* 464), referring indirectly to Karl Bleibtreu whose theory of Shakespeare Stephen cites in Scylla and Charybdis (9.1073–77; *U* 214). The actual postal district for the street in Berlin was W.15 between 1910 and 1922 and, one might assume, for 1904. The district is correctly listed as 'W.15' in the novel at 4.199 and 17.1700. In the 'Textual Notes,' Gabler writes 'the present reading would call for emendation were it not for an undercurrent of numerology particularly noticeable in this episode that raises the possibility not of an inadvertent error, although this seems more likely, but of an intended change' (G 1748). This confusion and failure to alter the text for the sake of sustaining numerological conformity suggests various inconsistencies in textual practice at odds with the editorial principles of the work. Gabler's defence of the inconsistent spelling of Rudolf versus Rudolph in Ithaca (17.1869) or, more importantly, his 'editorial conjecture in accordance with the stylistic mode of the [Eumaeus] episode' concerning the revision of a construction in Rosenbach which he rejects, are two other examples.

Why, furthermore, does Gabler choose to insert 'By juxtaposition' in answer to the question how 'was a glyphic comparison of the phonic symbols' of Hebrew and Gaelic orally made, when the phrase appears only in a marginal addition to the Rosenbach manuscript? It did not appear in the first or second typescript and was not re-inserted at any later stage. The editor could not know if it was omitted accidentally from the first typescript or deleted by Joyce (17.733; *U* 688). These examples are acts of editorial discrimination that consistently jeopardize the rigour of computer accuracy and affect the validity of the entire text. Just what, one begins to ask, is the meaning of 'correct' in Gabler's stress on a 'corrected text' of *Ulysses*?

Gabler's 'Textual Notes' furthermore confirm the poetics of deconstructionism. Questioning the use of a question mark after 'it' preceding a comma at 16.294 (Eumaeus), Gabler writes 'R's [Rosenbach's] punctuation would seem an instance of immediate graphic expression of the undecidedness of the episode between spoken and written speech' (G 1749). The theoretical questions of trace, of erasure and of *differance* in the text, appear in an applied manner in the 'Textual Notes' and their careful reading would provide a workshop for the application of Derridian grammatology (cf for example, 3.181, G 1731; 5.156, G 1733; 8.496–97, G 1736–37; 10.634, G 1740). The critical rather than mechanical establishment of text remains, then, a debatable if not controversial dimension of the Garland *Ulysses*; a variety of passages in the text have readings noted less for their accuracy than for their interpolation. Or, as certain commentators have asked, how much did it really cost Bloom for his cake of 'Fry's Plain Chocolate'? (see 17.1472; G 1752).

In sum, a series of questions may focus objections, or at least queries, about the Garland *Ulysses*:

1. Is the readmission of early-draft and textual elements into printed versions of *Ulysses* legitimate?

2. Is it correct to give the 'Continuous Manuscript Text' a double status of both a reconstituted text, actually a computer generated text, and a copytext, in turn edited to create 'the critically edited text' (G 1896)?

3. Is it valid to reject the corrected eighth impression of the 1922 1st edition – the second edition of 1926 – as copytext?

4. Is it valuable to include rejected or deleted readings in the 'Continuous Manuscript Text?' And if deletions are not included in the 'Critical Reading Text', should not additions have the same status? If not, why not?

5. What principles have guided the notion of authorial intention and has Gabler been presumptuous in determining Joyce's final intentions, including in the 'Continuous Manuscript Text', autograph notations, overlays, corrections, revisions and additions?

6. Is it valid to base a critical edition of *Ulysses* on a text

131

Joyce himself never saw? Is it not sufficient only to state that Joyce wrote every word of the novel by hand because, by careful selection among drafts, any editor can produce a version which, while in the author's hand, he [the author] might repudiate as opposed to his intent?[12] The need is to prove that Joyce attributed a privileged status to his autograph notations, revisions or additions as assumed by the editors.

These matters relate to another subject that requires even greater attention if we are to understand the nature of Joyce's texts and their formation. That subject is the phenomenology of error, the first topic Freud addressed in his 1915–17 lectures at the University of Vienna and published in English in 1920 as *A General Introduction to Psychoanalysis*. Errors, Freud argued, have meaning and occur as 'mental acts arising from the mutual interference of two [or more] intentions.' What, we may ask, is the nature and significance of Joyce's errors? What do they mean and how do they relate to the analysis of his work? Methodologically, how do we evaluate mistakes Joyce made in manuscript as opposed to errors made by others (and Joyce) in typescript, *placards* or page proofs – and failed to correct? Why, in fact, did he let some errors stand? Neglect, oversight, forgetfulness? Is it legitimate to propose a philosophy of error for Joyce, accepting the notion of Christopher Ricks, writing of Pater and Arnold, that nothing literary gets into a text by chance? And if misquotation or errors of transcription are always revealing, even if the author was not himself aware of the error, what do these mistakes reveal about Joyce? Or do we have to accept the contention that literary error is so universal that psychological explanation is unnecessary? A possible response appears to be that in making errors we are, in a fashion, taking possession of what passes through our hands, leaving our mark. 'What may look like mere sloppiness' the writer Janet Malcolm has noted 'is in (unconscious) fact a studied assertion of personality.'[13]

Freud himself provides an interesting case study. In a letter to Wilhelm Fliess upon completing a reading of the proofs of *The Interpretation of Dreams*, Freud said he would make no more changes in the book 'even if it contained 2,467 mistakes.' Freud then goes on to analyse the apparently arbitrary number he gave following his principle that there is nothing 'arbitrary or undetermined in the psychic life.' His self-analysis shows cogent reasons for the number '2,467', recalling that at the age of 24 he was impressed by a general he met in a hospital during his one year of compulsory service and that a news account he had just read reported the general's retirement. Adding his present age as he writes the letter to Fleiss (43) to his age when he met the general (24), he obtains 67, the second number. This number, he suggests, is the age at which *he* wishes to retire, a response to his wife's question, at the time he read the story, as to when Freud thought of retiring? This comment set off his unconscious but significant reference to the possible number of errors in *The Interpretation of Dreams.*[14]

A study of the phenomenology of error in Joyce, based on his own corrections and comments during and after the composition and publication of *Ulysses* would be revealing. Gabler, providing us with the materials for such a study by including the traces and evolution of errors in Joyce's text, now makes it possible. The culmination of such a study would, of course, be *Finnegans Wake* because in that work, with its morphological and lexical distortions, 'error' is elevated to the status of the correct text. The intentional misspelling of words and their irregular syntax become their proper form in the text. Language, through dislocation, renews itself and 'error' becomes correction, a new method to establish meaning. As Joyce warns us, 'You are deepknee in error, sir, Madam . . . let me then tell you' since 'with each word that would not pass away the squidself which he had squirtscreened from the crystalline world waned chagreenold and doriangrayer in its dudhud' (*FW*, 67.23–4, 186.6–8). 'Erringnesses' (279.F05) are everywhere in the text and a gauge, I would suggest, of its understanding. Freud states that errors are '*compromise*-formations; they express part-success and part-failure for each of the two intentions' that formulate an error (*General Introduction*, p. 70). *Finnegans Wake*, with its neologisms, and private but decipherable language of deviation, embodies this concept. It seems likely, then, that Joyce's errors may be the very 'portals of discovery' Stephen refers to in his discussion of mistakes in Shakespeare (9.228–29; *U* 190).

It remains to examine the ease with which students and scholars can use the Garland *Ulysses* – and ask how workable is its system of diacritical marks and textual notes, lists of collation and other apparatus? As an example let us take a portion of the final sentence of the novel, what corresponds to 782.32–783.14 in the Random House and to 18.1588–1611 in Garland. The parallel texts of the Garland edition are visually quite different, with the coding of the synoptic text creating a visually complex page on the left, and slightly longer by some four lines than the text on the right. The marks, however, recreate the stages of development of the text, although we would need to refer to the list of symbols at the beginning of each volume for clarification. They record, for example, that in line 1 the phrase beginning ⌐²∧ and the Arabs' was an addition in the second proof stage within one document at the overlay level, while the phrase 'outside Larby Sharons' indicates an addition at the third proof level. Deletions are shown by <   > so that 'Moors' replaced 'Turks.' Perhaps the most interesting information is that at least nine of the thirteen 'yes's' on the final page, almost seventy per cent, were added in the third or later proof stage. The final and rhythmically important phrase 'yes and his heart was going like mad' was an addition at level B before the first *placards* while among the final four 'yes's', all were late additions, beginning with the second proof and extending to the third. The textual notes for the entire episode (G 1753) detail the source documents and refer us back to a discussion of the edition and general textual situation in the 'Afterword' (G 1885–91) where the editors provide a narrative of the episode's completion and correct the myth that Robert McAlmon rearranged some of the text with Joyce's approval (G 1886). If one wants to collate the critical passage with other editions, he must turn to the 'Historical Collation List' where symbols are also required to understand the changes.

A slight confusion may emerge, however, because the identification numbers in the collation list refer to the running line numbers of the 'Critical Reading Text' and not to the Synoptic edition, nor to page numbers of the edition. This discrepancy will make citation difficult and create problems for scholars who must identify which edition they are using.

Locating our section, however, 18.1588–1611, we note the following absences from earlier editions: the number '2' following 'posadas' (18.1595; *U* 782.40) and the article 'the' preceding 'pink and blue and yellow houses' (18.1600; *U* 783.4). The collation also reveals that the placement of 'Joyce's signature', his place and dateline, at the end of the novel had shifted. Originally, in the 1922 and 1926 editions, a comma followed 'Trieste-Zurich-Paris' with the dates; in the 1932 Odyssey Press edition this was continued but with the addition of an umlaut over the u in 'Zurich', a practice followed in the 1961 Random House edition. The first edition italicized the dates to conform with the printing of the place names but in 1926 switched to roman. The first edition also had the dates on a separate line; in 1932 and from 1936 through 1961 they appeared on the same line as the place names.

The Garland *Ulysses* partially restores the 1922 format, using a non-italicized, no comma, non-umlaut form with the dates on a separate line. However, the manuscript of the Penelope section, as photographed in the Rosenbach facsimile, does not show the dates flush left as Gabler has printed them. Indeed, neither the typescript, *placards*, page proofs nor facsimile of the 1922 first edition show the dates as flush left. In fact, it was only in *placard* E of this section, dated November 1921, that Joyce actually shifted his 'signature' from the right to the left side of the text, restoring the position it had in the original manuscript.[15] Gabler, it appears, contradicts Joyce's intention to place the dates under the place names and flush left in opposition to centring them under the place names as in the Rosenbach facsimile. There is, surprisingly, no comment on this movement nor change in the textual notes, nor note that the 1934 first American edition contained, some twenty-five lines below the final line of the text, the bracketed phrase ' [THE END] ', flush left, with the 'signature' placed one line above and flush right, italicized, without the umlaut, with the dates following a comma after 'Paris,' unitalicized, with a period at the end. This may have been taken from Roth's pirated edition or from the 1932 Odyssey Press edition which included, following the dates, the phrase in caps 'THE END.' Ironically, even Joyce's final 'signature', its placement, appearance, spelling and typeface have been subject to distortion, misrepresentation and error.

Details such as these are now generally available to students of *Ulysses* in an orderly and largely accurate manner. With the Joyce Archive, Rosenbach facsimile, and now Garland *Ulysses*, it is possible for readers to witness the process of Joyce's composition. But despite the gathering of an extraordinary amount of data in the new *Ulysses*, despite the scrupulous collation, and computer reliability, a good portion of the final editorial readings depend on judgement and not on external evidence. Textual decisions are not as indisputable as they may at first appear. These decisions will require continued analysis by scholars parallel to the reformulation of textual criticism as McGann has outlined before acceptance of the synoptic and critical text as definitive takes place.

Furthermore, a crucial question emerges: the dynamic relation between readers and the text and how the textual history of *Ulysses*, now elaborated as never before, will effect its critical reception. Will readers feel compelled to revise their understanding of the text because of new additions and changes? Will they have to revaluate the novel's prominence in the modern canon because of its formerly corrupt state and now well-documented provenance? Will they become permanently sceptical of any textual reading, turning to facsimiles and archives to confirm a word or a passage? The path of the text, traced in detail by Gabler, will now begin a new Odyssean journey, returning to sources not formerly available as readers reassess, judge, evaluate and decide the quality of the textual changes for themselves. Finally, can we expect future editions of Joyce's work to match the detail of the Garland *Ulysses*? With approximately three times the amount of errors, will a new *Finnegans Wake* be appearing in multiple volumes, a new *Portrait*? No doubt in time they will, but their importance will only be as a means to understanding Joyce's work more fully after having first recovered his texts. Bloom, contemplating his 'inverted volumes improperly arranged' near the end of Ithaca (17.1358), reflects on 'the insecurity of hiding any secret document behind, beneath or between the pages of a book' (17.1413–14). The Garland *Ulysses* confirms his suspicion, for where a document does not exist, it manages to invent one, and where a text has been lost, it has now been found.

Stemma for the Garland *Ulysses*

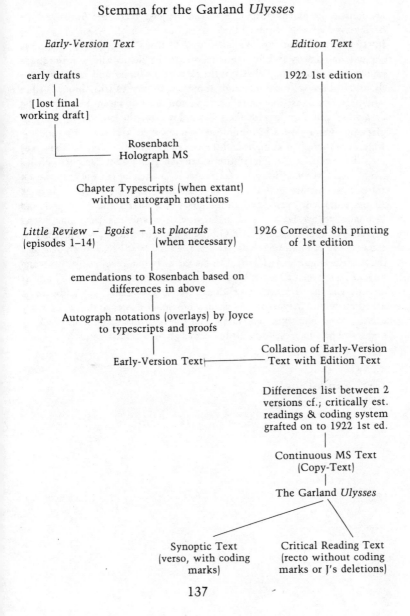

Early-Version Text   *Edition Text*

early drafts   1922 1st edition

[lost final
working draft]

              Rosenbach
              Holograph MS

      Chapter Typescripts (when extant)
        without autograph notations

Little Review – Egoist – 1st *placards*   1926 Corrected 8th printing
(episodes 1–14)   (when necessary)   of 1st edition

        emendations to Rosenbach based on
            differences in above

    Autograph notations (overlays) by Joyce
        to typescripts and proofs

              Early-Version Text├——————— Collation of Early-Version
                                          Text with Edition Text

                                Differences list between 2
                                versions cf.; critically est.
                                readings & coding system
                                grafted on to 1922 1st ed.

                                  Continuous MS Text
                                    (Copy-Text)

                                  The Garland *Ulysses*

        Synoptic Text   Critical Reading Text
      (verso, with coding   (recto without coding
          marks)   marks or J's deletions)

auctions in the morning the Greeks and the jews ⌐^and the Arabs and the
devil knows who else from all the ends of Europe and Duke street^ and the
fowl market all clucking ⌐outside Larby Sharons⌐ and the poor donkeys
slipping half asleep and the vague fellows in the cloaks asleep in the shade
5 on the steps and the big wheels of the carts of the bulls⌐ and ⌐the old castle
thousands of years old ^yes^ and⌐ those handsome ^⟨Turks⟩ Moors^ all in
white ⌐and turbans⌐ like kings⌐ ⌐asking you to sit down in their ⌐little⌐ bit
of a shop and Ronda with the old windows ⌐of the posadas⌐ ⌐[two] 2⌐
glancing eyes a lattice hid ⌐for ⟨the⟩ her lover to kiss the iron ⌐and the
10 wineshops half open at night and the castanets⌐ and the night we ⌐[stayed]
missed the boat at Algeciras⌐ the watchman going about serene with his
lamp⌐ and O that awful deepdown torrent O and the sea the sea crimson
sometimes like fire and the glorious sunsets⌐ and the ᴮfigtrees in theᴮ
Alameda gardens ⌐yes⌐ ⌐and all the queer little streets and ⌐the⌐ pink and
15 blue and yellow houses and the rosegardens and the jessamine⌐ ᴮand
⌐geraniums and⌐ cactusesᴮ and Gibraltar as a girl where I was a ⌐[flower]
Flower⌐ of the mountain ⌐yes⌐ ᴮwhen I put the [ᴵred] rose in my hair like
the Andalusian girls used ⌐or⌐ shall I wear a ⌐[white rose] red⌐ᴮ ⌐yes⌐ and
how he kissed me under the Moorish wall and I thought well as well him as
20 another and then I asked him with my eyes to ask again ⌐yes⌐ and then he
asked me would I ⌐yes⌐ to say yes my mountain flower and first I put my
arms around him ⌐yes⌐ and drew him down to me so he could feel my
breasts all perfume ᴮyes and his heart was going like madᴮ and ⌐yes⌐ I said
⌐yes⌐ I will ⌐[yes.] Yes.⌐

25 Trieste-Zurich-Paris
1914-1921

Greeks and the jews and the Arabs and the devil knows who else from all
the ends of Europe and Duke street and the fowl market all clucking
outside Larby Sharons and the poor donkeys slipping half asleep and the   1590
vague fellows in the cloaks asleep in the shade on the steps and the big
wheels of the carts of the bulls and the old castle thousands of years old yes
and those handsome Moors all in white and turbans like kings asking you
to sit down in their little bit of a shop and Ronda with the old windows of
the posadas 2 glancing eyes a lattice hid for her lover to kiss the iron and   1595
the wineshops half open at night and the castanets and the night we missed
the boat at Algeciras the watchman going about serene with his lamp and O
that awful deepdown torrent O and the sea the sea crimson sometimes like
fire and the glorious sunsets and the figtrees in the Alameda gardens yes
and all the queer little streets and the pink and blue and yellow houses and   1600
the rosegardens and the jessamine and geraniums and cactuses and
Gibraltar as a girl where I was a Flower of the mountain yes when I put the
rose in my hair like the Andalusian girls used or shall I wear a red yes and
how he kissed me under the Moorish wall and I thought well as well him as
another and then I asked him with my eyes to ask again yes and then he   1605
asked me would I yes to say yes my mountain flower and first I put my
arms around him yes and drew him down to me so he could feel my breasts
all perfume yes and his heart was going like mad and yes I said yes I will
Yes.

Trieste-Zurich-Paris   1610
1914-1921

                                                                        1727

FROM TELEMACHUS TO PENELOPE: EPISODES ANONYMOUS?

PATRICK PARRINDER

> One of the chief occupations of critics of this book is making
> parallels between the sections and characters of *Ulysses*, and the
> *Odyssey*. The chief reason for this performance is that the author
> exhibits a notebook with all these parallels and many other
> symbolical explanations.
>
> Mary Colum, Freeman, 19 July 1922[1]

Should the Homeric names of the episodes be restored in
future editions of *Ulysses*? That it was Joyce's intention that
each episode of the printed text should begin silently and
anonymously is amply documented. Indeed, it may be said
that one cannot 'restore' what was neither present nor
intended to be present in the text as long as Joyce controlled
it. But if the word 'restored' in my opening sentence is
tendentious, so is the word 'episodes'. If the parts of *Ulysses*
are anonymous, what warrant have we for referring to them as
episodes rather than as chapters or sections?

To ask whether the episode-names belong (so to speak) to
Ulysses is to reveal a stark contradiction between
conventional editorial principles, on the one hand, and the
universal assumptions and practice of Joyce criticism and
scholarship on the other. There is no Joyce critic writing today
who does not regard *Ulysses* as a modern epos divided into
eighteen named episodes. The vast majority of scholars and
explicators take familiarity with the episode-names for
granted. One of the first things any teacher of *Ulysses* is
obliged to do is to teach the names of the episodes; and the
reader or student who does not know them is denied access to
the whole of the advanced scholarly literature. Yet up to now
trade editions of *Ulysses* have respected Joyce's wishes. It is
within this climate that the Garland *Ulysses*, based on a
principle of scrupulous fidelity to the 'ideal text' (G 1892)

reconstructed from study of the author's documented intentions, has been produced. Gabler has devised an ingenious but equivocal and (necessarily) temporary way of dealing with the problem of the status of the episode-names. The effect of his edition is not, I believe, to solve this problem but to reopen it for discussion. In this paper I shall review the historical and pragmatic arguments for and against preserving the anonymity of the episodes in future trade editions. Not only are these arguments more complex than they at first appear, but their implications for textual editing and interpretation stretch well beyond the intrinsic interest of the rather technical matter under discussion.

I shall begin by looking at Gabler's edition, which is in fact the first text of *Ulysses* in the English language in which the names of the episodes have been printed. What is more, the names are used as running titles on every double-page spread of the text. However, they appear at the bottom of the left-hand page (the synoptic text), and not on the right-hand page (critical text). A trade edition based strictly on Gabler's critical text as it stands at present would not, therefore, contain the names of the episodes, though they would be numbered.

The layout of the *Critical and Synoptic Edition* is as follows (the example taken is G 418–19):

Left-hand page (synoptic edition)	Right-hand page (critical edition)
Text	Text
———	———
Notes	Notes
418 11.6. SCYLLA AND CHARYBDIS	EPISODE 9 419

We are at liberty to suppose that editorial scruple has restricted the naming of the episodes to the left-hand (synoptic) page. But if Joyce did not wish his episodes to be named in the published text of *Ulysses*, neither did he wish them to be numbered – the only authorised number-divisions in *Ulysses* being the three 'books', usually known as Telemachiad, Odyssey and Nostos – nor did he necessarily wish them to be called episodes. Gabler's 'left-handed' solution presupposes that, in future, the number if not the names will become integral to the text of *Ulysses*. The proof of this is in the new standard system of textual reference that he advocates – a system in which 'Henceforth, the text of *Ulysses* may be referred to not by page and line number, but by episode (1 to 18) and line number of this critical edition. Thus, 15.3562 will mean line 3562 of episode 15 ('Circe'), (G 1903). Here the episodes have been numbered against the wishes of the author, but for the convenience of the reader – but this principle has not been unequivocally extended to the names. 15.3562 would mean line 3562 of episode 15 in a trade edition based on the right-hand page, but the name Circe still appears in parenthesis, and must be sought in the synoptic edition (left-hand page) marked, as it were, 'For scholars only'.

I would claim that the muddle here is not Gabler's fault, but that it lies with the principle of authorial intention. But were not Joyce's intentions, as I have already suggested, entirely straightforward? Despite Joyce's use of them as working titles, the episode-names appear neither in the *Egoist* and *Little Review* serialisations of *Ulysses*,[2] nor in the Rosenbach manuscript, nor in the first edition. The care that Joyce habitually gave to such matters is indicated by his letter to Harriet Shaw Weaver of 22 October 1917 concerning a new edition of *A Portrait of the Artist*, in which he specified that the chapter-headings, 'Chapter I', etc., should be replaced by bare numerals, and also that the words 'The End' should be deleted.[3] The question of the episode-names in *Ulysses* specifically arose in 1933, when Bennett Cerf of Random House, Joyce's prospective American publisher, tried to persuade him to permit the inclusion of an explanatory chart based on the schema which had already been published by Stuart Gilbert.[4] Joyce, through his intermediary Paul Léon, refused permission even though this brought him into conflict with the publisher who was on the verge of victory in his tenacious campaign to establish the legality of *Ulysses* in the United States. Joyce did so on the grounds that 'if it needs explanations these belong to the class of critical and historical writings, not to the book itself' and that '*Ulysses*' text must stand on its own feet'.[5]

These letters written by Paul Léon on Joyce's behalf are the basis of a *caveat lector* issued by Phillip Herring in his selection of notes and early drafts for *Ulysses* from the Buffalo collection (1977). Herring warns, as other critics and scholars have done, against excessive preoccupation with Joyce's schemata:

Even if their validity is incontestable on all grounds, we should ask ourselves whether or not we were really meant to plunge into the novel armed with 'catchwords' and directions as to what to look for. Apparently Joyce was in no doubt about this, for he deleted the Homeric titles as chapter headings and wished to supply only a few critics with clues to the correspondences he had so patiently covered with the strata of Dublin.[6]

Herring's ordinance is not, as it happens, self-denying. He uses the Homeric names of the episodes throughout, just as every scholar does. Nor is the construction he places on Joyce's intentions a coherent one. General publication of the Homeric correspondences has, Herring says, 'caused confusion and has blurred into one [Joyce's] roles as writer and critic'; however, 'Joyce's culpability is minimal' for this (122). (By 'minimal' Herring does not mean 'zero'.) Joyce's action of showing to a selected few critics what he had decided to withhold from the multitude is explained as being due to a loss of confidence – 'he wished to show commentators what they were meant to see, as if no longer confident that his fictional realm was lucid' (122) – and also by a determination to restrict this knowledge to his immediate circle: 'Joyce's schemata were not circulated as recipes from the cook but were served as postprandial stimulants for a selected few guests' (123). My understanding of Joyce's actions is quite different from this interpretation, with its implicit suggestion (not unwelcome to some Joyce scholars) that a true understanding of the puzzles of *Ulysses* was always meant to be the prerogative of a small coterie or elite. On the contrary: Joyce both deleted the episode names and made quite certain, even before the book was published, that the existence of detailed Homeric parallels would have entered the public domain. Like a crossword, these parallels were perhaps meant to take the form of a code which everyone was independently capable of breaking. At the same time, it seems likely that Joyce had overestimated both the capacity of readers and the potential goodwill of contemporary critics and reviewers.

From 1917–18 Joyce invariably referred to the episodes by their Homeric names in his private correspondence. (It took him, however, some time to decide how many of them there would be.) Serialisation began in the *Little Review* in April 1918, and a letter to Harriet Shaw Weaver in the following month suggests that he had reached his final decision on the anonymity of the published episodes; for he stipulated that if the Telemachiad were published as a separate volume, its title should simply be *Ulysses I*.[7] When the first edition came out in February 1922, it was indeed merely divided into parts I, II and III, and hostile critics made much of the confusion induced by this. Holbrook Jackson complained that '*Ulysses* is a chaos', mentioning – amid strictures on the lack of quotation marks and capital letters, and the eccentricity of Joyce's punctuation and sentence-construction – that its 'chapters have no apparent relation to one another, and neither numbers nor titles'.[8] Shane Leslie in the *Quarterly Review* reported that he had discovered 'a thin parallelism with the movement of the Odyssey, for the episodes of Circe, Aeolus, Nausicaa, are visible amongst others less easily traceable'.[9] How then did it come about that, three months before Leslie's review was published, Mary Colum was able to observe in another journal that 'One of the chief occupations of critics of this book is making parallels between the sections and characters of *Ulysses*, and the *Odyssey*'?[10]

The answer lies in the publicity provided at Joyce's instigation by his friends, especially Valery Larbaud. There is no question here of 'postprandial stimulants'. Larbaud's public lecture on Joyce, in which he described the existence of detailed Homeric parallels as the 'key' to *Ulysses*, was delivered on 7 December 1921, two months *before* the publication date. The lecture was given in Joyce's presence at Sylvia Beach's bookshop.[11] The text of Larbaud's lecture appeared in the *Nouvelle revue française* for April 1922, and the relevant section was translated as 'The *Ulysses* of James Joyce' in the first number of T. S. Eliot's *Criterion* the following October. But Larbaud's lecture had attracted notice outside France almost as soon as it appeared in print. Arnold Bennett, the leading English reviewer of the day and scarcely one of Joyce's 'selected few', reported on it in the *Outlook* on 29 April:

According to Valéry Larbaud the day was very elaborately planned and organized. James Joyce loved the *Odyssey* in his youth, and the spirit of Homer presided over the shaping of the present work, which is alleged to be full of Homeric parallels. It may be so. Obviously Valéry Larbaud has discussed the work at length with the author. I should suspect the author of pulling Valéry Larbaud's leg, were it not that Larbaud has seen with his own eyes the author's drafts . . .[12]

The situation in which a living author's unpublished drafts entered public debate at the same time as his finished book is unparalleled in literary history; that is the oddity of the problem with which we are concerned, for it points to the contradictory nature of Joyce's 'intentions'. He did not publish the episode-names, but he always intended them to be discussed. Edmund Wilson considered the Homeric parallels in the *New Republic* of 5 July, arguing that Joyce had made a mistake in following the structure of the *Odyssey* so closely.[13] Ezra Pound, in a 'Paris Letter' for the *Dial* the previous month, both named some of the episodes and coined the metaphor of 'scaffolding' which dominates critical discussion of the schemata and correspondences to this day.[14] It will be evident from my argument that, whatever we make of Joyce's schemata, the idea of them as scaffolding which the author meant to be discarded is misleading, and perhaps intentionally so. The true analogy is with plans or blueprints, which are normally preserved because they contain important information which retains some of its usefulness when the building is completed.

The rest of the historical evidence may be presented quickly, for it is much more familiar to students of Joyce than are the events of 1921–22. At least one episode of *Ulysses* was published under its Homeric title in Joyce's lifetime: this was

'Protée', translated by Auguste Morel and Stuart Gilbert, which appeared in the *Nouvelle revue française* in August 1928.[15] It was with the publication of Gilbert's *James Joyce's 'Ulysses'* in 1930 that the detailed Homeric parallels became widely disseminated for the first time; once again, for the majority of Anglo-American readers, the commentary came in advance of the book itself. Gilbert's book, while clearly a critical study rather than an authorised appendage to *Ulysses*, was nevertheless written with Joyce's full approval. Later Joyce listed the episodes of the central section of *Ulysses* in suitably disguised form in *Finnegans Wake* (229.13–16). It took some time, however, for the use of the Homeric names in criticism and scholarship to become universal. A. Walton Litz, for example, rather self-consciously draws attention to the practice in the preface to his influential study *The Art of James Joyce* (1961). By 1970 this mode of reference had become so routine that the Joyce *Critical Heritage* volume edited by Robert H. Deming cites the early reviewers of *Ulysses* as quoting from named episodes of Joyce's book even where the names were unknown to them. Phillip Herring's warning against taking the Homeric titles too seriously occurs, as we have seen, in a book which makes use of the titles throughout. To learn these titles, however, the novice reader must still turn to introductory works of criticism and commentary rather than to the generally available text of *Ulysses* itself.

The aim of the *Critical and Synoptic Edition* is to establish an 'ideal text freed of the errors with which *Ulysses* was first published' (G 1892.). Such errors would not normally include 'mistakes' of the author's deliberate contrivance.[16] But if manifest authorial intention were the only principle followed in establishing a text, then any scholarly or annotated edition would appear illegitimate. Joyce himself cannot be said to have endorsed a variorum edition of his book. Even before the Garland edition, with its editorial apparatus, Joyce's distinction between the book itself and 'critical and historical writings' had been breached by Richard Ellmann's historical essay printed as an afterword to the Penguin edition – and it is obviously right that this should be so. Greater liberties have routinely been taken with older texts, such as the division of Shakespeare's plays into acts and scenes and the rewriting of

146

the stage directions in these plays.[17] If it is accepted that other principles besides authorial intention should control the form in which a text is transmitted – the more so the further we get from the original point of publication[18] – then it would seem that the question whether or not to include the episode-names is not one of editorial obligation but of editorial choice. Indeed, as soon as the period of copyright on Joyce's original texts is over one can foresee the likelihood of different editions embodying different decisions. In any case, the crossword-puzzle aspect of the Homeric structure of *Ulysses*, which Joyce somewhat experimentally inflicted on his early readers, has a wholly different meaning now to that which it had in 1922. Then it offered, or was thought to offer, an interpretative puzzle which everyone could tackle on equal terms – a puzzle to which, as Larbaud's lecture announced, there was a key. Today the propagation of a text without any indication as to the episode-names inserts an unnecessary barrier between the struggling first-time reader and the text as it is known and understood by critics and scholars. Gabler, at this moment in time, has given us eighteen numbered episodes; will he supply the names, as well, in the coming 'definitive' text of *Ulysses*? Or – for the uninitiated – will the basic structure of Joyce's book continue to baffle, lurk illegibly, and be anonymous?

SOME CRITICAL COMMENTS ON THE TELEMACHIA IN THE 1984 *ULYSSES*

CHARLES PEAKE

The edition of *Ulysses* published in 1984 has presented Joyce's readers with so many changes in a familiar text that, not surprisingly, many have responded with uneasiness and some with hostility. I am referring not to the specialised bibliographical disputes, which lie outside my field of competence, but to the reactions of critics and scholars, long aware that all texts of Ulysses were notoriously defective, but not prepared for the numerous and radical revisions offered by Hans Walter Gabler and his colleagues (hereafter referred to, collectively, as 'Gabler').

Two much-discussed examples illustrate the problems. According to all printed texts, in Hades, Bloom, referring to the gas emitted by decaying bodies, thinks 'One whiff of that and you're a goner' (U 104). This characteristic example of Bloom's earthy humour and colloquial idiom is challenged by the new edition's insistence that the last word should be 'doner' (6.612), a word with which most readers are quite unfamiliar: the footnote reference to the English Dialect Dictionary does little to reduce the shock of seeing a felicitous and long-enjoyed phrase wiped out. But the Rosenbach manuscript unquestionably has 'doner', so does the typescript, and so did all proofs until the sixth, when, in some hand not Joyce's, it was replaced by 'goner'. Here, Partridge's Dictionary of Historical Slang helps: it explains 'doner' as 'One who is done for, ruined, fated to die: lower classes', and, although it gives a similar explanation for 'goner' ('One who is undone, ruined or dead'), it adds, 'orig. (1847), U.S.; anglicized ca 1880'. This suggests that what may have happened is that, although Joyce imagined Bloom in 1904 using the still-current slang-word 'doner', by 1921, when the

148

word of American origin had replaced 'doner', the printer's reader, believing that he had spotted a literal, 'corrected' the proof. Of course, those who dislike the removal of 'goner' may argue that Joyce raised no objection to the word and perhaps instructed the scribe who made the change, but there are many errors in the printed editions which Joyce overlooked and there is no evidence of any such instruction. The issue cannot be finally settled, but the balance of probability, on which many editorial decisions necessarily depend, seems to lie with Gabler.

Similarly the much-quoted insertion in Scylla and Charybdis, where Stephen identifies 'Love' as the 'Word known to all men', has upset those who feel that this explicitness removes from the novel an important element of uncertainty and even mystery. Clearly Joyce did not think so when he wrote the manuscript: the lines have been omitted by the typist, either as a result of authorial instruction or because his/her eye skipped two short paragraphs in the manuscript. The insertion adds something to the continuity of the dialogue, and it makes good structural sense that Bloom and Stephen, both given to thoughts about the nature of love, should equally fail in their characteristic ways to define what they mean by the word, Bloom by his inept 'the opposite of hatred', Stephen by the garbled and incomplete reference to Aquinas in this insertion. There are *pros* and *cons*, but, again, on balance, I take Gabler to be justified.

But the real point made by these two examples from outside the chapters I propose to discuss is that they illustrate how, repeatedly, bibliographical and critical judgements are interdependent. Without Partridge, 'doner' might be plausibly attributed to a slip of the pen when Joyce was making his fair-copy manuscript: if the inserted lines could not be justified critically in their immediate context and in relation to the novel as a whole, it would be reasonable to suppose that Joyce omitted them in preparing the 'lost final working draft' given to the typist.

But if, in some places, critical argument may be offered in support of Gabler's editorial decisions, it may, in other places, challenge them. Gabler's general policy is to give preference to what Joyce can be shown to have written: he views with varying degrees of suspicion deviations from the manuscript without autograph (or implied autograph) support, whether they originate in typescripts, proofs or editions. It is hard to disagree with this as a general policy, and, indeed, the vast majority of changes in the new edition improve on current texts; but, as Gabler is very well aware, no rule of thumb works consistently for all the complexities of the *Ulysses* text, and it is precisely where critical judgement (taking into account the bibliographical information Gabler supplies) may prefer the version without unchallengeable manuscript backing to the version derived from the manuscript that the most interesting editorial problems arise.

The *Telemachia* chapters form a limited and more or less consistent group in which to examine some of these problems: all three were typed by Joyce's friend, Claud Sykes, they have similar (though not identical) documentation, and they raise a representative variety of the editorial questions provoked by the new edition. I shall concentrate on Telemachus, where the reasoning behind Gabler's decisions is complicated but clear, and the occasions for disagreement comparatively frequent and significant.

According to Gabler, the documentation for the chapter is as follows. Of the typescript in triplicate prepared by Sykes in late 1917 from Joyce's fair copy (the Rosenbach manuscript) nothing survives, but, from the printed versions derived from the typescript, Gabler concludes that Joyce initially corrected only two copies of each page, mixed the pages so that each set contained corrected and uncorrected sheets, sent one set each to *The Little Review* and *The Egoist* in 1917, and, in 1921, sent the last set, after re-examining it less systematically, to the printer. To these initial documents – the Rosenbach manuscript (*R*), *The Little Review* printing (*LR*), *The Egoist* galley proofs (the chapter was not published) (*Eg*) and the printer's first *placards* (or galleys-in-page) (*Pl*) – there have to be added postcards and letters sent by Joyce to Sykes, during typing, asking for certain changes to be made; autograph amendments to the proofs; the errata lists, autograph and printed, prepared after the appearance of the first edition in 1922; and subsequent changes introduced by editions published during Joyce's lifetime.

Comments on the Telemachia in the 1984 Ulysses

On his examination of the original documents, Gabler bases two crucial editorial decisions: first, if any two of the early printed versions (*LR*, *Eg* and *Pl*) concur against the third in 'substantive variants', the probability is that the variant in two versions is a correction made in two copies of the typescript in 1917 and, therefore, likely to be authorial: second, if all three printed texts agree against the manuscript in substantive variants, it merely indicates typing errors, present and uncorrected in all three sets of typescript:

Without exception, then, the agreement of two printed texts against the third (and/or the fair copy) reveals an authorial correction or revision of the typescript, while a triple LR-Eg-Pl agreement against R represents an uncorrected typing error. (G 1872)

These two editorial decisions seem related, almost two aspects of the one decision, but they are not, and the specific choices they lead to differ in character and in critical acceptability. This will become evident when the substantive variants occurring are considered in groups.

There is no need to spend time considering the three variants with *LR-Pl* concurrence, since Gabler accepts all three and, therefore, agrees with all the published editions, which derive, of course, from the *placards*.

There are seven substantive variants arising from *LR-Eg-R* concurrence against the *placards*. (In the following lists, an asterisk marks Gabler's choice. The last figure in the Garland reference numbers the word on the line. A question mark indicates absence from the relevant edition.)

Group A	LR-Eg-R	Pl	
(1)	quick	great	(1.86.5; *U* 5.14)
(2)	wholly*	(absent)	(1.248.9; *U* 9.32?)
(3)	beneath*	behind	(1.249.5; *U* 9.33)
(4)	alone*	above	(1.250.3; *U* 9.34)
(5)	He crammed his mouth with fry and munched and droned.*	(absent)	(1.385.1–10; *U* 13.23?)
(6)	the*	(absent)	1.428.16; *U* 14.32?)
(7)	and lips*	(absent)	(1.694.1–2; *U* 22.9?)

With the exception of (1), which is a special case, Gabler consistently chooses the *LR-Eg-R* variants, and rejects the *Pl*

151

variants as due to typing errors in the uncorrected sheets or to printing errors. There can be little doubt that he is right: the autograph Errata list corrects (4) to 'alone'; the second edition restores (5) and (7), omitted from the first; context shows (3) 'beneath' to be correct; the idiom of 'Are you from the west, sir?' demands the definite article in (6). The restoration of (2), 'wholly,' in 'A cloud began to cover the sun slowly, wholly' may seem less necessary, but it marks the correspondence in time between this chapter and Calypso, where exactly the same words occur, a correspondence further emphasised a little later by 'warm running sunlight' (Telemachus) and 'warm sunlight came running' (Calypso). Gabler supposes that Joyce indicated on the printer's typescript that he wanted 'grey' instead of (1) 'quick', but his instructions were misread and 'great' was introduced instead: in his autograph list of errata to the first edition, Joyce again asked for 'grey' (to replace 'great'), but whoever typed out the list provided a wrong line-reference, with the result that, since the second edition, readers have found 'grey sweet mother' instead of 'great sweet mother', and 'great searching eyes' instead of 'grey searching eyes'. In each case, critical examination confirms the rightness of Gabler's choice, even though in four of the seven instances he departs from all previous editions of *Ulysses*.

The four places where *LR-Eg* concur against *Pl* and *R* are less consistent in character and produce less consistent choices from Gabler.

Group B	LR-Eg		Pl-R	R	
(1)	on*		by		(1.3.8; *U* 3.3)
(2)	and I	an I		and*	(1.194.7; *U* 8.14)
		[Amended to 'and I']			
(3)	hauled		haled*		(1.329.5; *U* 12.1)
(4)	I'm	We're*		(illegible)	(1.562.1; *U* 18.18)

Curiously, the most certainly correct of these choices is (2), where Gabler rejects Joyce's autograph emendation of the first *placards*. His argument is that the 'and' of the manuscript was misread by the typist as 'an I' (visually plausible, but making no sense); that Joyce assumed a 'd' was missing and inserted it in the typescript sheets sent to *LR* and *Eg*, but failed to amend the printer's copy; and that, in 1921, seeing the same 'an I' in the *placards*, he again added a 'd'. This may seem an overingenious explanation, but the restoration of 'and', instead of 'and I', is necessary and important: all printed editions have oddly informed us that, when Mulligan was making tea in his house, it was Stephen who 'went across the landing to get more water', whereas what Joyce wrote in his manuscript and what makes much better sense is that Mulligan went for more water and consequently met his mother on the landing. The choice of (3) 'haled' is also well justified; that is unquestionably the word in the manuscript, and it is easy to imagine a typist replacing it with the more familiar 'hauled' (though 'haled' is not a common word, it is not, as Gabler calls it, 'obsolete'); Joyce presumably missed the change when checking the typescript in 1917, but spotted it in his rereading of 1921 and restored 'haled' to the printer's copy. It is hard, however, to see why this logic doesn't apply equally to (1) 'by': the manuscript has 'by', the typist could easily have mistyped 'on', and Joyce might, as with 'haled', have restored the correct reading in 1921. But I suspect that here Gabler has been misled by what looks like a similar expression in Oxen of the Sun, referred to in a footnote, where 'sustained' is followed by 'on', not 'by'. There is no real parallel: in Oxen of the Sun a veil of gossamer is 'sustained on currents of the cold interstellar wind'. Gossamer can be 'sustained on' a 'wind', but a dressinggown cannot be sustained on 'mild morning air': it is merely sustained or raised 'gently', as Mulligan moves, 'by' the air. I am also surprised by Gabler's departure from his own principle in (4). In a manuscript which is normally very easy to read, the word is illegible: if one can say with some certainty that it is not 'I'm', one can say with equal certainty that it is not 'We're', because the initial is totally unlike Joyce's 'W's, and, in fact, resembles his 'M's and 'N's. However, to a careless eye, it looks more like 'We're' than 'I'm'. It would, then, be reasonable to suppose, on Gabler's own principle, that the typist's 'We're' was corrected to 'I'm' on the typescripts sent to *LR* and *Eg*, but left uncorrected on the printer's copy (as in the case of (2)). Nowhere else does Stephen refer to himself in the plural; there is no suggestion that Mulligan, like Stephen, is 'always tired in the morning'; and there is no autograph evidence that Joyce ever wrote 'We're'.

However, on this examination of the application to substantive variants of Gabler's first editorial principle for Telemachus, it appears to work very well: in nine out of eleven instances, it makes what seems, to a critical eye, the right choice.

It is about the application of his second principle – that *LR-Eg-Pl* concurrence against *R* 'represents an uncorrected typing error' – that I begin to feel very doubtful.

Group C	R	LR-Eg-Pl	
(1)	out*	up	(1.6.11; *U* 3.7)
(2)	land*	country	(1.10.10; *U* 3.11)
(3)	slow*	low	(1.24.9; *U* 3.26)
(4)	Connolly*	Conolly	(1.128.11; *U* 6.21)
(5)	It is	It's*	(1.206.10; *U* 8.28)
(6)	pantomime*	pantomine	(1.258.3; *U* 10.2)
(7)	(after 'briskly')*	to and fro (after 'hearth')	(1.314.5–7; *U* 11.25)
(8)	breasts	paps*	(1.398.7; *U* 13.37)
(9)	(absent)*	only	(1.411.4?; *U* 14.12)
(10)	– Look at that now, she said.*	(absent)	(1.417.1–6; *U* 14.18?)
(11)	That's a shilling*	(absent)	(1.444.9–11; *U* 15.10?)
(12)	any*	(absent)	(1.490.4; *U* 16.16?)
(13)	out*	(absent)	(1.547.9; *U* 17.40?)
(14)	birdsweet*	birdlike	(1.602.9; *U* 19.23)
(15)	He is	He's*	(1.605.7; *U* 19.26)
(16)	There is	There's*	(1.614.1; *U* 19.36)
(17)	ferule*	ferrule	(1.628.3; *U* 20.16)
(18)	a*	the	(1.638.3; *U* 20.27)

In all but four instances, Gabler, applying his principle, adopts the manuscript variant, and about those four there can be little doubt. Concerning the three elided forms in (5), (15) and (16), he declares that 'they were introduced by the typist', but accepts them as 'changes conforming to Joyce's colloquial styling of speeches in this episode' (G 1729). But it would be very remarkable if three casual innovations of the typist came closer to Joyce's 'styling' than did his own manuscript: it seems much more likely that the changes were made on Joyce's instructions, in which case one has to suppose communications with Sykes in addition to the extant postcards and letters. The replacement of 'breasts' by 'paps' is, of course, covered by a postcard to Sykes requiring the change: if it were not for that postcard, Gabler says, 'it would follow that all *ER-Eg-Pl* concurrences against *R* showing no positive trace of error' would have to be accepted. This is an overstatement: there could still be overlooked typing errors which would have to be assessed critically. But the assertion shows why Gabler cannot afford to accept for instance, (2) 'country' as authorial; it would complicate his handling of this group of variants.

There are two other undeclared assumptions concealed in the principle guiding Gabler's decisions in this group: first, that all the relevant correspondence with Sykes survives, and, second, that, when making his corrections to the printer's copy in 1921 (however 'unsystematic'), Joyce never made the same amendments that he had made to the *LR* and *Eg* typescripts in 1917. The latter cannot be proven one way or the other, but I would have thought that in all probability some of the 1921 corrections would have been the same as those made earlier. As for the Sykes correspondence, there are a number of reasons for supposing that what survives is not all that was sent by Joyce. On one postcard, Joyce wrote,

The reason I trouble you so often is that I make notes on stray bits of paper which I then forget in the most unlikely places, in books, under ornaments and in my pockets and on the back of advertisements. (*Letters* II, 415)

The reference to such a variety of notes and hiding-places, and the expression 'trouble you so often' seem to imply many more changes requested than are accounted for by the extant correspondence – two postcards containing two amendments (and one planned amendment) for Telemachus and three postcards with six amendments for Nestor, spread over about four weeks. Moreover, on a postcard summarising corrections to Nestor already requested (*Letters* II, 415), Joyce refers to the correction, 'department', as having already been made by Sykes: in fact, the typist has, in two places in the chapter, replaced 'group' by 'department', but there is no request for this in any of the extant cards: this alone implies that there was at least one other communication to Sykes. Finally, as I've already suggested, the introduction of the elided forms in (5), (15) and (16) is probably due to instructions from the author, but there is no card asking for these elisions to be made. Thus, in my view, the probability is that Joyce sent Sykes more amendments than are accounted for by the two mentioned in the extant postcards – 'paps' and 'plunged and rummaged': I think we should *expect* to find more than those two differences between the manuscript and the typescript.

Of course, this argument cannot justify attributing all the discrepancies between *LR-Eg-Pl* and *R* to non-surviving instructions to Sykes: it means only, as Gabler himself says, that 'each individual instance must be critically weighed', and that the *LR-Eg-Pl* variants should not be too readily attributed to typing errors.

There are some fairly evident typing errors; for instance, the misspellings of (4) 'Connolly', and of (6) 'pantomime' (corrected in the second edition). I am also inclined to agree with Gabler about (10) and (13): the omission of the old woman's remark on learning that Mulligan was a medical student can reasonably be attributed to the typist's eye skipping a line, and its restoration helps to explain why 'Stephen listened in scornful silence' as metaphorically 'She bows her old head'; equally, the omission of (13), 'out,' looks like a typing slip – to make out reasons is idiomatic and to make reasons is not.

This leaves ten places where Gabler's choice of variant can be challenged (and, no doubt, defended) on critical grounds. Concerning (1), (2) and (3), which all occur on the first page, there are some general arguments to be considered, which must have been rejected by the editorial team. First, a typist, especially a typist like Sykes with literary interests, would be less likely to make three substantive errors on the first page than on any other. Second, a typescript-checking author would be less likely to miss three substantive errors on the first page than on any other, especially if the first check was followed by a later, though less systematic, one (and yet another if one counts the preparation of the errata list in 1922). Third, if all

156

three typing changes on the first page are even arguably improvements, it is extremely improbable that they are casual slips: such slips can easily produce absurdity, but it is very unlikely that all three would be arguably as good as, let alone better than, the original.

With these considerations in mind, the remaining variants can best be examined in order.

(1) out*/up

To call out down 'dark winding stairs' is possible, 'out' then meaning no more than 'loudly'. But there is something a little clumsy about it; 'out' would be more appropriate if Mulligan had been calling over the parapet or into the air, rather than into an interior. To call up is 'To summon, from some lower region or place (e.g. from Hades)' (*OED*), and this is precisely what Mulligan is doing. The suggestion of a conjuration in 'Come up, Kinch! Come up, you fearful Jesuit' is reinforced by 'call up'. I think it more likely that Joyce, feeling a little dissatisfied with 'out' and perceiving the force of 'up', made this change, probably by instructing Sykes, than that, as Gabler conjectures, the typist anticipated the 'up' in Mulligan's call.

(2) land*/country

This does not seem to me like an accidental typing replacement. Joyce may have realised that, when speaking of a Martello Tower close to the shore, it was inapt to refer to 'the surrounding land'. 'The surrounding country' is less specifically earthy and can include land, shore and offshore waters. It seems a clear improvement and authorial in origin.

(3) slow*/low

Gabler takes 'low' to be a 'well-meant, but mistaken' typist's correction, and argues that 'Mulligan's preceding request for "Slow music, please" . . . clearly conditions the repetition of the adjective.' But the matter is not settled so easily. If, as 'a long . . . whistle' suggests, Mulligan whistles a sustained note, I find it difficult to understand what 'slow' could mean: a long sustained whistle can be high or low, but not slow. Moreover, on the proofs, Joyce added, 'Two strong shrill whistles answered through the calm'. Remembering that, working on the proofs, Joyce had 'low' before his eyes, it seems likely that 'shrill' is deliberately placed in contrast, and that what Joyce is describing is an odd but not uncommon echoic phenomenon. I quote from *Chambers's Encyclopaedia* (1967) IV, 752:

Harmonic Echo – The pitch and timbre of an echo sometimes appear to differ from those of the original sound. Thus the echo from a clump of trees may sound an octave higher than the signal . . .

I don't know whether this phenomenon occurs (or used to occur) at the Martello Tower, but it seems to be the only explanation of 'shrill', and 'shrill,' as I've said, seems deliberately contrasted to 'low'. (If 'low' is replaced by 'slow', it is doubtful whether an editor can retain the sentence added in proof, written when Joyce had 'low' in front of him.) With this, as with the other two variants on the first page, I think that the balance of probability, both documentary and critical, suggests that Joyce asked Sykes to make these changes in the typescript.

(7) to and fro (misplaced?)

The Rosenbach manuscript has 'moved briskly to and fro about the hearth, hiding and revealing its yellow glow.' In *LR*, *Eg* and *Pl* 'to and fro' follows 'hearth', and Gabler supposes this to be a typist's inversion. He quotes, in support of his case for restoring the manuscript sequence, Pound's comment on receiving the first seventeen pages of typescript in December 1917, observing the 'accidental rhyme' of 'fro' and 'glow' (*Letters* II, 414). But the fact is that, although Pound pointed out the rhyme, Joyce made no attempt to restore the manuscript order then or later: there can be no question of this being a typing error overlooked by Joyce. Personally, I think that the mimetic sway of 'to and fro, hiding and revealing' is precisely why Joyce told Sykes to amend the sentence order. His works are full of similarly mimetic patternings of syntax, often with rhyme or assonance: e.g. 'They moved in slow circles, circling closer and closer to enclose, to enclose. . . .' (*P* 141)

(9) (absent)*/only

As printed in previous editions, the if-clause in Mulligan's declaration – 'If we could only live on good food like that' – idiomatically expresses desire and regret for an unavailable condition, implying 'but unfortunately we can't, because it is not available or we can't afford it'. 'Only' is essential to the idiom, and not, as Gabler asserts, 'an eking out of an idiomatic phrase', for which the typist is responsible. Without it, the condition is an absurd one – 'If we could live on good food like that': of course we could live on good food. I suspect that Joyce accidentally dropped the word from his fair copy, and restored it in one of the two ways I have suggested.

(11) That's a shilling*/(absent)

Here Gabler's suggestion that the typist's eye skipped from the first to the second occurrence of the word 'shilling' is plausible; the problem is that instead of the omission of three words from the milkwoman's reckoning producing nonsense or incoherence, as one might expect, it is an improvement which exactly catches the way in which simple people like the milkwoman add up money. Since I doubt whether many improvements to Joyce's work were brought about by accidental error, I suspect Joyce told Sykes to omit the words, as he told him to omit similar groups of words in Nestor. (See *Letters* I, 109.)

(12) any*/(absent)

The manuscript has 'Would I make any money by it?': the printed versions are without the 'any'. This question to Haines makes Mulligan angry with Stephen: ' – You put your hoof in it now. What did you say that for?'. It is not that Mulligan is uninterested in money, but merely that he feels Stephen has been unnecessarily blunt. The *R* version makes Stephen ask whether he might get some money out of Haines's proposed collection of his sayings: the *LR-Eg-Pl* version is much blunter, since it implies that Stephen is uninterested in the collection except as a way of making money. This accounts better for Mulligan's annoyance, and seems echoed in Stephen's reply, 'The problem is to get money' – not 'some money'. Again, the omission of 'any' seems an improvement with which I would credit Joyce rather than a careless typist.

(14) birdsweet*/birdlike

At the end of the chapter, Mulligan's voice is referred to as 'sweettoned and sustained', and Gabler quotes this as confirming his choice of 'birdsweet'. But, in the immediate context, Mulligan is capering about pretending to be a bird, 'fluttering his winglike hands' and, according to the typescript, making 'birdlike' cries. It is, of course, possible that 'winglike' influenced the typist unconsciously into changing the later adjective, but the parallel forms may be meant to suggest the somewhat laborious attempt to amuse. My guess is that Joyce, looking over the chapter, decided that 'birdsweet' here was a little too cute and sugary.

(15) ferule*/ferrule

It is true that the *OED* gives 'ferule' as a nineteenth-century variant spelling of 'ferrule', but in the present sense of 'a ring or cap of metal put round the end of a stick', it is so rare that I have never, in fact, seen it. No doubt, the reason for this is that, in English, 'ferrule' and 'ferule' have different etymologies and different meanings, a 'ferule' being a rod or cane. Joyce was probably led to the misspelling by his familiarity with Italian *ferula*, a rod, but I believe an editor should correct such casual errors – as the typist did, whether instructed to or not, in 1917.

(17) a*/the

This seems a very small matter, but my reason for preferring 'the' is that it makes more certain the reference to Goldoni's play, of which the English title is *The Servant of Two Masters*. Stephen immediately adds, 'And a third . . . there is who wants me for odd jobs': he could have said 'three masters' in the first place, except for wanting to refer to the title of the play – a kind of retort to Mulligan's mocking application to him of the title of Captain Marryat's novel, *Japhet in Search of a Father*.

Thus of thirty-two substantive variants in the chapter, where the editorial choice has been shaped by the two principles governing discrepancies between *R*, *LR*, *Eg*, and *Pl*, I find grounds for disagreement with 12 of Gabler's decisions, and 10 of these are connected with his rule of regarding *LR* – *Eg* – *Pl* concurrence against *R* as attributable to typing error. That, in itself, seems to me to cast some suspicion on the validity of

the rule. Even putting aside the possibility that some corrections made by Joyce on the *LR* and *Eg* typescripts in 1917 were
repeated on the printer's typescript in 1921, ten alterations to
the manuscript (in addition to the two mentioned on extant
postcards) do not seem to me more than the apology to Sykes
for 'troubling you so often' would lead one to expect.

Two other places in the first chapter where Gabler deviates
from current editions deserve notice because, although of no
great importance in themselves, they derive from editorial
decisions with recurring effects.

There is no doubt that the Rosenbach manuscript, the
proofs, and the early editions refer to the 'barbacans' of the
Martello Tower both here (1.316.5; *U* 11.27) and in Proteus
(3.272.1; *U* 44.17). No modern English dictionary gives this
spelling, except the *OED* which lists it as a form current in the
15th–17th centuries. The 1932 editor noted the anomaly,
changed to 'barbicans' and has been followed in all succeeding
editions. Gabler, however, reinstates 'barbacans', presumably
because he believes it possible that Joyce deliberately chose an
archaic spelling. There is no point in archaism in either
context: a simpler explanation is that after years in Trieste and
Pola, both of which have castles, Joyce had become
accustomed to the Italian *barbacane*, and this led to
misspelling of the English word. I have already suggested a
similar reason for the misspelling of 'ferrule', and an even
clearer example is offered (in Calypso – 4.489.1; *U* 68.24 –
and Lestrygonians – 8.1084.3; *U* 180.42) by the mention of
Boylan's 'brillantined hair'. Not even the *OED* gives this as an
alternative spelling, and the obvious explanation of it is that
Joyce was familiar with Italian '*brillantina*' or French
'*brillantine*'. But without the 'i' the word cannot be correctly
pronounced in English, and, again, quite justifiably, the 1932
editor and subsequent editors have changed to 'brilliantined'.
Curiously, in some later places, Gabler shows awareness of the
effect of Continental residence on Joyce's spelling: in Ithaca
(17.165.10; *U* 671.4) he rejects Joyce's proof correction of
'filter' to 'filtre', as 'an apparent contamination by French
spelling' (G 1752), and he is the first editor to amend Joyce's
'pelosity' (influenced by Italian *pelosità*) (17.1202.3; *U* 703.14)
to 'pilosity'. Another illustration from the same chapter occurs

where the Rosenbach manuscript refers to a torn piece of toenail as a 'lacerated unghial fragment'. On the third proof, some scribal hand amended to 'unguial', which survived into the first edition: the printed list of errata and the editions from 1926 to 1961 changed the word to 'Unguical'; and Gabler goes further and introduces the correct English form 'ungual' (17.1491.6; *U* 712.9). Again, Joyce's original spelling was clearly affected by Italian *unghia* (nail). I am certain Gabler is right in choosing 'filter' and introducing 'pilosity' and 'ungual', but I cannot understand why the same principle did not commend to him 'barbicans', 'ferrule' and 'brilliantined'. A related point here is that 'lattiginous' (Ithaca – 17.1043.8; *U* 698.23), conjecturally explained in the Textual Notes as 'a nonce-form, derived from Eng. *latten* "alloy similar to brass" (*OED*) or from It. *latte* "milk" ', is, in fact, an anglicization of Italian *lattiginoso* (milky), although on the model of such forms as 'lactiferous', the anglicization should have been 'lactiginous'.

The last point raised by the new editing of Telemachus is totally different in kind. Where the Rosenbach manuscript, typescript and early proofs had '—We can drink it black, Stephen said', Joyce added on the third proofs (i.e. the second page proofs) 'thirstily'. But these proofs were not returned to the printer, and therefore 'thirstily' is absent from the fourth proofs and from all subsequent printings. Is the appearance of an addition (or an alteration for that matter) on an unreturned proof sufficient authority for including it, as Gabler does, in the text (1.340.8; *U* 12.16?)? Joyce presumably knew the set of proofs had not been returned to the printer, but made no later attempt to add the word. Did he have second thoughts? There is at least one occasion later when, having made a substantial addition to an unreturned set of proofs, he appears to have changed his mind and adapted the added passage to use in a completely different place. Here he may have realised that the adverb 'thirstily' occurs more effectively in Nestor where a woman at the races is remembered 'nuzzling thirstily her clove of orange' (2.312.6–11; *U* 32.28). Or he may have perceived that it was at odds with all the other adverbs applied to Stephen's behaviour in the first chapter – 'wearily', 'quietly' (twice), 'gloomily', 'coldly' (twice), 'gravely', 'listlessly', 'drily': in such unenergetic, withdrawn, melancholy company, 'thirstily' seems uncharacteristically avid and eager. In other words, there may be plausible critical reasons for supposing that Joyce changed his mind. This, of course, is a matter of general editorial policy, but it does seem to me a dangerous proceeding to include material which the author sent neither to typist nor printer, and which, therefore, may be first thoughts later abandoned.

I do not propose to discuss at length changes in the new versions of Nestor and Proteus, but merely to look at certain additional problems raised by them. For instance, in discussing 'thirstily', I questioned the validity of using materials never sent to typist or printer, and, as only one adverb is involved, the matter hardly seems important. But in Proteus more is at stake. To Richie Goulding's remembered greeting, '—Morrow, nephew', Gabler adds, from the unreturned third proofs (second page proofs), 'Sit down and take a walk' (3.79.3–8; *U* 39.5?); to the description of the sandflats' 'sewage breath', he adds, from the same source, 'a pocket of seaweed smouldered in seafire under a midden of man's ashes' (3.151.3–152.3; *U* 41.3?); at the end of the memory of Kevin Egan's talk about Ireland, ending at 'Arthur Griffith now', Gabler adds, from the same unreturned proofs, 'AE, pimander, good shepherd of men' (3.227.9–228.4; *U* 43.8?). These are substantial additions, each in its way characteristic of Joyce's treatment of such things as Richie's jocularity, Stephen's sense of decay and moribundity, and AE's occultism. Yet may it not be that the failure to add them to subsequent proofs is evidence that all three were passing ideas, later abandoned? It can be argued that Ritchie's remark is a feeble anticipation of his jocular threat about twelve lines later, '—Sit down or by the law Harry I'll knock you down'; that the seaweed passage is, perhaps, a bit pretentious and heavy-handed in its alliteration; and that the reference to Russell is out of keeping with the other items in the catalogue of Egan's topics. ('Pimander' was used later in Circe.) But it requires about as much editorial boldness to throw them out as it took to put them in. One relevant oddity in the chapter is that, according to the edition, the sentence, 'Unfallen Adam rode and not rutted' (3.386.1–6; *U* 47.28), was added on the same unreturned proofs, yet it has somehow survived into the printed editions. Is this simply an editorial slip? Did Joyce reinsert it on later proofs? I can find in the edition no explanation of the apparent discrepancy.

The remaining problems I want to consider arise from a slight difference in documentation: for the second and third chapters, *The Egoist* printing, instead of being based on a separate copy of the typescript, was merely a resetting of the version already published in *The Little Review*. Consequently *Eg* no longer has any separate authority, its concurrences with other documents have no evidential weight, and Gabler's editorial principles for dealing with substantive variants in *R*, *LR*, *Eg*, and *Pl* no longer apply. If Joyce continued his practice of correcting only two copies of the typescript (though this is 'less easily demonstrable' than for Telemachus), there would be three possible ways in which the typescript copies were distributed:

(a)   One corrected copy to *LR*, and the other unused; in which case the *LR* variant would have authorial support against *R – Pl* concurrence;

(b)   One corrected copy to the printer of *Pl*, and the other unused; in which case *Pl* would have authorial support against *R – LR* concurrence;

(c)   One corrected copy each to *LR* and the printer of *Pl*; in which case *LR – Pl* concurrence would have authorial support against *R*.

However, it would be equally possible that variants occurring either in *LR* or *Pl* were printer's errors, and that instances of *LR – Pl* concurrence were merely evidence of errors in the typescript. This is the position adopted by Gabler:

Editorially, the high potential of transmissional corruption in both LR – Eg and LR – Eg – Pl concurrences leads to the rejection of the variants from LR, Eg and Pl in all but a few critically compelling instances. (G 1874)

Again, Gabler follows his general rule – when in doubt, stick to what Joyce can be shown to have written, either in the Rosenbach manuscript, in correspondence with Sykes, or in autograph amendments to proofs; and, again, the rule for the most part produces critically convincing decisions. The area for dispute concerns, essentially, how 'few' are the 'critically compelling instances'.

Comments on the Telemachia in the 1984 Ulysses

Leaving aside for the moment the *LR* – *Eg* – *Pl* concurrences attributed to typing errors, there are two places where *LR* and *Pl* differ, both in Nestor and both with slightly odd features. In the Rosenbach manuscript, when the boy Armstrong tries to define a pier, he does so as 'A thing out in the water' – but it looks on the manuscript as though Joyce began to write 'waves' and changed it to 'water'. *LR* also has 'water' but *Pl* has 'waves', and Gabler's interpretation is that Sykes mistakenly typed 'waves', that Joyce corrected this on the *LR* copy, but that he failed to do so on the copy which went to the printer in 1921 (2.32.11; *U* 24.39). It does seem odd that the typist should have reverted to the word Joyce originally began to write (the manuscript now clearly reads 'water'), and it seems equally possible that, either in 1917 or 1921, Joyce decided, on second thoughts, that 'waves' was better. Preference between the two words has, then, to be decided on critical rather than bibliographical grounds. My own preference for 'waves' is based on two grounds, one local, the other less so. Armstrong, thinking of Kingstown pier, associates the word 'pier' with the sea, as opposed to a bridge which, for Comyn, 'is across a river', and 'waves' is more specifically marine than 'water': moreover 'waves' introduces a key-word in the chapter, picked up in the 'Lycidas' recitation (2.78.10; *U* 26.7) and in Stephen's thoughts (2.83.9; *U* 26.13), preparatory to its fuller development in Proteus.

The other example involves two places in the text, and here, surprisingly, Gabler goes against the Rosenbach reading. The manuscript refers to Sargent's 'tangled hair and scraggy neck' and, a little later, to his 'lean neck and tangled hair'; so, too, does *Pl*. But *LR* replaces 'tangled' in both places by 'thick' and Gabler accepts this reading, though rather uneasily:

The replacement of 'tangled' by 'thick' appears only in LR (+ Eg). The R reading, recurring in Pl, may seem more attractive. But the identical change in two instances supports the authority of the revision. (G 1732)

I think it likely that Joyce wanted the *LR* printer to get rid of the repetition of 'tangled'. But the two places, though so close, are significantly different. In the first, Sargent's hair and neck 'gave witness of unreadiness': 'tangled' gives such witness, 'thick' does not. Moreover, between the two occurrences, Stephen has begun to feel a certain pity for the boy: 'tangled' and 'scraggy' are pejorative adjectives: 'lean' and 'thick' are not. The most likely explanation is that Joyce asked *LR* to replace the second 'tangled' by 'thick' and that, due to some misunderstanding, both were changed. Critical argument here seems to me to favour strongly 'tangled hair and scraggy neck' (2.124.4–8; *U* 27.17), while accepting the *LR* emendation 'lean neck and thick hair' (2.139.4–8; *U* 27.33).

In all seven instances of *LR* – *Eg* – *Pl* concurrence against *R* where the editorial choice seems to me disputable, Gabler has opted for the fair copy version, but the cases are so various in kind and importance as to require individual consideration.

(1) *R* tissue*/*LR* – Pl tissues (2.24.2; U 24.29)
The manuscript assertion, that on Armstrong were crumbs which 'adhered to the tissue of his lips', seems to me pointless. To what other part of his lips could crumbs have adhered? Why not simply 'adhered to his lips'? But if Joyce had in mind the wet inner and dry outer tissues and wanted to suggest that crumbs stuck to both, 'tissues' would be significant. I suspect that Joyce accidentally dropped the 's' in fair copying, and either instructed Sykes to replace it or inserted it himself on the typescript.

(2) R their*/LR – Pl the (2.371.9; U 34.15)
As there are three 'theirs' in the sentence, I had better quote it in full: 'Their eyes knew their (the) years of wandering and, patient, knew the dishonours of their flesh.' Joyce may well have thought the manuscript sentence was clumsy. The typed version has a firm chiasmic construction. 'Their . . . the . . . the . . . their', which is so plainly an improvement that I am reluctant to attribute it to a typing slip. As this occurs on the only surviving sheet of typescript, one would have to suppose that Joyce instructed Sykes to make the change.

(3) R human*/LR – Pl (absent) (2.380.14; U 34.27?)
In Mr Deasy's assertion that 'All human (?) history moves towards one great goal', 'human' is not so much unnecessary as mistaken. 'The ways of the Creator' apply to all history, not

just human history, and Mr Deasy is replying to Stephen's declaration that 'History is a nightmare'. The sentence is improved by the omission of the adjective, and, as this, too, occurs on the extant sheet of typescript, I would attribute the improvement to Joyce's instructions to Sykes.

(4) *R* awhile*/*LR* – *Pl* a while (2.387.8; *U* 34.35)

To justify the manuscript form, Gabler refers to '*OED* sv Awhile'. But, in fact, the *OED* says of the word used substantively, 'Improperly written together, when there is no unification of sense, and *while* is purely a substantive', and gives the very phrase in question, 'for awhile' as one illustration of this improper form. Irrespective of whether the change was made on Joyce's instructions or not, the typist corrected a simple error, and I see no point in restoring it to a text where it has never before appeared in print. The additional oddity here is that, in a postcard to Sykes (*Letters* II, 415), Joyce wrote 'Please change the word "captive" in phrase "Mr Deasy held his nose captive for a few moments" etc to "tweaked".' But in the Rosenbach manuscript from which Sykes was typing (and on which, in pencil, he made the required change), the words were 'held for awhile the wings of his nose captive'. Presumably Joyce was quoting from his own rough copy of the chapter, and then it would seem that 'awhile' was an error which slipped in while he was making a fair and slightly amended copy.

(5) *R* upon*/*LR* – Pl on (3.51.4; *U* 38.17)

Idiomatically, the form familiar from all earlier printed editions (deriving originally from the *placards*), 'Warring his life long on', is correct, as in 'to make war on'. 'Upon' looks like a slip in the fair copy, corrected on the typescript.

(6) *R* written*/*LR* – *Pl* (absent) (3.141.4; *U* 40.34?)

For Stephen to refer to his epiphanies as 'written' on green oval leaves seems unnecessarily specific. In the self-mockery, the epiphanies might be imagined as incribed in some far more pretentious ways. The omission marginally improves the sense and was, I suspect, authorized by Joyce.

(7) *R* His arm. Cranly's arm.*/*LR* – *Pl* (absent) (3.451.9–12;
U 49.23?)

Gabler suggests a typist's 'eyeskip' to account for this
omission, but there are no local circumstances that would
support the explanation. There are, however, two plausible
reasons for supposing that Joyce asked Sykes to omit the words
or that he deleted them himself from the typescript: in the first
place, he had used precisely the same two sentences in
Telemachus, and, in the second, following immediately after
'Wilde's love that dare not speak its name', the words suggest
a homosexual relationship more explicitly than the author, on
second thoughts, may have desired.

In all these cases, some more important than others, Gabler's
choice requires alterations of the versions given in previous
editions. My contention is not that he is wrong in preferring
variants with manuscript support, but that there are more
instances where 'critically compelling' reasons can be given
for accepting the *LR* – *Eg* – *Pl* variants than the 'few' he
recognises.

One last point concerns two of the 'Textual Notes' on the
first three chapters. In a note on Stephen's mental listing of his
debts, 'Mulligan, nine pounds, three pairs of socks, one pair
brogues' (2.255.1–10; *U* 31.1–2), Gabler observes,

Episode 1 at 8.14–21 indicates that neither were the (black) brogues
Mulligan's, nor had Mulligan procured them for Stephen (see note
74.17). (G 1730)

But the passage referred to in Telemachus doesn't refer to
'brogues' at all, but to 'breeks' (1.113.7). This is probably a
mere slip, but, unfortunately (as the reference to note 74.17
indicates), it leads to a more significant misunderstanding of a
sentence at the beginning of Proteus, 'My two feet in his boots
are at the ends of [my two] his legs, *nebeneinander*' (3.16–17).
Both the mention of 'one pair of brogues' and the substitution of
'his' for 'my two' were apparently written into a lost printer's
copy of the typescript, and this leads Gabler to suppose that
Joyce had forgotten the distinction made in Telemachus
'between the black trousers of unspecified origin which Stephen
is wearing and the grey ones with hairstripe offered him by
Mulligan'. In fact, there is no evidence that Joyce had forgotten.

Comments on the Telemachia in the 1984 Ulysses

I hope it is evident from this discussion of the Gabler versions of the *Telemachia* chapters that the objections I have raised in no way constitute a complaint about the edition itself. Having looked at all the substantive changes in the text, I find the vast majority to be improvements, and where, for critical reasons, I have suspected the Gabler versions, I have had to turn to the bibliographical information supplied by him and his colleagues to find textual justification for my suspicions. All readers of Joyce, not themselves bibliographers, now have available to them a mass of information about the novel and its development which it is unlikely that any of them previously possessed. The nature of this paper puts emphasis on points of disagreement, but the new edition, through the whole course of the novel, corrects errors, clears up difficulties, adds valuable new material, and, in general, makes for the restoration of what the late Jack Dalton called 'this hideously corrupt text'.[1]

Even in the first three chapters, I recall at random the satisfaction of seeing Swinburne and Milton at last correctly quoted, the confusion about Mulligan's teamaking cleared up, 'Los *demiurgos*' italicized so that now it unmistakably refers to Blake's figure and not to some mysterious Spanish entities, '*amplius*' replacing '*nimium*' in the apostrophe to the baldhead, 'Nother' instead of 'Mother' in the telegram Stephen considered a 'curiosity to show', 'moomb' instead of 'womb' in Stephen's attempt at versifying. Many of these have been noted by earlier commentators but, at last, they appear in an edition, the first edition to have given to the preparation of the text the time, care and thought it deserves.

It has been said that this edition demonstrates that no definitive edition of *Ulysses* will ever be possible. If by 'definitive', one means a text where every word is beyond dispute, the statement is, of course, true – but it would be equally true of Shakespeare's plays and of all literary texts of any bibliographical complexity. I think it would be wrong to throw up our hands in despair at the magnitude and multiplicity of the problems. I see no reason, given rational discussion and debate, why it should not be possible to reach agreement about a large proportion of the disputed matters, so that, in the not too distant future, there might be one accepted text with variant readings, within which various editors might operate, providing their own decisions about and interpretations of unsettled problems. That is all a definitive text can ever be, and Gabler's edition is a major step towards it.

CURIOS OF SIGNS I AM HERE TO REDE[1]!

C. GEORGE SANDULESCU

After Joyce, Gabler has created most.[2]

1. In the present paper I wish to propose an *alternative theoretical approach* to the *Ulysses* multitext. For what we are faced with is one resultant of an ordered set of subtexts (which had by a complicated process been collapsed into one). This multitext is, within the present theory, the equivalent of the 'continuous manuscript' idea that Gabler propounds. Secondly, its components are sequentially organized (hence the ordered set), and there again my views largely coincide with those of Gabler. However, these subtexts, which are the very members of the ordered set, are not in themselves arranged on a proper diachronic dimension. It is there that I strongly disagree with Gabler's notion of 'diachronic text', which is a flagrant contradiction in terms . . .

2. But let us begin at the beginning. If a text is a multitext in the sense that it is simultaneously derived from several other texts – which here I name subtexts (a term which has nothing to do with Stanislavski's notion), and which Gabler calls 'documents' – , then its status is that of an output text, which in the last analysis is a common denominator of all component texts.

As this is but the sketch of a theory, I do not wish to take up the theoretical question 'When does disparity become text?', that is to say, at what particular point in time does a jumble of jottings-down, totally unconnected in appearance, acquire the fundamental textual feature of connectedness (as defined in topology). The reason I do not want to take up this question is in order not to have to deny (at this early stage of the discussion) the status of subtext, i.e. component text, to Joyce's notebooks.

3. In quite another respect, there are several major *operations* that can be performed on a text or subtext, though

171

NOT (emphatically!) on disparate jottings-down which have not yet acquired the feature of connectedness. Incidentally, it must be said in passing that these 'operations' are more or less the same as the so-called 'transformations' which may apply on kernel sentences, on an obligatory or optional basis, as part of any transformational-generative grammar, particularly one of the first generation, i.e. characterizing pre-1965 developments, as outlined, for instance, by Emmon Bach.[3]

There are six such operations (or transformations) that can be performed on a text; more importantly, there are no other conceivable possibilities. Further, these six operations fall in fact into pairs, the first pair being the most important, as the second pair is easily reducible to the first. The third and last pair of textual operations poses more delicate problems and is less relevant to the present sketch of a theory; however, within the framework of a complete and exhaustive theory, a lot more attention would have to be paid to it.

4. The *six operations*, here defined by means of the standard TG formalizations employed by Emmon Bach, are the following:

A 1.	Deletion	$a \longrightarrow \emptyset$
A 2.	Insertion	$\emptyset \longrightarrow a$
B 1.	Substitution	$a \longrightarrow b$
B 2.	Permutation	$ab \longrightarrow ba$
C 1.	Reduction	$a + b \longrightarrow a'$
C 2.	Expansion	$a \longrightarrow a' + b$ (or $a' + b'$)

It is to be noted that Insertion is sometimes called Addition, and Substitution is sometimes called Replacement. The twin term 'deletion and replacement', used by Gabler in the chart of Symbols (on page x of Volume One, and page vi of Volumes Two and Three, lines 10 and 30) is flagrantly ambiguous even in a most elementary approach, as the term *replacement* contains the notion of 'deletion' in its own semantic structure.

Group A, containing the operations of Deletion and Insertion, is made up of two *elementary* changes, or transformations, or operations, or processes. They are 'elementary' in that they cannot be further reduced; in exchange, the two operations making up Group B are easily reducible to the very first two: Substitution is made up, first of a Deletion, then of an Insertion (in the empty slot thus created). In a context-free approach,

$$a \longrightarrow b \qquad
\begin{array}{ll}
(1) & a \longrightarrow \emptyset \\
(2) & \emptyset \longrightarrow b \\
(1 \ \& \ 2) & a \longrightarrow b
\end{array}$$

there is first a deletion of a, followed by an insertion of b, which is indeed tantamount to a substitution or replacement. In a context-sensitive approach, the formalization would be the following (with x and y denoting foregoing and subsequent context respectively):

$$xay \longrightarrow xby \qquad
\begin{array}{ll}
(1) & xay \longrightarrow x\emptyset y \\
(2) & x\emptyset y \longrightarrow xby \\
(1 \ \& \ 2) & xay \longrightarrow xby
\end{array}$$

Operation B 2, called Permutation, should from the start be formalized within a context-sensitive approach, as it is the most complex by far of the first four textual operations. Part of its complexity also lies in the fact that in addition to foregoing and subsequent context there can also be some (optional) medial context; these three types of contexts are here denoted by x, y, and z (corresponding to initial, medial, and final positions). The breaking down of a permutation of this kind requires four different stages, as follows:

(1)	$xaybz \longrightarrow x\emptyset ybz$	(Deletion of a)
(2)	$x\emptyset ybz \longrightarrow xbybz$	(Reinsertion of b)
(3)	$xbybz \longrightarrow xby\emptyset z$	(Deletion of second b)
(4)	$xby\emptyset z \longrightarrow xbyaz$	(Reinsertion of a)

Alternatively, in another type of sequentialization, the number of stages can even go up to seven, if successive deletions and successive insertions are envisaged separately; also, when more substantial context segments are taken into account, or if one wishes to foreground context segments more prominently, the three corresponding symbols are capitalized:

(1)	$XaYbZ \longrightarrow X\emptyset YbZ$	
(2)	$XaYbZ \longrightarrow XaY\emptyset Z$	
(3)	$X\emptyset YbZ \longrightarrow X\emptyset Y\emptyset Z$	Deletion in output of (1)
(4)	$XaY\emptyset Z \longrightarrow X\emptyset Y\emptyset Z$	Deletion in output of (2)
(5)	$X\emptyset Y\emptyset Z \longrightarrow X\emptyset Y\emptyset Z$	Matching of outputs (3 & 4)
(6)	$X\emptyset Y\emptyset Z \longrightarrow X\emptyset YaZ$	Reinsertion of a.
(7)	$X\emptyset YaZ \longrightarrow XbYaZ$	Reinsertion of b.

173

All this is no theoretical speculation: it is what happens on the actual text in a case of permutation. And this is precisely the situation in Episode Ten, line 183. As a result of a 'revision at first overlay level' (indicated by a pair of carets), the sentence –

.A homely and just word.

becomes –

.A just and homely word.

This is precisely an instance of permutation of the kind formalized in the preceding paragraphs. It also has the extra advantage of containing a medial context. The advantage of treating it as permutation lies in the fact that the correct identification of the phenomenon under scrutiny makes it so much simpler to pass on to an analysis of the poetic reasons for the switch: it is more than probable that this particular permutation occurs in order to have the shorter adjective first, the two-syllable one afterwards. As such, it is a clear instance of switch.

5. During the 1979 session of the Joyce Symposium, which took place in Zurich, and which was devoted to a collective scrutiny of the little volume tabled by Gabler under the title *Prototype*[4], I outlined on the blackboard in front of the entire audience the exact relationships existing between the above discussed four operations A 1 and 2 as well as B 1 and 2: Gabler refused to see the theoretical point that was being made. Tucked away somewhere in the middle of page 1901 of Volume Three, this is all Gabler has to say on perhaps the more than fundamental taxonomy of textual operations:

The diacritical system is a notation in symbols of the dynamics of the textual development in the continuous manuscript as deletion, addition, and deletion + addition = replacement, the three aspects under which all revisional operations at the author's hand may be subsumed.

In the first place, Gabler fails to include the fourth fundamental operation, called Permutation; its existence is among others proved by the symmetry of formalization in the description of the two operations belonging to Group B. Failing

174

to do that, he is forced to treat all permutation in a way which is not only cumbersome but also grossly misleading poetically. Thus, the above discussed example appears in Gabler's Synopsis (page 480, line 18) as –

.A (OPEN CARET, OPEN POINTED BRACKET) homely and just (CLOSE POINTED BRACKET) just and homely (CLOSE CARET) word.

The function of pairs of carets is to indicate 'the extent of additions and replacements' (sic!). The function of pairs of pointed brackets is to indicate 'currente calamo cancellations and deletions in revision'. It should be first noted that in spite of the fact that, by their very definition, symbols, particularly of the graphic kind, should stand in a one-to-one relation to their gloss, i.e. one symbol/one gloss, each of the above glosses of Caret and Pointed Bracket indicates two possible alternatives. Thus the propositions –

> (1) Pairs of carets indicate additions.
> (2) Pairs of carets indicate replacements.

are both equally true and valid. Given the fact that, as demonstrated above, Insertion (or addition) is an *elementary* operation, and substitution (or replacement) is a *compound* textual operation, the symbol creates grave confusion by its ambiguity. Pointed brackets, too, simultaneously have two semantic alternatives: (a) currente calamo cancellations, and (b) deletions in revision. The most extraordinary and paradoxical outcome of all this is that, between them, the carets and the pointed brackets manage to convey ALL four fundamental textual operations. Quite in accordance with the definitions given in the chart of SYMBOLS placed at the beginning of each of the three volumes –

(1) Pairs of carets insert (i.e. indicate 'additions').
(2) Pairs of carets substitute (i.e. indicate 'replacements').
(3) Pairs of pointed brackets delete (i.e. indicate 'deletions in revision').

And last but not least,

(4) Carets and pointed brackets have in conjoined use the function to permute.

175

as in the example above discussed. How then can one speak of accuracy and adequate placement on a scale of ideal delicacy in subtext description, when all the four fundamental textual operations are at first reduced to three (as in the statement on page 1901), and afterwards marked by two symbols only?

As part of the alternative solutions to be offered within the present sketchy outline of a theory, I first propose that the four fundamental operations, if accepted, should each have its separate symbol in the chart. Secondly, leaving aside all constraints on space, they should be denoted by the computer-type instructions DELETE, INSERT, SUBSTITUTE, PERMUTE. This is at least a solution to be adopted in the preliminary stages of multitext scanning. The main purposes of the exercise are: (a) to keep the four phenomena, thus identified, in watertight compartments, and (b) to avoid the instances of ambiguity now too often characterizing the chart of SYMBOLS.

A minor point worth making before closing this part of the discussion is that what as part of the above quotation from page 1901 is correctly labelled 'deletion + addition = replacement' is strangely distorted on lines 10 and 30 of each chart of symbols so as to become '(deletion and replacement)', placed in parentheses. Not having yet got round to page 1901, the average reader may not be at all able to disambiguate the phrase: he is quite likely to interpret it as 'deletion-and-replacement', whereas it should be read within the parentheses as (deletion, and replacement) or even (deletion; and replacement), to say nothing of (deletion; replacement). In the last analysis, such regrettable ambiguities in the chart of SYMBOLS could only be ascribed to the compiler's lack of familiarity with lexicographic conventions.

6. There are also the changes which surface not within one particular subtext, but rather in the passage from one to the other. All the above four operations can apply equally well, therefore, not only in what Gabler calls 'intra-textual' situations, but also in 'inter-textual' ones. It goes without saying that *textual* is here taken in the sense of *subtextual*. Intra-textual changes are always explicit. Inter-textual changes are usually derived by inference: they are, in other words, obtained by implication.

176

7. From quite another point of view the changes affect either the language *segment* as such, or they are simply *parasegmental*. The language segment is made up of lexical items, commonly called words, and the textual operation can focus either on one particular one, or on a group of them, forming a phrase, a clause, or a sentence. However, if the changes are not geared to a particular sequence of words, then their focus usually lies beside the segment; rarely can they lie above or below it. Hence, the name of parasegmentals given here to markers such as paragraphs (or more precisely, paragraph indentation), dialogue dashes, and their exact positioning within the symmetry of the run-on graphic text; further, punctuation marks, italics, and quotation marks of all kinds as well as parentheses and specific aside markers. All these elements, though they are obviously present in the graphic text for everybody to see, are totally aberrant on the surface of a *phonic* text. (It is these elements that, for the sake of simplification, I called *visuals* in the spoken version of this paper given at the Monaco Seminar.)

The main point to be made here is that segmentals and parasegmentals are not at all on a par as regards their specific weight within the overall economy of the text. Thus, a study dealing with the use or non-use of, say, italics is of somewhat less far-reaching significance than a study dealing with the possible insertion or possible deletion of one particular language segment, be it at word, phrase, clause, or sentence level. In consequence, and from that particular point of view, there are two fundamental types of possible changes in a subtext:

(1) segmental changes;
(2) parasegmental changes.

The two types of changes are thus hierarchically organized, with the segmental changes holding a position of dominance over the parasegmental ones. This elementary truth was not accepted by Gabler at all, who, in reaching the figure of 'over 5,000 emendations', goes on counting changes indiscriminately.

In their turn, parasegmentals too are hierarchically organized in that some types of parasegmentals, such as proper-name spelling, are more significant than others. Let us take the following examples:

(1.a) (The 1960 Bodley Head, p. 45, lines 28–29)
.Sounds solid: made by the malet of *Los Demiurgos.*
(1.b) (The 1984 Garland 'Reading Text', Episode 3, lines 17–18)
.Sounds solid: made by the malet of Los *demiurgos.*
(2.a) (The 1960 Bodley Head, p. 235, line 21)
– Monsieur de la Palisse, Stephen sneered,
(2.b) (The 1984 Garland 'Reading Text', Episode 9, line 16)
– Monsieur de la Palice, Stephen sneered,
(3.a) (The 1960 Bodley Head, p. 250, lines 30–31)
　L'art d'être grand . . . 　　　(FOREGOING CONTEXT)
　– His own image 　　　　(SUBSEQUENT CONTEXT)
(BETWEEN THESE TWO CONTEXTS, GARLAND INSERTS 43 LEXICAL ITEMS)
(3.b) (The 1984 Garland 'Reading Text', Episode 9, line 426 ff)
　L'art d'être grandp. . . . .
　– Will he not see reborn in her, with the memory of his own youth added, another image?
　　Do you know what you are talking about? Love, yes. Word known to all men. *Amor vero aliquid alicui bonum vult unde et ea quae concupiscimus* . . .
　– His own image

It must be clear here that I am not at all asking the question whether Gabler is right or wrong in operating the (b) changes in the above instances (1), (2), and (3). What I am exclusively concerned with here is the question 'How important is one change, whichever you wish (of the given three) in the above examples, over the other two?'. The change is of course being defined by the overall discrepancies existing in each case between the (a) instances and the (b) instances. The first change involves parasegmentals, the main question at issue being the deitalicization of LOS. The second change involves intra-proper-name micro-segmentals (PALISSE v PALICE), whereas the last change involves the insertion of no fewer than 43 lexical items between given foregoing and subsequent contexts. However, what is worth pointing out most emphatically is that such changes are but seldom limited to one single phenomenon, the one in the focus of the scrutiny. In the first example, by the side of the deitalicization, there is also the twin phenomenon of decapitalization of DEMIURGOS in the stably italicized LOS foregoing context. In the second instance, by the side of the respelling of a proper name (what's in a name?), we witness the flush-left displacement of the dialogue dash. Lastly, by the side of the insertion of forty-three lexical items, some in English, some in Latin, there is also the insertion of at least ten different parasegmentals (punctuation marks, dialogue dash, paragraph marker, italics, capitals etc.); more importantly, foregoing context ITALICIZED GRAND PLUS THREE DOTS becomes in the Garland version ITALICIZED GRANDP PLUS FIVE DOTS, with not only a P after GRAND, but also two extra dots inserted. Thus, the foregoing context of one change becomes another phenomenon of change in itself, consisting of two distinct modifications. However, the insertion of LOVE WORD KNOWN TO ALL MEN shines so brightly, precisely because it is a *segmental* change, that it outshines all the rest: the great danger is that the average reader, blinded by it, tends to send the rest of the insertion, particularly the Latin segment, into the background, and totally ignore the two changes in the foregoing context. By the side of all other possible hierarchies, one obtains a hierarchy within the segmentals, which, by its very essence, falls outside the scope of the present discussion.

The sketchy analysis of segmentals and parasegmentals here undertaken was, among others, meant to point to the necessity of keeping descriptive stages quite separate from axiological operations. It may be quite safe to state by way of principle not only that minute description always precedes value assignation, but also that the two operations are quite independent of each other. However, the other conclusion is that the axiological significance of a theoretical problem is also related to the relative frequency of occurrence of the phenomenon under scrutiny: the graphic positioning of the dialogue dash becomes an overwhelmingly important problem, given the extremely high incidence of dialogue-marking parasegmentals (it is worth noting that monologue sequences, e.g. Chrysostomos, etc., are marked on an exclusively semantic basis, or in plain words, not marked!). Also interesting to analyse in relation to the dialogue dashes and monologue sequences is the graphic positioning of verse: monologued lines of verse never go flush left in the 1984

Edition, whereas dialogued verse invariably does. The direct outcome is that a hypothetical feature labelled [± FLUSH LEFT] can tell the two apart with absolute certainty: a disambiguation devoutly to be wished . . .

8. The *multitext* is the abstract embodiment of an ordered set of subtexts, which is either open or closed (depending on the status accorded to so far lost or as yet undetected, and undiscovered, component items). In consequence, the relationship these subtexts have to one another can be analysed in terms of the set theory in mathematics and general linguistics. It is important to note in this connexion that each element of a set can in its turn be or become a set. In its simplest formal (or formalized) description, a multitext can therefore be made up, derived from, based on, etc., a set of subtexts as follows:

$$mt \longleftrightarrow st_1 \quad st_2 \quad st_3 \ldots st_n$$

This is the formal relation in which Gabler's 'documents', chronologically sequentialized on a mini-, or micro-, time dimension, stand with regard to Gabler's 'continuous manuscript' idea. There is a complex relationship of overall equivalence (which it would take a lot more space to formalize) between the elements on either side of the equivalence symbol. Depending on the actual and concrete circumstances, a set may have a minimum of one member, where the relationship of equivalence becomes $mt \longleftrightarrow st$ (or even be an empty set, a possibility not explored here), or on the other hand, a maximum which remains indefinite and unspecified. An open set is by definition open-ended, though for practical purposes, particularly so in *Ulysses* studies, the maximum number of subtexts required for the complete description is, again according to Gabler, made up of under twenty members.

The multitext is made up of a stable number of eighteen episodes (too often given Homeric names), numbered from 1 to 18 horizontally, and, on the other hand, it is vertically made up of a variable number of subtexts for each of the eighteen episodes. By a strange coincidence, the highest number of subtexts for one single episode (Episode Twelve) is again 18!

It is worth noting that the 1922 published edition of *Ulysses* is taken as one such subtext, here denoted as P (for

Published). At the other end of the ordered set stands the R subtext, which is Gabler's own abbreviation for the Rosenbach manuscript. The following diagram shows that P and R do not at all have symmetric positions in the eighteen ordered subsets constituting the eighteen episodes of Joyce's novel:

Chart of P & R Correlations

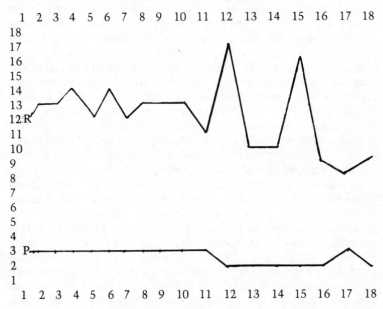

Total:

12 13 14 14 13 15 13 14 14 13 13 18 12 13 17 10 8 9

Note One: The ordered set of EPISODES is indicated on the horizontal dimension.

Note Two: The ordered set of SUBTEXTS is indicated on the vertical dimension:

The letter R denotes the Rosenbach manuscript;

The letter P denotes the 'Published' 1922 Edition.

Note Three: The horizontal 'TOTAL' line at the very bottom of the Chart indicates the total number of subtexts per episode.

The first major conclusion derived from this chart is that the 1922 edition is a subtext, or 'document', which lies at position three in the vertical subset for the first eleven episodes of the novel; it is then at position two for the subsequent five; there are again changes as regards the last two episodes.

The positioning of the Rosenbach manuscript within the ordered set is far more complex, as the chart clearly shows. Diagramming its place within the ordered set it belongs to is clearly like following the day-to-day evolution of the US dollar on the Paris Stock Exchange in late 1985 and early 1986 . . . For practical purposes in particular, it would have been far simpler to keep both the Rosenbach and the 1922 Edition at the same level of description; the introduction of, say, certain empty subsets could perhaps have helped. The 1922 Edition could have thus constantly been at level three (in both description and notational conventions, with zero subtexts introduced wherever it happens to appear at level two. On the other hand, the Rosenbach would constantly be at level 17 (the highest level of actual occurrence in the ordered set).

Against this formalized background, the instruction 'INSERT AT FOURTEEN' would always and invariably mean that the segment, or parasegment, in question is inserted at the level of the fourteenth member of the subset. The same simple procedure would also apply to the other three operations of deletion, permutation, and substitution. Further, a similar formal convention will have to be devised for the phenomena of inter-document changes. The very important outcome of this proposal would be that the novel *Ulysses* would in the formal description be treated as a *unitary* whole, instead of a jumble of disparate episodes painfully emerging out of a jumble of subtexts as is the case now.

9. Another weak point regarding the existing strategies of information display is Gabler's highly subjective theoretical notion of *synopsis*: for how can a synopsis be objective when out of the eleven Editions extant (see Bibliography, vol. III, pp. 1855–56), only the First Edition is part and parcel of the above diagrammed and discussed ordered set of subtexts? Had there not been the two lists of errors after the First Edition, there is a more than average chance that no printed edition would have been taken up as a subtext at all. Then, why not include all

editions published in Joyce's lifetime? Perhaps some subsequent lists of errors may have been lost, or which is worse, never put on paper. It must be emphatically stated at this stage that in a rigorously formalized approach, circumstance does not count.

In accordance with the elementary rules of information display, and equally elementary definition of the term *synopsis*, the left-hand pages of the 1984 Edition, called by Gabler *The Synopsis*, give the average reader but a partial synthesis of the information carried in the ordered set of subtexts. First, on account of the questionable space constraint imposed from the very start ('The length of line of synoptic text should be equal, or near-equal, to length of line of reading text') a lot of more than vital information overflows into the footnotes; then, the footnotes on the left-hand page flood the bottom of the right-hand page. But that is not enough: information is further split into two types: (a) footnote information, and (b) textual-note information, with the latter kind being relegated to end of Volume Three. So far we deal with mere overflow which does not derive from the theory. But what does derive from the theory is that information obtained from all editions other than the first one should be kept out of sight (largely on the strength of the proverb bearing the same name!), and relegated to what is termed *Historical Collation List*, again at end of Volume Three.

Imagine a researcher focusing exclusively on a close analysis of the first three episodes of *Ulysses* only (in 1983 Mondadori really turned this hypothesis into reality by publishing the one-volume *Telemachia*). Not sufficiently familiar with the 1984 information display, and going by the semantic features intrinsic to the word synopsis, he would assume, quite wrongly, that what he needs is to be found in Volume One, and take it home accordingly . . .

The label Historical Collation List is a misnomer: it concedes that in some way, particularly in the very essence of the term 'historical', its subtexts as well as those of the Synopsis all belong together; they are all part and parcel of the same ordered set (for a precedent had been created by the insertion in the set of the First Edition). It is indeed one of those Wilde paradoxes that, though the Historical Collation

List should in the theory not be confused with the Synopsis (as it is defined at G 1901 ff.), it is nevertheless included in the SYNOPTIC (sic!) 1984 ULYSSES! There is then reason to wonder in how many meanings does SYNOPSIS circulate in Gabler's theory of text change.

10. Each of the 5,000 or so proposed changes, as advanced by Gabler, should form the object of individual *case studies*, the way this is currently done in medicine, psychoanalysis (notoriously by Freud himself), and also in sociology and even linguistics. Such case studies should be carefully formalized in order to give explicit information on at least ten different points:

(1) TYPE OF MATERIAL under operation
   (segmental, parasegmental, combined etc.)
(2) TYPE OF OPERATION
   (Deletion or Insertion; Substitution or Permutation.)
(3) If intra-textual, SUBTEXT IDENTIFICATION (from 1 to 18).
(4) If inter-textual, IDENTIFICATION OF at least TWO SUBTEXTS.
(5) Specification of MATERIAL IN CONTEXT-FREE situation.
(6) Specification of MATERIAL IN CONTEXT-SENSITIVE situation.
(7) Degree of EDITORIAL INTERVENTION explicitly described.
(8) Degree of RELIABILITY OF THE CHANGE regardless of editorial intervention.
(9) Degree of RELIABILITY OF EDITORIAL INTERVENTION
   (a) objectively; (b) subjectively.
(10) Status of subtext in point of AVAILABILITY:
   (a) available, (b) 'lost', (c) hypothetical existence.

Further information may need explicit specification in the process of drafting the actual case studies. In the last analysis, the structure of a case study is not so very remote from the display of information in any good news items drafted for a newspaper (or for the telex of any news agency); for such an item, in order to deserve its name, must needs provide answers to the questions WHO? WHAT? WHEN? WHERE? HOW? and, as much as is humanly possible, WHY?

Information leading to the construction of such case studies is in the process of being provided by Gabler himself, in reply to queries in public – at conferences and conventions – , or merely in private (in a letter to a friend or over a pint of beer).

Editorial hesitations over the possible insertion of, say,

another period somewhere in the middle of Molly's monologue (as expressed in public by Gabler himself at the Sorbonne Conference in mid-May of 1985) should most certainly be included in the case studies, not only on account of their intrinsic value, but also on account of the fact that they provide a 'diachrony' of the Editor, and his shifts of decision, in much the same way in which the Editor's self-defined job in the Synopsis is to provide a 'diachrony of the Author' and of 'the shifts in HIS decisions'. For it is at this very point that the Editor comes closest to the Author and 'creates', as the epigraph to this contribution says, together with him. As the Author lingers, fumbles, and hesitates before a change (and the Editor is keen to provide that by way of striptease entertainment!), so does the Editor too linger and fumble and hesitate. Is it not his moral duty to make the two kinds of phenomena equally public?

11. This passing Author-Editor analogy in the process of text production occasioned among others the deliberate introduction of the term *diachrony*. In the above lines I used it with deliberate humorous intent: on the other hand, Gabler used it very much in earnest in his article 'The Synchrony and Diachrony of Texts: Practice and Theory of the Critical Edition of James Joyce's *Ulysses*'[5]. More than half the article (twelve out of twenty pages!) is devoted to the analysis of a story by Faulkner and a poem by Milton. (Why Faulkner before Milton in a discussion of diachrony?)

In looking at the prose of Faulkner and the verse of Milton, Gabler's aim is to point to the objective necessity of deriving a multitext out of an ordered set of subtexts. He then turns to the mountain achievement that is *Ulysses* only to emphasize the increased necessity of the same correlation. Seven of the eight remaining pages of this article expound the procedures of 'synoptically' displaying the information contained in the multitext (which passively mirrors the primary subtext existence of the given phenomena). The discussion is based on the sardines-on-the-shelves paragraph of Episode Eight, which had occurred on page 25 of the *Prototype* (cf pp. 362–63 of the 1984 Edition), a booklet which was distributed to the participants in the 1979 Zurich Symposium on Joyce (and afterwards withdrawn).

It is only in the half page conclusion of his Diachrony article that Gabler comes round to tackling genuinely theoretical problems when he states, somewhat dogmatically, that –

the work of literature possesses in its material medium itself, in its text or texts, a diachronic as well as a synchronic dimension. The act of publication which confers upon it a synchronous structure does not at the same time have the power to obliterate the coexisting diachronous structure of the work, to which the discrete temporal states of its text coalesce by complex hierarchical interrelationships. The synchronous and diachronous structures combine to form the literary work in the totality of its real presence in the documents of its conception, transmission and publication.

This chunk of text from Gabler's article is important as it contains all the theory that lies behind the construction of the 1984 Critical and Synoptic Edition of ULYSSES. Moreover, the passage is important as practically all the theory contained in it is wrong. The synchronic/diachronic distinction was first made by Ferdinand de Saussure[6] in 1907, and published in 1916. But the only thing Saussure had in mind was the *system* of the language, never the *structure* of the text. Saussure's starting point is that a change in the system of phonemes triggers other changes which affect the various language compartments differently:

Le système de nos phonèmes est l'instrument dont nous jouons pour articuler les mots de la langue; qu'un de ces éléments se modifie, les conséquences pourront être diverses, mais le fait en lui-même n'intéresse pas les mots, qui sont, pour ainsi dire, les mélodies de notre répertoire.

It so happens that the system of phonemes is a paradigmatic phenomenon; whereas the structure of a text is a syntagmatic phenomenon. The above passage from Saussure as well as his analogy with the playing of an instrument point to the clearcut distinction he makes between the paradigmatic and the syntagmatic axes.

Another fundamental distinction within Saussure's theory of language is that between 'Langue' and 'Parole':

Le tableau suivant indique la forme rationnelle que doit prendre l'étude linguistique:

Langage	Langue	Synchronie
	Parole	Diachronie

The above diagram shows beyond any shade of doubt that the Synchrony/Diachrony distinction only applies to Langue within Saussure's theory, never to Parole. And Text is always and invariably an instance of Parole; or of performance, as part of Chomsky's terminology (never of competence!). Gabler totally ignores and dismisses the fact, most clearly established by Saussure, as above, that the Synchrony/Diachrony distinction is not applicable to Parole phenomena.

12. Literary historians and text emendators would do well to read Saussure 'by the hour', as Joyce used to peruse Skeat, and then ask themselves the question – If the theory (Gabler's, not Saussure's of course), goes so wrong at such an early stage in its development, how can the practice be so very right? This discussion has been a mere preface to the issue as to why genetic studies, particularly those of late Joyce, are in my opinion badly in need of solid theorizing before passing on to the practice.

ULYSSES BETWEEN CORRUPTION AND CORRECTION

in a way that might be read as yes, ay, or no (16.612; *U* 629.34)

Proper evaluation of the new edition will be a task for the experts, for those schooled in the stringent methods of textual criticism, who are not always, rumour has it, the mildest mannered lot. The critical and non-synoptic remarks offered here come from one wholly untrained in textual scholarship, from a consumer, a Joycean reader of some experience. I will report, subjectively, on my on-going weaning process, as one trying to switch editions in the middle of research.

Our reading becomes a different experience, and this literally because of the way the letters are arrayed on the page, or rather, and that is part of the novelty, on *two* facing pages, one of which is not for reading anyhow but for slow extricative scrutiny. The different visual appearance, the change of externals – type, line length, placement on the paper – is in itself, I think, all for the good. To be shaken out of our habits is a stimulation we need. We all get too settled in our ruts. We are now enabled to see signs that were not there before, or not quite as they were, and even those that are essentially unchanged appear otherwise. This sensation is Ulyssean, a new challenge. It also delays us. Even finding an old familiar passage (whose location on the pages of Random House, Bodley Head, or Penguin we remember instinctively) now sets us back. We could of course speed up the process by writing in helpful, time-saving cross-paginations, but we may hesitate to deface the expensive paper of the handsome, sturdy volumes with our marginal scrawls.

So our work will take longer, or at least we have to put in some effort for an apprenticeship that may save us other efforts and much time later on. This always happens when a new system is introduced: the harvest will come considerably later; then our research will be facilitated. One such gain is

188

immediate, in my opinion (I have heard others): the introduction of a reference system in accordance with classical procedure. We have always been able to refer to Plato or Homer by pagination or foliation independent of the particular book in use (unfortunately there are still those who prefer the execrable parochialism of citing one specific edition rather than the conventional norm of ubiquitous accessibility, '*Odyssey*, p. 186' for example). Now, thanks to Gabler, even future editions, as long as they stick to the same lineation (which computer tape can easily ensure), will carry the same references. So, ever after, something like '*Autontimorumenos*' can be found effortlessly at '9.939', that is line 939 of the ninth episode (whose Homeric designation, Scylla and Charybdis, is appended in the Munich edition at the bottom of the synoptic page – outside of the text itself, a wise compromise). Such a referential agreement will assist us across continents and copyright areas. Until now, European users of the Penguin or Bodley Head editions had to convert their pagination to the critically established American usage, a needless waste of time.

In theory it is the left hand page that constitutes the real pioneering achievement, the one generally less looked at. It is a panorama of the accretive, hazardous growth of *Ulysses* through its seven years of gestation. It telescopes, by a meticulous diacritical code, various stages; it condenses time. It is, candidly and intentionally, a montage of what was never in existence at any one stage. In its ambition it entails ALL extant documents, and some conjectural ones as well. What before could be inspected, laboriously, in volumes of facsimiles by extensive leafing and collation, is now squeezed economically on to the left hand pages, a text studded with an impressive array of brackets, carets, letters and numbers and other elevated signs that can be – laboriously once again – deciphered by those in the know. How to do this is set out on pp. x–xiii of Volume One and pp. vi–ix of Volumes Two and Three, entitled 'SYMBOLS'. And here I raise my one major lament: I cannot bring those symbols to serviceable meaning. This may merely reflect my own obtundity. But a comparative study of groans with other Joyceans has convinced me that I am not alone in having thought, naively, that the edition was also meant for the likes of us. There must be users who can take in at a glance, and remember, that '1' is 'type-set reading in proofs defined as level 1 substratum'; but for those who don't I wish there were a more clear-cut way of putting it across. Perhaps that is the way it has to be; the matter may be labyrinthine beyond the reach of outside communication, the price that must be paid for a synoptic digest. Or, perhaps we may still learn in time. I fear some users may be frightened off.

Textual critics seem to experience a real, intrinsic difficulty in addressing the uninitiated outside the temple. If you work long and microscopically with all those multiple drafts, notebooks, fair copies, typescripts, *placards*, galleys and all the rest – to say nothing of lost final working drafts – all this will mean something to you once you give it a name; it is something individual, concrete, identifiable, memorable. But when all of this is put into words for those without, the result may well be an erudite blur. What textual scholars deal with are documents, not too far removed from factual things, and they write on the whole with step-by-step lucidity. It is all the more ironic that the accumulation of such short range lucidity is experienced as the utmost turgidity, even obscurity – the rightful domain of those operating at the other extreme of the spectrum, the theorists. I don't know what could be done or advised to ensure transparency about complicated matters. This being so, I would advise, however, that in future reprints Garland Press announce in the largest possible capital letters, in several conspicuous places, the most important principle adopted. We can find it buried in a long, thorough, informative, exacting Afterword. It could also be taken from the Foreword (as it is here); but it should be displayed so that no one can ever overlook it:

This Edition IN THE MAIN DOES NOT FOLLOW THE DEPARTURES OF TYPESCRIPTS AND PROOFS FROM THE TEXT IN AUTOGRAPH (G viii)

It is vital that this be committed to memory. It is what will incite most of the coming argumentation; it justifies most of the decisions. Whether you agree with the principle or with any of the individual decisions, at least you *know* the principle. And much idle criticism would be forestalled, concerning, for example, the absence of certain variants in the reading text as well as on the synoptic page. So it is otiose to complain that the former second occurrence of 'Agenbite of inwit' in every prior edition (you find it at *U* 17.3 after 'clean handkerchief') is not to be found anywhere in the Telemachus chapter. It has disappeared completely, and rightly so according to the premise. It is considered a mistake (and I concur) and should never have got where it was in the first place. It has no legitimacy in either of the two supplementary spreads that try to reproduce faithfully *what Joyce wrote*. We do find this wayward 'Agenbite of inwit' where it belongs, in the Historical Collation List in the third volume, where it is characterised briefly and correctly as *'MISPLACED INSERTION'*. This accident in the composing room of Darantière in Dijon, attended by an authorial oversight, need not be perpetuated in the functional texts.

Editors feel no responsibility to carry on, or signal prominently, mere misadventures, but they acknowledge them nevertheless. 'Agenbite' is still part of the edition, but relegated to an apparatus at the back. The Historical Collation List, a detailed delinquency report, takes up one hundred closely printed pages. This is where we go to transcribe the 5000 changes into our old editions. For practical purposes, of course, these 5000 errant readings are out of reach, in the attic, so to speak, accessible all the time, but requiring the exercise of a special, small, effort. I do not know how else the problem could have been handled.

Let me now take up this 'Agenbite of inwit' as the first of a handful of examples out of my personal experience. It is part of a paragraph that shows Buck Mulligan, watched by Stephen Dedalus, dressing and talking. I am not sure I can determine what Mulligan is actually speaking aloud or what perhaps Stephen only imagines or remembers him saying, or what Stephen himself could be thinking. In the sequence

> he called out for a clean handkerchief. Agenbite of inwit.
> God, we'll simply have to dress the character . . . (*U* 17.2–4)

I was always intrigued to find the Middle English phrase of remorse echoed in Mulligan's refracted monologue (it needn't be; we might still attribute it to Stephen's intrusive association). Would this mean, most likely (it is always a matter of probabilities), that an oversensitive Stephen at one point confided his obsession to non-sensitive, mocking Mulligan? This had puzzled me all along, and so I was relieved when the facsimile of the page proof made clear how it all came about. Joyce had added a short paragraph to the text and put it at the bottom of the galley; he then added an addition to that, 'Agenbite of Inwit', after 'They wash and tub and scrub' (*JJA* 22.18, see 1.481). This insertion was so placed, however, that a compositor could erroneously put it after 'clean handkerchief.' This chanced to be in the bottom line of the already printed version. In the next revision Joyce caught the absence of his phrase in the place where he wanted it, and he reinserted it. But he had no reason to check a passage that he had left untouched. So he didn't perceive the inadvertent intrusion. Having been a professional proofreader for many years, I can testify to such capricious mixups that often wreak unforeseeable havoc in the old movable-type letter press. One parenthetical observation is to note how many words have to be marshalled to give an idea, inadequate still, of what probably occurred. No edition could afford so much verbiage; it has to resort to shorthand and the casualties of abbreviations and 'Symbols'.

What I wanted to point out is that in one particular case my own feel for the passage was supported by the decision in Gabler's *Ulysses*. The decision, the evidence of the page proof, and my bias coincided. This will not always happen. I know that the deletion of 'Agenbite of inwit' is a serious loss for other readers of *Ulysses*. The point is that we all tend to respond emotionally, subjectively, according to preconceptions that we want to see confirmed. It is important that we know this. Many forthcoming textual discussions will be, basically and covertly, an airing of predilections, and will turn around how we want *Ulysses* to be read. Already many of the published reactions to 'Love', word, perhaps, 'known to all men' (9.429), have borne this out.

A textual editor cannot, must not, rely on his or anyone's subjective likings. Inevitably some of our most cherished readings will have been corrected out of existence. I cite two instances of wholly justified corrections and my contrasting responses to them. At the opening of Circe we have what used to read 'lumps of coal and copper snow' (*U* 429.7). The 'coal' has now been restored to 'coral' (15.6). The most plausible conjecture is that a copyist misread a word, or simply missed an 'r' and thereby substituted a different word. What Joyce wrote, demonstrably, is the 'better' reading, a more sensible one. Literary precedent may come to mind: 'her coral lips, her snow-white dimpled chin' (*Rape of Lucrece*, 420) offers a similar constellation. But even so we were not unduly worried before about the 'coal . . . snow' in Circe, because of the episode's non-realistic latitude, where such oddities can pass easily.

In the same stage direction of Circe there were 'Rows of flimsy houses' (*U* 423.9). This adjective, 'flimsy', always struck me as perfect; it expressed the insubstantiality of stage scenery (the French translation followed a similar notion: 'maisons de carton'). But no, the new text now says 'rows of grimy houses' (15.3), which is to me far less exciting, but it is what Joyce put down, no question. If we care to look up the Rosenbach facsimile we can check this and can also see that the word might well have been misread as 'flimsy' (Gabler's footnote labels this a 'MISREADING'). So *grimy* it must be, as I concede with just a twinge of irrelevant regret.

But, someone might argue, and arguments of this kind are sure to emerge, didn't Joyce perhaps notice the misreading and accept it? Perhaps he did, but no edition can be based on what Joyce perhaps approved of. It is one of the overriding principles of the Garland *Ulysses*, and a departure from bibliographical practice, that 'passive authorisation' on the whole is not admitted. Joyce's or Sylvia Beach's signature on a 'bon à tirer' constitutes legal approbation, but it does not confer the stamp of authority on the wording.

The close scrutiny of available documents in Munich has eliminated countless such misreadings and Joyce's inattention. We have to be grateful for those corrections, some of which had for some time been known in scattered publications. Take this passage in Sirens, towards the end of Dollard's singing of 'The Croppy Boy'. Bloom muses (or, rather, has mused, until 1984):

Pity they feel. To wipe away a tear for martyrs. For all things dying, want to, dying to, die. For that all things born. (*U* 286.5–6)

Not that we could not always construe some sense out of the

narrative orchestration of this chapter; I don't remember anyone ever voicing doubt about an irregularity here. One difficulty of an editor of *Ulysses* is that conventional grammar, rationality, or other norms no longer present a valid test. The Critical and Synoptic *Ulysses* now gives us a much clearer, a more plausible, a very Bloomian reading:

Thrill now. Pity they feel. To wipe away a tear for martyrs that want to, dying to, die. For all things dying, for all things born. Poor Mrs Purefoy. Hope she's over. Because their wombs. (11.1101-03)

The facing page informs us in its abbreviated manner how the rearrangement of the words took place. An experienced synoptic may deduce the process from this representation:

⌈ᴮ⌉[The thrill.] Thrill now.⁽ᴮ⌉ Pity they feel. ⌈ᴰTo wipe away a ^⟨tear. And⟩ tear for^ martyrs ^that^ want to, dying to, die.⌉ For all things dying, [⁽ᴮ⌉dead⟨,⟩:] for all things born. Poor Mrs Purefoy. Hope she's over. Because their wombs.

The congenitally dim-sighted among us may validate the rectification by looking at a page reproduced in the *James Joyce Archive*, from a typescript that Joyce revised, not too clearly:

It is possible to guess what went wrong. Joyce added something and then changed the addition. The relative conjunction 'that' is an insertion within an insertion (the case of 'Agenbite of inwit' is similar), but it could look as though it was meant to go between 'for' and 'all' in the typescript, and a compositor must have put it there, understandably. The Historical Collation List, tackling the issues one by one, cannot of course make the dislocations visible, but only articulate them serially. But the reading text gives us a satisfactory wording that makes immediate sense.

194

It is human nature that we nonchalantly accept all such improvements, but instantly quibble at changes that go against our bias. So I now pass on to cases where the emendations contradict vested interests of mine. To be carried away, hermeneutically, and then to be brought to a halt, textually, is sobering, but it is one of our risks. So I ask for tolerance. My extended toying with a phrase at the very beginning of *Ulysses* is illustrative. In all the previous texts we had read that Buck Mulligan

. . . peered down the dark winding stairs and called up coarsely:
—Come up, Kinch, Come up . . .

He peers *down* and calls *up*. For years I asked everybody in sight how they understood the apparent contradiction and the use of what ought to be, but isn't there, a transitive verb with an object. No one consulted had a convincing answer at the primary level, but there was no lack of secondary elaboration. The Critical and Synoptic *Ulysses* simply reverts to what Joyce had written in his own hand, an unproblematic 'and called out' (1.6). A footnote explains the troublesome 'up' as 'ANTICIPATION': a copyist ran ahead and unthinkingly moved the 'up' from Mulligan's shout to the sentence before: 'up' came up one line. The indubitable facts are that we have, in Rosenbach: 'called *out*', and then in the next stage, which is a first *placard*, 'called up.' What happened in between? Nobody knows. We can speculate. Now I had been aware of the former version 'called out' but taken the later one on trust as an authorial improvement, a more engaging phrase. Worrying at 'called up' quite a bit, I came to see it in the context of many transformations going on – dislocutions I would now call them. Since gold points in a mouth can be translated into 'Chrysostomos', the disquieting 'called up' might be similarly hellenised: the result would be 'call' = *kalein*, 'up' = *epi*. Greek *epikalein* means everything that 'call up' does (to summon, to appeal, to invoke, etc.), but it also means to nickname: 'come up, *Kinch*'! The noun *epiklesis* meant, among many other things, the invocation of the Holy Spirit in the mass (which Mulligan is mocking). Philologists used it for the invocation of an epic, like the first ten lines of the *Odyssey*. So the translation tantalises me as almost a perfect union of significant overtones, a combination of ancient Greece and the Church. I am also cautious enough to wonder how on earth Joyce could even be aware of these meanings. Whether he was or not, in 1904 he referred to what later became his much touted 'epiphanies' as 'epicleti' (*Letters* I, 55). A case can be made for *Ulysses'* being epikletic, but I do not invite anyone here to follow me into such dislocutory bypaths (it would suffice to see 'called up' simply as meaning to evoke, both epically and ecclesiastically); but most Joyceans will empathise with the captivation of interpretative processes. If Joyce, however, never intended 'up' to be there, all my seductive invocations go by the board; the phrase is reduced to a relatively trite shout (and makes me feel silly). Naturally I still prefer 'called up' (the preposition becomes very potent in the course of the book), but I cannot prove that it should be there. Nor can anyone that it should not be. What we have are principles and potential evidence.

Again we are left with the probability of, on the one hand, an authorial change that is not recorded, and, on the other hand, an author who, after a despairing struggle, finally sees the first galleys of his works, set up in type (the *placard* with 'up' is dated 11 June 1921, two and a half years after 'out' was put down), and misses a clerical error in one of the first lines. This was a writer who was distracted, overworked, frantic, with poor eyesight, who was proofreading, revising and creating at the same time, a writer who attestably overlooked the most glaring of errors. To be creator, scribe and proofreader may well be too much for one man. Very often much turns on just how bad a proofreader Joyce may have been. Authors are poor proofreaders. Very often we have one wording in Joyce's own hand (as a rule the Rosenbach fair copy, whether that is considered in the direct line of transmission or not) and then, in a later document of transmission, a different version. The Munich team's principle is to go back to the earlier, assured, reading. Other solutions would have been conceivable. The point is to be aware of the issue. Chances are that in our future work we will handle alternative readings and strategically settle on those that will suit our purposes and biases. The new edition gives us ample scope.

Textual scholars, we now learn if we didn't know before, no

matter how circumspectly they proceed, cannot simply determine readings according to the precepts of the craft and aided by technology. Considerations that are critical in the sense of criticism (never, even at its best, an exact science) cannot be avoided. We had hoped, some of us, that an 'accurate', 'correct', 'non-corrupt' text might finally give our interpretations at least a sure footing. But editorial decisions in respect of such a text are reciprocally co-determined by interpretation: it is a vicious circle from which we cannot break. This wouldn't do in logic. For better or worse, we have to err on an incommodius vicus of recirculation. One dilemma is that we are left with too many documents of the various stages of composition, and become dissatisfied with traditional bibliographical procedures, though again not quite enough to describe the changes with accuracy. The continuity of the Continuous Manuscript Text is intermittent, we have gaps, omissions, lacunae, silences, *Leerstellen*, not just gnomons – in a gnomon at least we know with Euclidian precision what it is that has been left out. Our foundation here too is 'upon the void. Upon incertitude' (9.842). This is not because any one particular editor decided for this rather than that.

The Critical and Synoptic edition acknowledges a strong, persistent, perhaps debatable temporal streak, its emphatically diachronic nature being in keeping with Joyce's transformative urge. It conflates readings from 1917 to January 1922 and compresses them into a conceptual presence which never existed synchronically. Joycean too, without intention, is the polarity of the two facing pages. A clear, established, authoritative text, at least in the sense that it is likely to become commercially dominant, in neat spatial order, impeccable, is to be found on the right hand. Confronting it, on the sinister side, we find something puzzling, obscure, muddled, unruly, many different stages and times collapsed into one. Our reading will consist in an interaction between the visible Shaun side and the unreadable Shem texture. We even have footnotes.

So somehow even the logically disturbing circularity seems to fit. In practice we will simply have to evaluate all the textual evidence provided – it is one great benefit that the new edition offers this – and then give it a fair trial. It is difficult to judge impartially, so we will all set our priorities. One of my present concerns is the narrative handling of successive and simultaneous time. *Ulysses* in its early chapters seems to pay close attention to sequential order, often in a cinematographic fashion. When Stephen is observing a dog on the beach – and for once not metamorphosing the dog, but giving it its own canine due – this is what we see and read:

> Along by the edge of the mole he lolloped, dawdled, smelt a rock and from under a cocked hindleg pissed against it. He trotted forward and, lifting his hindleg, pissed quick short at an unsmelt rock. (*U* 46. 35–39)

What strikes me is a deadpan scrutiny of the dog's doings and movements, without a governing mind verbally interfering (as Stephen's mind often does at other times): each single moment is seen for what it is. Now in the new edition there is one word added, retrieved from Rosenbach ('ABSENT' explains the Historical Collation List). Please pay attention to the difference (here underlined):

> . . . He trotted forward and, lifting *again* his hindleg, pissed. (3.358)

Such an 'again' is easily skipped in copying handwriting (we can imagine a typist being slightly shocked by the description). The resulting narrative difference is not negligible. Now an explicit comment on repetition puts a distancing comprehension where there was a more naive immediacy. Some consciousness is keeping track of the various leg-liftings: there is less direct sensation and more intellect. The muted difference is remarkable. I find the phrasing without 'again' superior, and more in line with Joyce's development away from officious narration (compare also the impassive prose of Wandering Rocks). In a draft version of the chapter Joyce had originally written: 'from under a heaved hindleg pissed . . . heaving again his hindleg, pissed' (*JJA* 12.292). The change from 'heave' to 'lift' is away from a Stephenesque, bookish, verbal consciousness towards more realistic reticence; I see the hypothetical deletion of an instrusive 'again' as part of the same process. But what I am doing is clutching at exegetical straws to defend a reading that suits much better a thesis I am developing and that I simply like better for aesthetic reasons. As against such merely intuitive and perhaps unarguable judgement, I have also come to wonder, on rereading, whether

198

the dog's 'lifting again his hindleg' may not in part echo the observation from the preceding paragraph, that the cocklepickers 'waded, . . . soused their bags and, *lifting them again*, waded out.' This would justify 'again', and it would do so aesthetically. Contextual evidence points either way. But any one reader's idiosyncratic response or disputation must not be a textual editor's criterion. Given the editor's stated premise, the decision was right and inevitable—'lifting again'. The critical issues raised become fascinating: the new Garland text provokes by the questions it must raise.

Decisions *are* decisions, not compelling logical conclusions. We can argue the basic principles, but the principles very often can't help us: they tell us more about themselves than the text. One of my questions is just how much Greek Joyce might have known and used. A clue appeared to offer itself. In the library discussion Stephen thinks of himself as

Autontimorumenos. Bous Stephanoumenos. (9.939)

This is how Joyce spelled the first word in 1918; we find it in the Rosenbach manuscript. In the subsequent typescript just one vowel was changed: 'Autontim*e*rumenos' (*JJA* 12.167); this becomes the reading in all editions from 1922 to 1984. The typescript shows corrections by Joyce; for example he underlined the Greek composite words but left the first 'e' untouched: '-timoru-' had become '-tim*e*ru-'. There is no doubt but that the o-form is correct. Terence's play is called *Heautontimorumenos*, nearly as Joyce wrote it first: the 'Self-Tormentor' (*heauton* or *auton*, 'self'; *timorein* 'take vengeance'). The *e* is an error. Except that there is a Greek verb with a root *time* (*timao*, also a noun *time*), whose meaning is to honour, to worship. The mistake might be a Wakean overtone with a characteristic ambivalence. Stephen, who with his obsessive mind torments himself, also proudly honours his own person with narcissistic energy. Too subtle and also unnecessary for unhellenised Stephen or Greekless Joyce, perhaps, and no more than a transmissional error and a coincidence. The errors of a genius may be portals of discovery, but scribes may be pointlessly fallible and proofreaders merely inattentive. I could never use a wrong vowel as evidence for Joyce doing to Greek what he often does to English. I can just claim feebly that a mere passive oversight is somewhat less likely for a difficult, long, foreign word where we all know mistakes occur easily. One might give them particular care.

Of course when Joyce was inattentive, as thousands of errors that have been corrected now make him appear, those many oversights by themselves become an issue, something to deal with. When so many errors, slips, misunderstandings in *Ulysses* are artistically contrived, what about those accidents that escaped the author's attention? Often a reading is now reinstated that Joyce must have forgotten at some time, or simply no longer cared about enough. We also know that in his proofreading he did not have his manuscripts to check galleys against; it had to be done from memory, often a defective memory. A passage in Eumaeus, for example, had been very cryptic, appearing to be more than the typical loosening of narrative strings of the chapter:

Marble could give the original, shoulders, back, all the symmetry. All the rest, yes, Puritanism. It does though, St Joseph's sovereign . . . whereas no photo could, because it simply wasn't art, in a word.

(*U* 653.11–14)

Perhaps this simply isn't art the way it was intended. Something may have gone wrong. A great deal of critical effort went into the new version which, established as follows, is still cryptic:

Marble could give the original, shoulders, back, all the symmetry, all the rest. Yes, puritanisme, it does though Saint Joseph's sovereign thievery alors (Bandez!) Figne toi trop. Whereas no photo could because it simply wasn't art in a word. (16.1451–55)

The changes derive from the Rosenbach manuscript (Eumaeus, fol. 40) and are accounted for in a long Textual Note (G 1750–51). I have no quarrel with them: this is an extremely tricky problem. The point is that a text could become as corrupt as it was in 1922 only if Joyce either simply forgot what he once had in mind, or was too sloppy to make a new effort. But how are editors to evaluate slips, failures of memory, omissions, in a postFreudian age? Can they be treated as mere absences to be filled with material from an antecedent stage? Again, I see no general solution. The emendations offered above seem to have a bit less validity than most others (the

200

editors would probably agree). Surely, just as I would be on shaky ground basing a view of Joyce as a manipulator of Greek semantemes on a questionable '*Autontimerumenos*', some reading which turned on '(Bandez!)' or 'Figne toi trop' hardly has a more solid basis. As it happens, 'Figne' is now a printed part of *Ulysses* and may await interpretation.

Decisions are decisions.

The ruling of the new edition retrieves much that, in the chancy genesis of *Ulysses*, had fallen by the wayside, whether by oversight, as has been assumed, or else by judicious, but unrecorded excision (Joyce has been known to do this, though rarely). Maybe the more doubtful recoveries could have been marked by take-it-or-leave-it signals. Those would not have solved anything and merely shifted the circumference of uncertainty somewhere else. But they would have given warning of the caution that we must exert throughout. Each reclaimed fragment – if it ought to be included, by whatever criteria – has its own valuable story to tell us about what must have been part of the author's intention at one time. In Eumaeus, a chapter that has now been most significantly corrected, the talk at one point is about Katherine O'Shea, the villainess in an Irish drama. 'That bitch, that English whore', she is called, but one customer concedes:

Fine lump of a woman all the same; . . . and plenty of her. *She loosened many a man's thighs.* I seen her picture in a barber's. (16.1354–56)

The sentence in italic has not appeared in any previous printed edition of *Ulysses* (see *U* 650.26). It disappeared in the typescript made from the Rosenbach manuscript. This typescript is interesting. It pointedly leaves some blank space for the sentence (which was legible enough); the respective line is incomplete. It is easy to imagine a copyist being squeamish: a few lines above, 'that English whore' was also replaced by a blank. But there Joyce wrote it in again, as he did 'bosom' further down the page (16.1411). He did not fill in the gap between 'of her.' and 'I' (which began on a new line, *JJA* 15.395).

It is instructive at any rate to know that 'She loosened many a man's thighs' did at one stage belong to the chapter. The sentence makes the speaker, who in his other sayings is not rhetorically remarkable, a bit more of a Dublin wit and gives him a classical background. The allusion deflects a Homeric tag for war and death to sex. Killing in the *Iliad* is sometimes metaphorically a loosening of the heroes' knees. In the *Odyssey* it is Eumaios who curses Helen, the runaway wife, the source of all evil, who '. . . *pollon andron hypo gounat' elyse'* (*Odyssey* 14.69) – 'she loosed the knees of many men,' as A. Buckley literally translated in the nineteenth century; 'she caused the loosening of many a man's knees' is what Butcher and Lang say. Zeus, incidentally, caused the same thing (*Odyssey* 14.236). In the context of Parnell's adultery, knees have become thighs. The analogy is very close – Helen and Kitty O'Shea are paired, a quotation is minimally distorted, the location is the Eumaios episode – it fits well, too well. Perhaps this was why it was taken out in the revision. The Homeric direction might have seemed too obvious, laid on with an unJoycean trowel. But it does show, most clearly, that Eumaeus strains towards an epic style and towards literary stereotype: it is the chapter which frequently borrows its diction from (translations of) Homer.

The loosening of the texture has other consequences as well. It becomes a problem for the editor who has to come to graphic terms with the serial fate of a text on the genetic synopsis. The left hand side of our paragraph is photocopied here:

—Fine lump of a woman all the same, the *soi-disant*° townclerk° Henry Campbell remarked, and plenty of her. She loosened many a man's thighs. I° seen her picture in a ⁵[shop.] barber's.⅂ The husband was a captain or an officer.

This conflates all the relevant stages for our convenience; in this case they are a) Rosenbach; b) typescript (not differentiated here because identical with a) except for the omission mentioned which, as a transmissional interference, goes unmarked); c) the *placards* and page proofs of Darantière (only level 3 needs to be mentioned). At this final stage there is just one change from 'shop' to 'barber's' (this was a page proof, *JJA* 27.104). In the subsequent set of proofs Joyce finally put 'I seen her picture . . .' right after 'of her.', which up to that time had been the end of the half-line which the typist had created by leaving out the sentence with the 'thighs': the gap had been left standing. Joyce also deleted an erroneous dash before the 'I' (the footnote in the edition, G 1420, mentions this latter change).

All this is difficult enough to describe (I remember my own harsh words about lucidity and turgidity earlier on) or to condense into a few synoptic lines. And an illusory touch is made to intervene by the text's composedly carrying along the sentence that was not there most of the time. When Joyce changed 'shop' to the more specific 'barber's' – or when he, in several rounds of correction, did nothing to this passage – it did not contain at those stages 'She loosened many a man's thighs.' But the presentation on the page might suggest to us that it did: additions or substitutions are marked, but not absences. No amount of *syn-opsis* (a seeing all together) could have called up to inspection what was not there. So the 'Continuous Manuscript Text', at least in one sense of the term, was not continuous, did not contain what maybe should have been there, but wasn't. Restored parts are a jump across time, anachronistic spectres. Which merely proves the precariousness of all our concepts (Joyce could have told us that, and did). The linear tracing of a developing, strandent-wining, but also eroded, and sometimes neglected, text is graphically impossible, at least on two dimensional paper, no matter what. An irritant element of dyschronicity must – appropriately, as I believe – discomfit the best laid schemes.

What the author wrote down in his own hand carries great weight, as we have seen, and it can create problems. But it would be wrong to assume that Joyce's own hand, even when his authorship is indubitable and when the writing is legible, automatically prevails. When Bloom in the Ithaca episode drops from his area railing and falls to the ground, the Newtonian fall is given in a profusion of data, including the astronomical terms that serve to determine the movable feasts for the church: 'golden number 5, epact 13', etc., including:

Roman indication 2 (*U* 669.2)

I remember when I came upon those words and figures in *Thom's Directory* for the year 1904 and found, as others have done, that the correct term is 'indiction' – (the form in *Ulysses* is a clear misprint, I thought, an unwitting slip from an unaccustomed 'indiction' to a more familiar 'indication', is an almost routine event in typing or typesetting), and I eagerly saw to it that the German translation then in progress would read, correctly, '*Indiktion*' and not, as before '*Indikation*'. The same inference may have guided the new edition, which reads:

Roman indiction 2 (17.98)

An improvement of sense, no doubt. But as we can now verify, Joyce actually and clearly wrote 'indic*a*tion', very late in January 1922 (*JJA* 27.140). The editors naturally consulted the page proofs too, and they consider Joyce's spelling one of two 'plain errors to be emended' (G 1752; the other error is 'MXMIV' when 'MCMIV' is meant). Joyce had no further opportunity to rectify this, which was done in a hasty finish against an imminent deadline. So the decision is in favour, not of what Joyce wrote, but of what he meant to write. That may lead us to wonder what other parts Joyce perhaps intended to put down and somehow didn't bring off – all of which is outside the jurisdiction of any editor.

Plain error, or, as a textual note labels an opposite view, 'speculation on the intended subtlety of the forms "indication" and "MXMIV" in Joyce's notation' (G 1752) – these are the poles between which, not only here, editors as well as interpreters have to move. Unless we are convinced beforehand, how do we argue this? Does the very fact that Joyce wrote *two* glaring errors in the same one sweep indicate that he lapsed because of exhaustion, or does this make an intention more probable? The French translation, for what it is worth (there was a possibility to consult the author), faithfully reproduced the mistakes in the twenties. As readers we don't have to decide, but it is good to be alerted to the problem. We are offered the option in the clear reading text; we also have the variant 'indication' in three different places: a footnote, the historical collation, and a textual note. We can give priority to what Joyce wrote *or* to what he, presumably, had in mind. To shift the ground, we can accept the version in tune with the chapter's aim at scientific precision (therefore 'indiction') *or* the one in accordance with the chapter's frequent failure to attain this aim (in which case 'indication'). 'Guesswork', thought Bloom on another occasion, 'it reduced itself to eventually', only to add aloud:

There was every indication they would arrive at that. (16.1293–95)

In a critical edition this guesswork has become highly erudite and scholarly, at times a Sherlock Holmesian weighing of probabilities, with the cards all laid on the table. The table meanwhile consists of two facing pages and the tabulations of Textual Notes and the Historical Collation List as well as the densely packed Afterword. One main problem is, as Hans Walter Gabler puts it in relation to conflicts between two successive autographs, to distinguish between 'authorial commissions' and 'scribal omissions'. 'The critical task is to distinguish intended revisions from unintended copying mistakes or oversights' (G 1865–67). Joyce, like Shakespeare (who is 'all in all, boy . . . mature man, . . . bawd and cuckold,' 9.1018 ff), like HCE or like you and me, plays more than one role. 'In copying, he was both author and scribe' (G 1864). Creator, he also became rereader, reviser, proofreader, only begetter and lonely forgetter, or to employ metaphors that were becoming current at the period of writing, there was an *ego* side and an *id* side to all such combined activities. This is all as it should be: it is what *Ulysses* is about. The composite author of *Ulysses* is the one who composed, serially, the following sentence with its stratified grammatical subject:

In Lionel Marks's antique saleshop window haughty Henry Lionel Leopold dear Henry Flower earnestly Mr Leopold Bloom envisaged (battered) candlestick(s) melodeon oozing maggoty blowbags.

(11.1261–63)

(The parentheses signal the difference between the inclusive new edition and those that preceded it, as *U* 290.17.) There is not one single tune, nor one unified Bloom. As we envisage the passage earnestly and synoptically, we find that the author of a fair copy had written 'battered candlesticks'; a typist had typed 'candlesticks'; a Dijon typesetter had put down 'candlestick'. All of this was successively intended and changed by a revising author, or else overlooked by a preoccupied proofreader. Some of us will from now on use '*battered* candlesticks' – maybe aware that *Ulysses* is full of battered objects and that a similar Bloom had passed 'Wine's antiques' and 'Carroll's dusky battered plate' (11.87–88) –

205

while others will stick to the one unbattered candlestick – perhaps judging that 'battered' was withdrawn from circulation in a careful reappraisal. Because of the ways in which the multiple co-authoring subjects became entangled, with the Munich editors being the last link in the chain, *Ulysses* is an intrinsically battered text.

In many instances, the majority it would seem, the newly established text will stabilise the wording. In others it will not. We will be all the more inclined now to juggle the variants that have been brought to light. New diversification will be a result. The Critical and Synoptic Edition will not just harmonise us in scriptural unison, but also intrigue us with 'its variety of forms', its 'variety entertainments', and the 'various different varieties' it presents (17.215, 17.665, 12.106). We may finally reveal the word known to all textual critics, as we are enabled now to 'fingerponder nightly each his variorum edition' (9.1062–63). But the text adds wisely, uncorruptedly and with Ulyssean caution, 'ware of wiles.'

ULYSSES IN SPANISH

FRANCISCO GARCÍA TORTOSA.

In Spanish there are two complete translations of *Ulysses*. The first was published in Argentina in 1945 and the second in Spain in 1976. The Argentinian edition, as is widely known, was extensively criticised from the date of its publication, which demonstrated the need for a new translation to make up for the defects, errors and omissions of Subirá's. However, there are not many translators who dare to confront a text as complex as Joyce's in Spanish or in any other language, because of which the long awaited authorised version had to wait 31 years. Finally, one daring translator emerged who seemed to combine all the necessary requirements at least to produce a proper and accurate version, having a long and prestigious record as a translator behind him. Before tackling *Ulysses*, he had undertaken such a task with authors considered as the most untranslatable in several languages, and since the highly respected José Ma Valverde, professor of ethics at the University of Barcelona, was not daunted by languages, German, French, Italian or English, these were minor obstacles for him. Professor Valverde had, moreover, another advantage: he is a published poet and prolix essayist. Most ambitious writers would envy such a copious list of publications, but they lack such a fertile muse. According to Valverde's own confession, he did the translation in a short period of time, since the rhythmical aspect of Joycean prose and the translator's own sense of Spanish prose rhythm obliged him to carry out his work under pressure. Acting as if it were a symphony, he did not want any blank spaces to damage the musicality and cadence of the sentences, although it is true that in some passages he succeeds in transferring the musicality of Joycean prose to the Spanish. I would emphasise, as a stroke of luck, the beginning of episode 14, where it is not necessary to know Spanish to appreciate the aptness of this rhythmical translation:

207

Deshill. Holles Eamus. Deshill Holles Eamus. Envíanos, tú luminoso, tú claro, Horhorn, fecundación y fruto del vientre. Envíanos, tú luminoso, tú claro, Horhorn, fecundación y fruto del vientre. Envíanos, tú luminoso, tú claro, Horhorn, fecundación y fruto del vientre. ¡Aúpa, es ñiño ñiño, aúpa! ¡Aúpa, es ñiño ñiño, aúpa! ¡Aúpà, es ñiño ñiño, Aúpa (p. 21, vol. II).

Even so, Subirá is every bit as good, and I would even say that, Valverde's obsession with rhythm apart, he excels him. Just compare the earlier passage with the Argentinian version:

Deshill. Hollis Eamus. Deshill. Hollis Eamus, Envianos, ¡Oh brillante! ¡Oh veloz! Horhorn, fecundacion u fruto del vientre. ¡Hoopsa, varón un varón, hoopsa! ¡Hoopsa varón un varón, hoopsa! ¡Hoopsa, varón un varón, hoopsa! (p. 405).

However, in spite of partial successes and the praise that any effort to translate *Ulysses* deserves, Valverde has not managed to set Spanish speaking Joyceans at ease, as several reviews, some of them particularly harsh, and criticism, like that which appeared in the newspaper *El Pais* a few months after its publication, have already emphasised.

To begin with, one would have to say that Valverde is not free of the errors that were frequent in Subirá, although it is true that he avoids some that the Argentinian translation falls into; but he introduces others which, as I see it, stem from the lack of a scholarly knowledge of Joyce in particular, and English in general. It is well known that the primary requirement that the reading of Joyce demands is a high degree of familiarity with the history of the English language, as well as with its colloquial and dialectal registers. In the second place, Valverde follows the much abused Argentinian translation too closely, much more than some commentators have pointed out. It is true that some Argentinian idioms are castilianised in Valverde's *Ulysses* and that one is sufficiently aware of his persistent desire to differentiate, to get farther away from it, which is too strong in my opinion. Even so, the differences affect vocabulary exclusively and hardly ever the syntactic structure. Valverde, like Subirá, adopts the principle

208

of literality, perhaps the only possibility in any translation of Joyce, but this contrasts with the hermeneutic emphasis that he has adopted on other occasions. This represents another indication of the attention Valverde has paid to the Argentinian translation. The most suspicious aspect lies in the fact that lexical differences invariably occur in a sequence of synonyms, as if trying to disguise the attention paid to Subirá, although it is precisely in the disguise that the fault is revealed with greater clarity.

For all these reasons, in a strict sense in Spanish there is no more than one translation of *Ulysses*. Although the translators do not indicate the text or edition they follow at any time, it is clear that Subirá used the Random House edition of 1934 (and only that), while Valverde's case presents a few complications: on the one hand, it is made clear that he knows and handles more than one edition, since his translation shows many departures from any existing one; on the other, for reasons incomprehensible to me at present, he changes from one to the other without any apparent motive, and not always with good judgement, as when he accepts the erroneous Gregorian transcription of the 'gloria in excelsis Deo' of episode 9, which is taken from the Penguin edition, among others, avoiding that which appears in the Random House or Shakespeare and Company editions, which is correct. This indicates, among other things, that Valverde's encyclopaedic knowledge does not encompass Gregorian music. The difficulty in ascertaining the original text or texts used by Valverde becomes insuperable on occasions, especially when he introduces words and even sentences that are non-existent in any of the extant editions of *Ulysses* (in episode 9, one sentence in French); or when he omits sentences without any justification (in episode 7, the second part of the title which begins 'Sophist wallops . . .'). From this, we must deduce either that on occasion Valverde treats the text with a freedom which strongly contrasts with the literality of his usual practice, or that he is following other non-Spanish translations which have allowed themselves to take liberties which he later takes into Spanish. At this time I cannot confirm the existence of that hypothetical translation, but it is true that Valverde has used several editions of the original text as well as other non-Spanish translations, even when he has not always known how to profit as one would have hoped from such a variety of sources.

With the appearance of the Garland edition last year, whatever corrections may be accepted in 1986 or in the future, there is no doubt that the need for a new translation into Spanish becomes more urgent. It is not necessary to underline that after the publication of a text that corrects or makes additions on more than five thousand occasions, the image of the novel takes on new dimensions. The extent to which that image modifies the aesthetic or intellectual value of the work is not the object of my contribution here. However, I would like to point out the reshaping that the Garland edition would imply in any existing Spanish translations and the influence that this edition would have on any future Spanish translation, which would not be small as the effects of alterations in a given text appear in a different way in the target language. Any translation implies a process through unique and unrepeatable filters which modify the original text in an equally unique way, albeit always within the limits that the form and content of the latter impose.

The majority of corrections that the Garland text introduces appear in the area of punctuation, lexical changes and the insertion of new vocabulary. Punctuation varies very slightly from one language to another because, among other things, in all of them a high degree of flexibility is accepted, which allows the writer to vary, shape and emphasize the message or part of it depending on his personal perspective. Normally, the translator respects the punctuation of the original, with the minor exceptions which the conventions of the target language impose on him. In Spanish, these exceptions are limited to initial interrogation and exclamation marks, some cases in relative clauses and the division between the main and subordinate clauses which are not even universally accepted. So, on general lines, Subirá's translation follows the Random House edition and Valverde's, as we have already said, is a mixture of several.

In order to focus the comparative commentary on a single episode, episode 9 has been chosen, without suggesting that this is particularly problematic, or that the translation is better or worse than that of other episodes. Beginning with the changes in commas and choosing one example among many, I take the phrase 'that queer thing genius' (*U* 195) that appears in the Garland text without punctuation, while in earlier editions, a comma is inserted between 'thing' and 'genius'. In Subirá's it is translated as: 'Sí, creo que tiene eso tan raro, el ingenio' (p. 219) and in Valverde's: 'Sí, creo que tiene esa cosa rara, genio' (p. 324, vol. I). Forgetting about the suitability of the omission of the comma, which editorial reasons apart is endorsed by the context of the word 'genius' in *Ulysses* (which appears in the novel over a dozen times modified by adjectives or adjectival phrases), in the Spanish translation, the Argentinian as much as Valverde's, the adjectival nature of 'thing' is lost, which it undoubtedly acquires on deleting the comma. The translation of the Garland text ought to consider this aspect, and, doing it in this way, 'genius' would acquire the ambiguity that Joyce intended. Another case in which the Garland text would involve a revision of the Spanish translation is found some lines farther on in the same episode: 'Blushing his mask said,' which appears in Gabler's with a comma after 'Blushing.' The Argentinian translation gives the following version: 'Con la máscara sonrojándosele, dijo' and in Valverde's it becomes: 'Ruborizando su máscara, dijo en voz baja.' Notwithstanding the differences between the two and forgetting Valverde's unnecessary addition, both completely distort the meaning of the phrase, misled by a comma. It is true that in both cases the falseness of the 'Quaker librarian' is evident, but they distract the reader from the hypocrisy that the flattery to Stephen involves, since what Joyce intends to emphasize is not so much the librarian's honesty or dishonesty, but his duplicity in affirming that Stephen's theory seems 'most illuminating.' The meaning would be more or less: so, he (the librarian) blushing, his mask said.

There are eleven examples like these in this episode, where the Spanish translation gets Joyce's text wrong because of erroneous punctuation, some as serious as that which Valverde makes when he interprets a new paragraph as the beginning of the speech of a new interlocutor. What is made clear from this aspect of punctuation is that the errors in the original increase in the translation and what might be confusing in English becomes incomprehensible in Spanish.

In the Garland text there are three nouns in the plural, in this same episode 9, which in the earlier 1922 edition appeared in the singular form, with the function of collective nouns: *MIND/S, PALM/S,* and *DEPTH/S* (9.52, 9.132, 9.760). In the case of *MIND,* the two translators keep to the original, although using different words, *MENTE* in the first and *ESPIRITU* in the second, and accept the English collective noun. However, the Platonic context in which it is inserted requires the plural and not the collective form, since only the plural is capable of suggesting the existential and vital duality of the Platonic world. Spanish accepts the plural of the other two words more easily than the collective counterparts. It is so obvious that in the Argentinian version, although it has been taken from a text where *PALMS* appears in the singular, the translator opted to interpret it in the plural form, since, in Spanish, 'spitting in his palms' is 'escupir en las manos' or 'en la palma de las manos.' With regard to vocabulary and added paragraphs in the Garland edition, it is only necessary to emphasize what has already been said in relation to punctuation: that the Spanish translation would have gained in clarity and precision with the corrections and additions to the new edition. Without making reference to the passage at 9.425–31, amply discussed by commentators, other corrections of minor importance contribute to a better comprehension not only of the text but also of the peculiar way in which Joyce wrote. The addition, for example, of 'last year' before '1903' (9.599) would help a not very attentive reader to remember the date on which the novel takes place; the replacement of *CONJUGAL* by *CONJUGIAL* (9.631) would demonstrate the allusion to Swedenborg, which does not exist in *CONJUGAL*: in the same way as when the possibility that ANN HATHAWAY would admit a lover in New Place becomes almost a certainty with the insertion of 'with her' (9.803). In the brief appearance of Bloom in this episode, some short and confused words are given to him, ending with an unmistakable interjection which betrays his insecurity and shyness: 'eh' (9.1140). However, in previous editions, owing to a typographical error, 'eh' becomes 'he' because of which, Bloom appears as if he were one more fellow in the gathering at the library and were referring to one of its number.

We could continue to comment on the other ten lexical innovations that appear in episode 9 of the Garland edition, which would confirm what is already clear, that is, that any change in the original, which involves clarification of the content and of the means and process of creation, will always have even greater repercussions in the translation, especially in the Spanish one which, up to now, is considerably defective. In the cases where I have been able systematically to compare the translations of Subirá and Valverde, the Garland edition appears in general to be a text which would invariably improve any translation into Spanish, mainly because it would make it more coherent than the existing ones and because it would make some passages of doubtful interpretation more explicit. Of course, I do not think it is necessary to add that I do not speak from an editorial point of view.

THE 1922 AND 1984 EDITIONS: SOME PHILOSOPHICAL CONSIDERATIONS

DONALD PHILLIP VERENE

In his university oration of 1708 concerning the proper methods of study, Giambattista Vico said he wished to assess the value of both sides of the quarrel between the ancients and the moderns regarding the best approach to knowledge. The controversy concerning the value of the 1922 and the 1984 editions of Joyce's *Ulysses* has some elements in common with the quarrel. At present the controversy concerning the text of *Ulysses* is very young; it is, in fact, just beginning. It could die young or it could last a long time. At one level this controversy concerns which of the thousands of corrections and adjustments in the 1984 Garland text should stand and which should be questioned. This is a technical matter, one that no general reader of Joyce can decide. Dispute over such specifics could result in some revisions of the Garland text itself.

At another level this controversy is not over what should or should not be corrected; it is a clash between two textual mentalities, perhaps even two senses of knowing. On this level a parallel exists between the controversy over the two editions and the quarrel between the ancients and the moderns. The 'continuous manuscript' of the Garland edition is arrived at by the most modern methods of treating texts. The Garland text depends upon a scientific mentality that attempts to construct the real object as it exists through its appearances. The appearances in this case are not various perceptions of an object in the external world, but the various versions and corrections that exist of the work. The real text is produced through the synthesis of this manifold. This synthesis and the production of the true or nearly true text is made possible by scientific methods. As Hugh Kenner says in his *TLS* review (13

214

July 1984]: 'Two technologies made that possible: facsimile reproduction and the computer.'

The ancients in this controversy hold out special respect for the importance of the original 1922 edition. The supporters of the 1922 edition are responsible for creating the controversy. To do so is to challenge science. This is difficult in an age that believes in the power of scientific thinking joined with technology to produce the real. There is no question that there are errors and omissions in the original printing. But the question is: how are we to respond to this fact and to the fact of Joyce's own changes and corrections? John Kidd in a recent paper to the Society for Textual scholarship (New York, April 1985) calls attention to the fact that the 1984 edition overrules Joyce's own revision of 'filter' to 'filtre' (17.165). The editor calls Joyce's correction in proof to the '-re' ending 'an apparent contamination by French spelling' (G 1752) and refuses to allow it. The arbitrary is always a part of scientific objectivity; but when it is discovered and pointed out, it is always shocking.

What can be said of the value of what I have called the 'ancient' versus the 'modern' approaches? Is there a way to balance the merits of one against the other? The case of the Garland edition seems almost to make itself. From this new, ideal text we know more than we did before. Richard Ellmann rightly emphasizes this in his review in *The New York Review* (25 October 1984). He points out that we can now know that 'the word known to all men' in the Circe episode is 'love'. To have this clarified after the various theories about it is quite important. To correct errors, rectify omissions, bring together various versions, and show changes are valuable aids to literary scholarship and general understanding. By so doing we know more about Joyce's meaning. But in another sense we know less.

From the standpoint of the ancient, the danger of the modern is the rationalizing, clarifying, and logical reordering of what is unique and particular. The Garland edition uses the most rational methods possible to achieve the ideal text. But through this approach we will find in Joyce's text only those elements that rational methods will allow, those that will combine to make the ideal. The real text is not the one that comes about at a particular time under particular circumstances and which preserves the elements of those circumstances for better or for worse as part of its reality. The quest for the ideal text involves the perspective of thought expressed in Hegel's famous dictum in the *Philosophie des Rechts*: *Was vernünftig ist, das ist wirklich; und was wirklich ist, das ist vernünftig* – the rational is the real and the real is the rational. Scientific thinking is always a kind of applied idealism that never leaves the particular alone, but desires its reconstruction as an ideal type through rational methods.

Against this desire for the real text, this Germanic sense for rational order and ideal truth, one can put Vico's Italian sense of rhetorical understanding of an event. In the *Scienza nuova* Vico states as an axiom: *Le dottrine debbono cominciare da quando cominciano le materie che trattano* (ax. 106) (Doctrines must take their beginning from that of the matters of which they treat). To understand something made by the human mind for Vico requires the narration of its history. To understand a particular event we must construct for ourselves a narration of the elements that the event itself narrates to us. The sense of the particular is preserved by the knower's reconstructing its sense as a narration, not by the knower's transforming the particular into an ideally constructed object.

From this Vichian sense of the truth of the particular, one might hold that the 1922 *Ulysses* is the real text. The reader must confront the text as Joyce did and, armed with Joyce's later corrections, the reader must develop his own understanding of it. What the reader may see by doing this, by producing his own narration of its meaning and reality, he will miss when confronted by the Garland—fully and rationally reconstructed—text.

In Vico's terms the text is a certain. It is born at a particular moment under particular conditions and it takes on a particular life. Our understanding of the text must begin with its own beginning and preserve this sense of the original with its perfections and imperfections. These are part of its essential reality. The text is a certain in the sense that it is something that is just what it is and not another thing. This sense of the certain as the particular is opposite to the sense of the certain found in the logical proposition. The logical, scientific conception of certainty derives from the need to formulate something that is indubitable. The quest for certainty in this sense is the quest for something that is perfect, finished, and beyond doubt. This is attempted by constructing from particulars that which is universal in them. The real object is searched for in the multitude.

The Garland edition seems to me to embody much of this logical spirit and I think the advocates of the 1922 edition are essentially attracted to what I have called the rhetorical spirit. By 'rhetorical spirit' I mean that sense found in the tradition of Italian humanism of approaching a text and each version of it as having its own natural validity. I have made the sides of this controversy more extreme than they really are. But this is only an attempt to magnify their differences to test whether a philosophical difference may lie at the bottom.

The conclusion is in one sense obvious. Both the 1922 original and the 1984 'continuous' texts are necessary for any scholar's study of Joyce's work. The problem is not that there are two fundamental published texts of the completed *Ulysses* – the original and the latest. The problem is that the latest will be thought to be truer than the original. My point is that the ground of the dispute between the validity of the two editions is not the nature of the corrections that need to be made in the original. There are two different senses of truth involved – the one is impressed with the true text as what can be rationally and scientifically reconstructed; the other is impressed with the true text as that which actually comes into being in a certain way and asks the reader to experience in its original and flawed form.

APPENDIX

THE FIRST INTERNATIONAL SEMINAR OF THE
PRINCESS GRACE IRISH LIBRARY – MONACO

'A *FW* APPROACH TO *ULYSSES* – A SCRUTINY OF
THE 1984 EDITION'
CONFERENCE PROGRAMME

[When papers have been included in this volume, with or without
revision, the titles are given in brackets.]

FRIDAY 24	10.00 to 11.15	REGISTRATION, Visit of the Library.
	10.15 to 12.30	Private guided Tour of the Palace of Monaco.
	12.30 to 14.30	Lunch at the CASTELROC Restaurant (place du Palais).
	14.45 to 15.45	FORMAL OPENING: Address by H.S.H. Princess Caroline. Brief ten-minute statements by R. ELLMANN, C. HART, F. SENN
	16.00 to 17.00	Fritz SENN: 'My own Experience with the New Edition'. ['*Ulysses* Between Corruption and Correction.']
	17.00 to 18.00	Clive HART (speaks on behalf of Academic Advisory Committee on the New Edition of *Ulysses*). ['Art Thou Real, my Ideal?']
	18.00 to 19.45	DISCUSSION of the afternoon contributions.
	20.15	Private Buffet-Supper, Italian-Style, offered by Signora Anne-Marie Sozzani (3, place du Palais, Monaco-Ville).
SATURDAY 25	10.00 to 11.00	Richard KAIN: 'Dublin 1904'. ['Dublin 1904.']
	11.00 to 11.30	Ira B. NADEL: 'Editorial

218

	Principles and Textual Practice'. ['Textual Criticism, Literary Theory and the New *Ulysses*.']
11.30 to 12.30	DISCUSSION of the morning contributions.
12.30 to 14.30	Lunch across the street at the FELIX Restaurant (22, rue Basse).
14.30 to 15.30	Richard ELLMANN (speaks on behalf of Academic Advisory Committee of the New Edition of *Ulysses*). ['A Crux in the New Edition of *Ulysses*.']
15.30 to 16.00	G. SANDULESCU: 'Visuals'. ['Curios of Signs I am Here to Rede!']
16.00 to 18.00	DISCUSSION of the afternoon contributions.
18.00 to 19.00	Supplementary paper: S. HENKE: 'A Deconstructive Approach to a Reconstructed *Ulysses*'. ['Reconstructing *Ulysses* in a Deconstructive Mode'.]
19.00 to 20.00	Journey back to Monte Carlo and the Hotels.
20.15	Private Buffet-Supper, German-Style, offered by Frau Christine RENKL (Le 'Sun Tower', 14th floor, 7, avenue Princesse Alice, Monte Carlo).
SUNDAY 26 10.00 to 10.30	Carla de PETRIS on *Telemachia* (Mondadori). ['On Mondadori's *Telemachia*.']
10.30 to 11.00	Carla MARENGO: 'Italics'. ['Italics in *Ulysses*.']
11.00 to 11.30	F. García TORTOSA: 'Gabler's Edition and Spanish Translations'. ['*Ulysses* in Spanish.']
11.30 to 12.30	DISCUSSION of the morning contributions.
12.30 to 14.15	LUNCH at the SAME Restaurant as yesterday.

14.15 to 15.15	Journey to Beach Plaza Hotel, 22 av. Princesse Grace (Top Floor).
15.30 to 18.30	ROUND TABLE DISCUSSION AT THE BEACH PLAZA HOTEL on '*FW* as Method: *ULYSSES* as object of Study' co-chaired by R. KAIN and G. SANDULESCU, with the participation of J. AUBERT, C. HART, Ch. PEAKE, F. SENN, D. NORRIS and D. HAYMAN on the Panel. (A small audience of Monaco residents has also been invited to attend the discussions.) [Supplementary paper: Donald Phillip VERENE, 'The 1922 and 1984 Editions: Some Philosophical Considerations.'] EVENING FREE
MONDAY 27 09.30 to 10.00	R.-M. BOSINELLI: 'Joyce the Scribe and the Right-Hand Reader'. ['Joyce the Scribe and the Right-Hand Reader.']
10.00 to 11.00	David HAYMAN: 'Pro and Contra – A Summation'. ['Balancing the Book, or Pro and Contra the Gabler *Ulysses*.']
11.00 to 12.30	DISCUSSION of the Seminar as a Whole.
12.30	END OF SEMINAR.
12.30 to 14.00	Lunch at the AURORE Restaurant (opposite).

Appendix

THE LIST OF PARTICIPANTS

Jacques AUBERT, Université de Lyon, FRANCE
Kathleen BERNARD, Paris, FRANCE
Rosa-Maria BOLLETTIERI BOSINELLI, Universitá di Bologna, ITALY
Gudrun BUDDE, West Berlin, WEST GERMANY
Giovanni CIANCI, Università di Genova, ITALY
Robert G. COLLINS, University of Ottawa, CANADA
Carla de PETRIS, Università di Roma, ITALY
Richard ELLMANN, University of Oxford, BRITAIN
Wilhelm FÜGER, Freie Universität Berlin, WEST GERMANY
Jean-Richard GASTAUD, Princess Grace Irish Library, MONACO
Michael Patrick GILLESPIE, Marquette University, Milwaukee, U.S.A.
Clive HART, University of Essex, BRITAIN
David HAYMAN, University of Frankfurt, WEST GERMANY
Suzette A. HENKE, State University of New York, U.S.A.
Inge JACOBSEN, Organizer of the forthcoming 1986 Joyce Symposium, DENMARK
Richard M. KAIN, University of Louisville, U.S.A.
Geert LERNOUT, Universitaire Instelling Antwerpen, BELGIUM
Samuel LEVIN, State University of New York, U.S.A.
Carla MARENGO VAGLIO, Università di Torino, ITALY
George MORGAN, Université de NICE, FRANCE
Mark MORTIMER, British Institute, Paris, FRANCE
Ira B. NADEL, University of British Columbia, CANADA
David NORRIS, Trinity College, Dublin, IRELAND
Patrick PARRINDER, University of Reading, BRITAIN
Charles PEAKE, University of London, BRITAIN
Jasna PERUČIČ-NADAREVIČ, University of Zagreb, YUGOSLAVIA
Poul Jan POULSEN, Organizer of the forthcoming 1986 Joyce Symposium, DENMARK
C. George SANDULESCU, Princess Grace Irish Library, MONACO
Reinhard SCHÄFER, Universität Frankfurt, WEST GERMANY
Luigi SCHENONI, Bologna, ITALY
Fritz SENN, The Zurich James Joyce Foundation, SWITZERLAND
Margaret C. SOLOMON, University of Hawaii, U.S.A.
Rudiger THONIUS, Universität Frankfurt, WEST GERMANY
Francisco García TORTOSA, Universidad de Sevilla, SPAIN
Donald Phillip VERENE, Emory University, Atlanta, Georgia, U.S.A.
Kathleen WALES, University of London, BRITAIN

NOTES

HOW THIS PARTICULAR FUNFORALL CAME ABOUT
C. George Sandulescu

1   'Closing Statement: Linguistics and Poetics' in: Thomas A. Sebeok, ed.,
    Style in Language (New York: M.I.T. and John Wiley & Sons, Inc., 1960)
    350.

JOYCE THE SCRIBE AND THE RIGHT HAND READER
R. M. B. Bosinelli

1   Jack P. Dalton, 'The Text of *Ulysses,*' *New Light on Joyce from the
    Dublin Symposium,* ed. Fritz Senn (Bloomington and London: Indiana
    University Press, 1972) 102.
2   Bernard Benstock and Shari Benstock, 'The Benstock Principle,' *The
    Seventh of Joyce,* ed. Bernard Benstock (Bloomington: Indiana University
    Press, 1982) 10–21.
3   Richard Brown, 'To Administer Correction,' *James Joyce Broadsheet* 15
    (October 1984) 1.
4   Paul Gray, 'Odyssey of a Corrected Classic,' *Time* (2 July 1984).
5   Brown 1.
6   Cesare Segre, *Semiotica filologica* (Torino: Einaudi, 1979).
7   Paola Pugliatti, 'Between Philology and Semiotics: The Work of Cesare
    Segre,' *Poetics Today* 5.1 (1984) 201.
8   Pugliatti 203.
9   Segre 66; Pugliatti 203.
10 Edgar Allan Poe, 'The Philosophy of Composition' (1846), in *Selected
    Writings,* ed. with an introduction by David Galloway (Harmondsworth:
    Penguin, 1984) 481.
11 Fritz Senn, ' "Ulysses" – neu, genauer, kritisch. Zur revidierten Ausgabe
    vom Joyce Roman,' *Neue Zürcher Zeitung* 197 (25–26 August 1984).
12 See, for example, John Kidd, interviewed by David Renmick, 'Jolting the
    Joyceans. John Kidd: A Young Scholar Squares Off Against Academics
    Over the New Edition of "Ulysses",' *The Washington Post* (2 April 1985).
13 Dalton 103.
14 Fritz Senn, *Joyce's Dislocutions: Essays on Reading and Translation,* ed.
    Jean-Paul Riquelme (Baltimore and London: Johns Hopkins University
    Press, 1984).
15 Fritz Senn, 'On Trying to Name One Joycean Characteristic.' Typescript
    draft of a paper delivered in Cesena, Italy, July 1982. (Unpublished.)

TYPOGRAPHY UNDERRATED: A NOTE ON AEOLUS
G. Cianci

1   Cf. Michael Groden, *Ulysses in Progress* (Princeton: Princeton University
    Press, 1977) 64–114.
2   Cf. F. T. Marinetti, 'Destruction of Syntax – Imagination Without
    Strings – Words in Freedom' (1913) in U. Apollonio, ed., *Futurist
    Manifestos* (London: Thames and Hudson, 1973) 104.

3 Marinetti 105. At the International Joyce Symposium held in Frankfurt, 1984, I read a paper on 'Futurist Joyce' (forthcoming in print).
4 A proper study of Joyce and the avant garde remains to be written. For a few suggestions, see Archie K. Loss, *Joyce's Visible Arts – The Work of Joyce and the Visual Arts, 1904–1922* (Ann Arbor: UMI Research Press, 1984).
5 See in particular Stuart Gilbert and Groden, *Ulysses in Progress.*
6 Cf. A. P. Berger, 'James Joyce, Adman,' *JJQ* 3 (1965) 25–33.
7 Cf. Hugh Kenner, 'Notes Toward an Anatomy of "Modernism",' in E. L. Epstein, ed., *A Starchamber Quiry – A James Joyce Centennial Volume 1882–1982* (London: Methuen, 1982) 34.
8 Cf. Fritz Senn, 'The Rhythm of "Ulysses",' in Louis Bonnerot, ed., *Ulysses cinquante ans après* (Paris: Didier, 1974) 34.
9 The third instruction in the final page proof, which the Joyce Archive reproduces but which is omitted from Gabler's textual apparatus, reads: 'Ce point doit être plus visible.' John Kidd, in a paper read at The Society for Textual Scholarship, New York, April 1985, pointed out this omission, commenting: 'Darantière carried out Joyce's final instruction, and a large dot, somewhat squarish, appeared in the first edition and ten subsequent printings. The 1984 *Ulysses*, however, reverts to a modern full stop far smaller than even the intermediate dot Joyce had insisted should be made more visible.'
10 Cf. 'Dichiarazione al Tipografo,' *Lacerba* (Firenze) 2.9 134.
11 Cf. F. K. Stanzl, *Narrative Situations in the Novel* (1955) (Bloomington: Indiana University Press, 1971) 124.
12 Cf. Marilyn French, *The Book as World* (1976) (London: Abacus, 1982) 93.
13 Cf. Karen Lawrence, *The Odyssey of Style in Ulysses* (Princeton: Princeton University Press, 1981) 61.

ON MONDADORI'S *TELEMACHIA*
Carla de Petris

1 Giovanni Cianci, *La fortuna di Joyce in Italia. Saggio e bibliografia* (1917–1972) (Bari: Adriatica Editrice, 1974).
2 James Joyce, *Scritti italiani*, a cura di Gianfranco Corsini e Giorgio Melchiori (Milano: Mondadori, 1978).
3 James Joyce, *Epifanie*, a cura di Giorgio Melchiori (Milano: Mondadori, 1982).
4 James Joyce, *Finnegans Wake H.C.E.*, trad. con testo a fronte di Luigi Schenoni, bibliog. di Rosa Maria Bosinelli (Milano: Mondadori, 1982).
5 *Letters*, I, 113 (18 May 1918).
6 Weldon Thornton, *Allusions in Ulysses* (Chapel Hill: University of North Carolina Press, 1968).
7 Don Gifford & Robert J. Seidman, *Notes for Joyce: An Annotation of James Joyce's Ulysses* (New York: Dutton, 1974).
8 I am indebted to David Norris for his assistance in making this particular point clear in session, by reciting the two lines aloud in a Dublin accent.
9 *The Critical Writings of James Joyce*, ed. E. Mason and R. Ellmann (London: Faber and Faber, 1959) 80.

UNANSWERED QUESTIONS ABOUT A QUESTIONABLE ANSWER
Claus Füger

1 Richard Ellmann, 'The Big Word in "Ulysses" ', *The New York Review of Books* (25 October 1984) 30–31.
2 Though those who wish to do so can always call in doubt Gabler's decision (since he prefers the reading of an early fair copy to a later typescript on account of the plausible though finally unprovable hypothesis of an eyeskip on the part of the typist, thus rejecting the idea of passive authorization as well as the possibility that Joyce may have omitted these lines deliberately or deleted the passage at the lost final-working-draft stage), most critics will certainly be ready to admit that there are good editorial reasons for restoring the passage.
3 The ensuing ten sets of rules and definitions are a systematically ordered survey of the summarized pertinent results of the following studies: H. Paul Grice, 'Logic and Conversation,' in P. Cole and J. L. Morgan, eds, *Syntax and Semantics* III: *Speech Acts* (New York: Academic Press, 1975) 41–58; Ferenc Kiefer, ed., *Questions and Answers* (Dordrecht, Boston, Lancaster: D. Reidel Publishing Co., 1983); Robin Lakoff, 'Questionable answers and answerable questions,' in B. B. Kachru *et al.*, eds, *Issues in Linguistics: Papers in Honor of Henry and Renee Kahane* (Urbana: University of Illinois Press, 1975) 453–67; Dieter Wunderlich, *Studien zur Sprechakttheorie* (Frankfurt: Suhrkamp, 1976) esp. chapter 5: 'Fragesätze und Fragen' 181–250.
4 As to these particular delimitations, cf. John Lyons, *Semantics*, 2 vols (Cambridge: Cambridge University Press, 1977) 593, 605–06; latest survey of research by Klaus Hempfer, 'Präsuppositionen, Implikaturen und die Struktur der wissenschaftlichen Argumentation', in Th. Bungarten, ed., *Wissenschaftssprache* (München, 1981) 309–42.
5 Michael Groden, 'Foostering Over Those Changes: The New *Ulysses*', *JJQ* 22.2 (Winter 1985), 137–59 (here: 130).
6 Ellmann, 'The Big Word,' 30–31.
7 Accordingly, speech-art theoretical analyses can be expected to contribute in various regards to the further elucidation of *Ulysses*, above all in the case of the Ithaca episode (I hope shortly to finish a paper on this topic.)

WHY DOES ONE RE-READ *ULYSSES*?
Patrick Gillespie

1 G. Thomas Tanselle, 'The Editorial Problem of Final Authorial Intention,' in his *Selected Studies in Bibliography* (Charlottesville: Published for the Bibliographical Society of the University of Virginia by the University Press of Virginia, 1979) 313.
2 Ellmann 400.
3 *Letters* II, 419; Ellmann 497.
4 Ellmann 442, 507–08.
5 The most detailed account of this process is in Michael Groden's *Ulysses in Progress* (Princeton, New Jersey: Princeton University Press, 1977); but see also Ellmann's biography and Noel Riley Fitch's *Sylvia Beach and the Lost Generation: A History of Literary Paris in the Twenties and Thirties* (New York: Norton, 1983).

225

6   See W. W. Greg's 'The Rationale of Copy-Text,' *Studies in Bibliography* 3 (1950–51) 19–23, for a discussion of the crucial role of the copy-text in editing.

7   See G 1876–1907. The best survey of modern editorial practices can be found in G. Thomas Tanselle's 'Greg's Theory of Copy-Text and the Editing of American Literature,' *Studies in Bibliography* 28 (1975) 167–230. For specific discussions of Gabler's method, see Philip Gaskell's *From Writer to Reader: Studies in Editorial Method* (Oxford: Clarendon Press, 1978).

8   Gaskell 235.

9   For an argument in support of this procedure, see Gaskell 4–5.

10 Gaskell 4–5.

11 Michael Groden, 'Foostering Over Those Changes: The New *Ulysses,' JJQ* 22.3 (Winter 1985) 139.

12 Groden, 'Foostering Over Those Changes' 150.

13 Groden, 'Foostering Over Those Changes' 153.

BALANCING THE BOOK, OR PRO AND CONTRA THE GABLER *ULYSSES*
David Hayman

1   See the comments of Hugh Kenner in 'Leopold's bloom restored,' *ILS* (13 July 1984) 771–72 and Richard Ellmann's 'A Crux in the New Edition' (28–34, above). Significantly, Ellmann's revised views, as expressed in Monaco, fly in the face of his earlier acceptance of the change which undermines his own long-standing opinion that 'love' is indeed the answer to the *book*. It is worth noting that many of us in Monaco found the addition disconcerting and some of us concluded not only that 'love' is an inadequate response, but that it tends to confirm the undecidable nature of the question, adding more darkness than light.

2   I would suggest but not insist that a comma after 'note' would further clarify the sentence.

3   For clarity and concision, I shall incorporate, where possible, Gabler's changes in the Random House version and *vice versa*, enclosing them in parentheses.

4   For an explanation see G 1742.

5   Here we may note in passing an error in the remarkably accurate Historical Collation: the listing of a nonexistent ',' after the 'de' in the Random House *Ulysses*.

6   A final word is in order about the procedures followed in compiling the data for this essay. Having been in Frankfurt during the year and far from my copy of *JJA*, I have been obliged to rely entirely upon the Garland edition and my judgement as a reader of *Ulysses*. But that is precisely the situation in which most readers will find themselves. Doubtless, the editor can and will respond in many instances by a call to textual authority, but it is not to the specific instance that I would refer. It is rather to the fact that there remain in this edition a goodly number of dubious and even incorrect details, many of which have been consciously added and with the best of intentions. It is not intentions that should concern us, however. It is results.

DUBLIN 1904
Richard M. Kain

1   Oliver St John Gogarty, *As I Was Going Down Sackville Street* (London: Rich and Cowan, 1937), 40.

2   Gogarty, *As I Was Going* 57.
3   *Joseph Holloway's Abbey Theatre: A Selection from his Unpublished Journal, IMPRESSIONS OF A DUBLIN PLAYGOER*, ed. Robert Hogan and Michael J. O'Neill (Carbondale and Edwardsville: Southern Illinois University Press, 1967; London and Amsterdam: Feffer and Simons, 1967).
4   *Holloway* xviii.
5   Joseph Maunsell Hone, *W. B Yeats, 1865–1939* (New York: Macmillan 1943) 213–14.
6   John Eglinton [= William Magee], *Irish Literary Portraits* (London: Macmillan, 1935) 135–36.
7   Stanislaus Joyce, *The Complete Dublin Diary*, ed. George H. Healey (Ithaca: Cornell University Press, 1971) 75.
8   Robert Scholes and Richard M. Kain, eds, *The Workshop of Daedalus* (Evanston: Northwestern University Press, 1965) 56.
9   *The Workshop of Daedalus* 56.
10 Oliver St John Gogarty, *It Isn't This Time of Year at All!* (London: Macgibbon and Kee, 1954) 87.
11 *Dana: A Magazine of Independent Thought* 1 (May 1904) 32.
12 *The Letters of W. B. Yeats*, ed. Allan Wade (London: Hart-Davis, 1954; New York: Macmillan, 1955) 434.
13 Richard M. Kain, 'James Joyce's Shakespeare Chronology,' *Irish Renaissance*, ed. Robin Skelton and David R. Clark (Dublin: Dolmen, 1965) 106–19.
14 Richard M. Kain, ' ''Your Dean of Studies'' and His Theory of Shakespeare,' *JJQ* 10 (1973) 262–63.
15 Richard M. Kain, 'Shakespeare in *Ulysses*: Additional Annotations,' *JJQ* 8 (1971) 176–77.
16 William H. Quillan, 'Shakespeare in Trieste: Joyce's 1912 *Hamlet* Lectures,'*JJQ* 12 (1974/75) 7–63, and ' ''Composition of Place'': Joyce's Notes on the English Drama,' *JJQ* 13 (1975) 4–26.
17 'Two Joyce Letters Concerning *Ulysses* and a Reply,' *JJQ* 15 (1978) 376–79.
18 Eglinton 148, 135.
19 According to Holloway's diary the first rehearsal at the Abbey Theatre occurred on 31 October 1904.
20 *The Workshop of Daedalus* 63.
21 Richard Fallis, *The Irish Renaissance* (Syracuse, NY: Syracuse University Press, 1977) 96.
22 Eglinton 133.
23 James Stephens, *The Charwoman's Daughter* (London: Macmillan, 1912) 20–22.
24 Eglinton 133.
25 Eglinton 134.
26 Eglinton 5.

TEXTUAL CRITICISMS, LITERARY THEORY AND THE NEW *ULYSSES*
Ira B. Nadel

1   Jerome J. McGann, *A Critique of Modern Textual Criticism* (Chicago: University of Chicago Press, 1983) 2, 41, 81, 68, 89, 93.

2 For a reproduction of Joyce's hand correcting the original statement in the page proofs of *Ulysses*, see Joyce, *Ulysses, Facsimile of Page Proofs for Episodes 16–18*, *JJA* 17.305. See for example Noel Riley Fitch, *Sylvia Beach and the Lost Generation* (New York: Norton, 1983) 65–92.

3 See for example Jack P. Dalton, 'The Text of *Ulysses*' (1966), *New Light on Joyce from the Dublin Symposium*, ed. Fritz Senn (Bloomington: Indiana Univ. Press, 1972) 99–119; Philip Gaskell, 'Joyce, *Ulysses*, 1922,' *From Writer to Reader* (Oxford: Clarendon Press, 1978) 213–44.

4 Stuart Gilbert, cited in Michael Groden, 'A Textual and Publishing History ,' *A Companion to Joyce Studies*, ed. Zack Bowen and James F. Carens (Westport, Conn.: Greenwood Press, 1984) 107; Gaskell, *From Writer to Reader* 244.

5 Dalton, 'The text of *Ulysses*.'

6 R. F. Roberts, 'Bibliographical Notes on James Joyce's *Ulysses*,' *Colophon* n.s. 1 (1936) 565–71; for a summary of the textual scholarship on *Ulysses*, see Michael Groden, 'A Textual and Publishing History,' 91–110, 119–21 and especially 121.n67; Dalton 'The Text of *Ulysses*' 99.

7 The following are the most pertinent: Hugh Kenner, 'The Computerized *Ulysses*,' *Harper's* 260.1559 (April 1980) 89–95; Michael Groden, 'Editing Joyce's *Ulysses*: an international effort,' *Scholarly Publishing* 12 (1980/81), 37–54; Hans Walter Gabler, 'Computer-Aided Critical Edition of *Ulysses*,' *ALLC Bulletin* 8 (1981) 232–48; Michael Groden, 'Foostering over Those Changes: The New *Ulysses*,' *JJQ* 22.2 (Winter 1985) 137–59.

8 Roland Barthes, 'Theory of the Text' (1973), *Untying the Text, a Post-Structuralist Reader*, ed. Robert Young (Boston: Routledge & Kegan Paul, 1981) 32, 36, 32, 33. All further references are to this edition.

9 Gayatri Spivak, 'Translator's Preface,' Jacques Derrida, *Of Grammatology*, trans. Gayatri Spivak (Baltimore: Johns Hopkins University Press, 1976) xlix. See also Paul de Man, *Blindness and Insight* (New York: Oxford University Press, 1971) 140. The creation of the Gabler *Ulysses*, a text now known by that name, also illustrates Derrida's notion of a 'grouped textual field' where the original author's work is altered in content as well as name to reflect the enlargement of the base text. Derrida, *Positions*, trans. Alan Bass (Chicago: University of Chicago Press, 1981) 42.

10 On the trace see Derrida, *Of Grammatology* 62, 70 and his essay 'Freud and the Scene of Writing,' *Writing and Difference*, trans. Alan Bass (Chicago: University of Chicago Press, 1978) 226, 229–31. The statement on text by Derrida is from *Untying the Text* 29; see also Derrida, *Positions* 33. Derrida also explains there that Grammatology is 'the science of textuality' (34).

11 Philip Gaskell, *A New Introduction to Bibliography* (Oxford: Clarendon Press, 1972) 340; G. Thomas Tanselle, 'Recent Editorial Discussion and the Central Question of Editing,' *Studies in Bibliography* 34 (1980) 64.

12 For an earlier discussion of this very point see R. M. Adams, 'Letter,'*JJQ* 61.1 (Fall 1968) 98–99, concerning the text of *Portrait* established by Chester G. Anderson.

13 Sigmund Freud, *A General Introduction to Psychoanalysis*, rev. ed. trans. Joan Riviere (1924) (New York: Washington Square Press, 1967) 63,

hereinafter cited in text as *General Introduction*. See also Freud's *Psychopathology of Everyday Life* and the question of errors. Joyce had a copy of this book in his Trieste Library. Christopher Ricks, 'Walter Pater, Matthew Arnold and Misquotation' (1977), *The Force of Poetry* (Oxford: Clarendon Press, 1984) 392–416; Janet Malcolm, 'The Unreliable Genius,' *NYRB* 32.4 (14 March 1985) 12. For Joyce on error see *FW*, esp. 120, 123, 279. On reading proof, Joyce once commented to Budgen that ' "galley proofs remind me of the persons of the Trinity. Get firm hold of one and you lose grip on the others." ' See Ellmann 665.

14   Freud in Philip Rieff, *Freud: The Mind of the Moralist* (Garden City, NY: Doubleday, 1961) 123–24.

15   Joyce, *Ulysses, Placards, JJA* 50.366. The first version of *placard* E shows the shift from the right to the left side of the page with the dateline approximately two spaces beneath the place names of the 'signature' and centred. Cf. *R* 2.783. The change in *placard* E restores the alignment in the Rosenbach manuscript although the spacing slightly differs.

FROM TELEMACHUS TO PENELOPE: EPISODES ANONYMOUS?
Patrick Parrinder

1   Mary Colum, 'The Confessions of James Joyce,' reprinted in *James Joyce: The Critical Heritage* I, ed. Robert H. Deming (London: Routledge & Kegan Paul, 1970) 233–34. This was one of the early reviews of *Ulysses* which pleased Joyce most, according to Colum.

2   Cf. Michael Groden, *'Ulysses' in Progress* (Princeton: Princeton University Press, 1977) 125: 'The *Little Review* episodes are numbered but not named.'

3   *Letters* II, 408.

4   Stuart Gilbert, *James Joyce's 'Ulysses'*, (London: Faber and Faber, 1930). Richard Ellmann, who reprints the schema in *Ulysses on the Liffey*, wrongly gives the date of first publication of Gilbert's book as 1934 or, alternatively, 1931. See *Ulysses on the Liffey* (London: Faber and Faber, 1972) xvi; Ellmann 521.

5   Letters from Paul Léon to Bennett Cerf, 21 October and 14 November 1933, in *The United States of America v. One Book Entitled 'Ulysses' by James Joyce*, ed. Michael Moscato and Leslie Le Blanc (Frederick, MD: University Publications of America, 1984) 278, 280.

6   *Joyce's Notes and Early Drafts for 'Ulysses': Selections from the Buffalo Collection*, ed. Phillip F. Herring (Charlottesville: University Press of Virginia, 1977) 122. (Subsequent page references are given in the text.)

7   *Letters* I, 113.

8   Holbrook Jackson, 'Ulysses à la Joyce,' in Deming I, 199.

9   Shane Leslie, '*Ulysses*,' in Deming I, 211.

10   See note 1, above.

11   Ellmann 522.

12   Arnold Bennett, 'James Joyce's *Ulysses*,' in Deming I, 220.

13   Edmund Wilson, '*Ulysses*,' in Deming I, 229.

14   Pound, 'Paris Letter,' in *Pound/Joyce*, ed. Forrest Read (London: Faber and Faber, 1968) 197. Cf. A Walton Litz, *The Art of James Joyce*, (London: Oxford University Press, 1961) 40, for an influential recent endorsement of the 'scaffolding' metaphor.

15 John J. Slocum and Herbert Cahoon, *A Bibliography of James Joyce 1882–1941* (London: Hart-Davis, 1953) 113.
16 However, there is the curious case of D. H. Lawrence's *Sons and Lovers,* where extensive cuts in the first edition proposed by the publisher's reader and accepted by Lawrence are to be restored in an edition to be published by Cambridge University Press.
17 Both processes were begun by the editors of the posthumous First Folio and continued by subsequent editors, though the substitution of literary for theatrical stage directions is still not complete. See Alfred W. Pollard, *Shakespeare Folios and Quartos* (London: Methuen, 1909) 124–25.
18 'Further' in linguistic as well as chronological terms. As the 1928 'Protée' shows, it is customary for translators of texts to be permitted a degree of licence not so readily granted in the original language.

SOME CRITICAL COMMENTS ON THE TELEMACHIA
IN THE 1984 *ULYSSES*
Charles Peake

1 'The Text of *Ulysses,*' in *New Light on Joyce from the Dublin Symposium,* ed. Fritz Senn (Bloomington and London: Indiana University Press, 1972) 114.

CURIOS OF SIGNS I AM HERE TO REDE!
C. George Sandulescu

1 Curios of signs (*FW* 018.17); Signatures of all things I am here to read (3.2); rede (*FW* 018.18 etc).
2 After God Shakespeare has created most (9.1028).
3 E. Bach, *An Introduction to Transformational Grammar* (New York: Holt, Rinehart & Winston, Inc., 1964) 69ff.
4 H. W. Gabler et al., eds, *Ulysses II.5, Prototype of a critical edition in progress* (München 1979). Printed manuscript.
5 H. W. Gabler, 'The Synchrony and Diachrony of Texts: Practice and Theory of the Critical Edition of James Joyce's *Ulysses*' in *Text: Transactions of the Society for Textual Scholarship* I (1981) (AMS Press, Inc. 1984) 305–26.
6 Ferdinand de Saussure, *Cours de linguistique générale* (Paris: Payot, 1969) 134 and 139 respectively.

NOTES ON CONTRIBUTORS

BERNARD BENSTOCK is Professor of Comparative Literature at the University of Tulsa, and Director of the Program in Literature and Society there, as well as Coordinator of the annual symposium in comparative literature. He has written three books on James Joyce (the most recent in the Literature and Life series published by Frederick Ungar), coauthored a fourth, as well as edited four volumes of essays on Joyce, and co-edited three others. He has recently completed (with Shari Benstock) *Narrative Con/Texts in Ulysses*, and they are now at work on *Narrative Con/Texts in Finnegans Wake*. His most recent publication is *Critical Essays on James Joyce*, and he has prepared the proceedings of the Ninth International James Joyce Symposium as *James Joyce: the Augmented Ninth* for publication.

ROSA MARIA BOLLETTIERI BOSINELLI is Associate Professor of English at the University of Bologna, Italy. She graduated with a dissertation on Joyce's Triestine years. As a post-graduate, she attended courses at Trinity College, Dublin. She was a Fulbright visiting scholar at the University of Laramie, Wyoming, and Cincinnati, Ohio, in 1976, and at Stanford University, Palo Alto, Ca., in 1984. She has contributed a number of articles on the works of James Joyce, mainly *Finnegans Wake*, to the *James Joyce Quarterly*, the *James Joyce Broadsheet*, *Comparative Literature Studies*, *Lingua e Stile* and *Paragone*. In the field of English Language teaching and cultural studies she has published works on the image of Italy in the U.S. press, the language of conflict in Northern Ireland, the analysis of political discourse in the U.S. presidential election 1984. Dr Bosinelli's work in progress is a study of the narrative techniques in *Finnegans Wake*.

GIOVANNI CIANCI is Professor of English Literature at the University of Genoa, Italy. He is the author of *La Scuola di Cambridge* (on the literary criticism of I. A. Richards, Empson and Leavis; Bari, 1970) and *La Fortuna di Joyce in Italia* (Bari, 1974). He edited *Quaderno 9* (a special issue on Futurism/Vorticism; Palermo, 1979) and an international collection of essays in *W. Lewis, Letteratura/ Pittura* (Palermo, 1982). He is currently writing a book on the impact of Futurism on the early English avant-garde.

CARLA de PETRIS was educated at the main University in Rome, where she has been teaching since 1971. She is now research assistant at the Department of Comparative Literature. She contributed monographic entries on Irish Literature to the Italian *U.T.E.T. Encyclopedia.* She is also the author of essays and articles on T. S. Eliot, H. Miller, J. D. Salinger and on Irish Writers such as S. O'Casey, B. Behan, C. Brown, B. Moore, S. Heaney and B. Kennelly, published in various books and periodicals. She is translating into Italian some works by major contemporary Irish poets. Dr de Petris provided the introduction and notes to the 'Telemachus' episode included in the volume *Ulisse-Telemachia*, edited by Giorgio Melchiori and published in 1983. She contributed an essay, an interview and new photographic material to the volume *Joyce in Rome – The Genesis of Ulysses* edited by Giorgio Melchiori. She is engaged at present on a study of Joyce's play *Exiles.*

RICHARD ELLMANN, Woodruff Professor at Emory University, and Goldsmiths' Professor Emeritus at Oxford University, is the author of *James Joyce* (rev. ed. 1982), *Ulysses on the Liffey, The Consciousness of Joyce,* and other books, and editor of Joyce's *Letters,* vols. II and III, and other writings of Joyce. He has written widely on modern writers.

WILHELM FÜGER received his Ph.D (1963) and his Venia Legendi (1970) from the University of Munich, and has been Professor of English at the Free University Berlin since 1973. His numerous publications range from Spenser to Beckett and include monographs on Daniel Defoe (1963), the English Prose Poem (1973), and Virginia Woolf (1980). He is the editor of a casebook of German criticism of Joyce's *Portrait* (1972) and of a concordance to *Dubliners* (1980). He contributed articles and notes on Joyce's oeuvre to *Anglia, arcadia, Archiv, AWN, DVJS, GRM, ITL,* and *JJQ.* Narrative theory is another field of research he has been working on. For more details, see: *Kürschners Deutscher Gelehrtenkalender 1976,* ed. by W.Schuder, Berlin and New York 1976, I, 823; *Neuer Anglistenspiegel,* ed. by Th. Finkenstaedt, Augsburg 1983, I, 218–22.

MICHAEL PATRICK GILLESPIE has been an Assistant Professor of English at Marquette University, Milwaukee, since receiving his Ph.D. from the University of Wisconsin in 1980. He has written *Inverted Volumes Improperly Arranged: James Joyce and His Trieste Library* (1983) and *An Annotated Catalogue of the Joyce Trieste Collection* (forthcoming). His present research includes a study of Joyce's stylistic development.

CLIVE HART was born in Western Australia and educated at the Universities of Western Australia, Paris, and Cambridge. He was

Notes on Contributors

Chairman of the Departments of English at the Universities of Newcastle, N.S.W. (1967–69) and Dundee (1969–72) before taking up his present post as Professor of Literature at the University of Essex. He is the author of several books on Joyce, including *Structure and Motif in Finnegans Wake* (1962) and *James Joyce's Ulysses* (1968). He is co-editor, with David Hayman, of *James Joyce's Ulysses: Critical Essays* (1974) and was co-founder, with Fritz Senn, of *A Wake Newslitter: Studies of James Joyce's Finnegans Wake* (1962–84). He is editor-in-chief of A Wake Newslitter press. In addition to writing on other aspects of modern literature, he has written a children's book and is the author of three books on the early history of flight.

DAVID HAYMAN was educated at New York University and the University of Paris. He taught Comparative Literature and English at the Universities of Texas and Iowa, before moving to the Comparative Literature Department of the University of Wisconsin. He also taught at the University of Paris and the Goethe Universität in Frankfurt. His published work includes over fifty articles in English, French, Spanish, and Portuguese on James Joyce, Gustave Flaubert, literary theory, as well as 19th and 20th Century English, French, and Spanish literature. Among his books are *Joyce et Mallarmé, A First-Draft Version of Finnegans Wake, Ulysses: The Mechanics of Meaning, James Joyce's Ulysses: Critical Essays* (edited with Clive Hart), 25 volumes of *The James Joyce Archive* (edited with Danis Rose), and *In the Wake of the Wake* (edited). He also edited and served on the editorial boards of seven journals including *Contemporary Literature, James Joyce Quarterly, The Iowa Review, TriQuarterly*, and *Formations*.

SUZETTE A. HENKE is Associate Professor of English at the State University of New York at Binghamton. She is author of *Joyce's Moraculous Sindbook: A Study of 'Ulysses'* (1978) and co-editor, along with Elaine Unkeless, of an essay collection entitled *Women in Joyce* (1982). Her work in modernist and feminist studies includes essays on such authors as Virginia Woolf, Samuel Beckett, Anais Nin, Dorothy Richardson, E. M. Forster, W. B. Yeats, Frances Farmer and John Cage. She is presently completing a book on *James Joyce and the Politics of Desire* and working on a study of autobiographical fiction by contemporary women writers.

Professor Henke has taught as a guest professor at Aarhus University in Denmark and Haifa University in Israel. She recently completed a round-the-world lecture tour that included India and Australia, and has spent a sabbatical semester in residence as a fellow at the Camargo Foundation in southern France.

RICHARD M. KAIN is Professor of English, Emeritus, at the University of Louisville in the United States. He also taught elsewhere, notably at Harvard, Northwestern, New York, Massachussetts, Washington, and Colorado. He was a Fulbright Professor in Venice, and taught for a while at University College, Dublin. The author of many articles, reviews, and contributions to books, Dr Kain's main publications include *Ulysses, Fabulous Voyager* (1947); *Dublin in the Age of William Butler Yeats and James Joyce* (1962); *Susan L. Mitchell* (1972); and, in collaboration, *Joyce, the Man, the Work, the Reputation* (with Marvin Magalaner, 1956); *The Workshop of Daedalus* (with Robert Scholes, 1965); and the introductory chapter in *Anglo-Irish Literature: A Review of Research* (1976). He is an advisory editor of the *James Joyce Quarterly*, and an honorary trustee of the James Joyce Foundation.

CARLA MARENGO VAGLIO is Professor of English at the University of Turin, Italy. She graduated in 1966 from the same university. In 1977 she published *Invito alla lettura di Joyce* (Milan: Mursa), and *An Introduction to La Grazia* (Milan: Rizzoli). More recently, she published 'Time Theme in Dubliners' in *Genèse et métamorphose du texte joycien* (Paris: Sorbonne, 1985) as well as 'Joyce and Metafiction: The Case of EUMAEUS' in *International Perspectives on James Joyce* (New York: Whitson, 1985). She has been a member of the Board of Trustees of the James Joyce Foundation at Tulsa since 1982, and her current research preoccupation is the linguistic analysis of *Finnegans Wake*.

IRA B. NADEL is Professor of English at the University of British Columbia in Vancouver. He was educated at Rutgers and Cornell. His publications include *Biography: Fiction, Fact & Form* (1984) and articles on Victorian autobiography and fiction. He has recently co-edited four volumes on Victorian novelists and poets for the Dictionary of Literary Biography, as well as a series for Garland entitled *The Victorian Muse, Selected Criticism and Parody of the Period*. He is presently completing a study of Joyce and his Jewish circle.

PATRICK PARRINDER was born in Cornwall and studied English at Cambridge, where he subsequently became a Fellow of King's College. He moved to Reading, where he is currently a Reader in English. His first book was *H. G. Wells* (1970), and he later edited *H. G. Wells: The Critical Heritage* (1972) and co-edited *H. G. Wells's Literary Criticism* (1980). He has also written *Authors and Authority* (1977), *Science Fiction: Its Criticism and Teaching* (1980), and *James*

Joyce, in Cambridge University Press's 'British and Irish Authors' series (1984). His next book, a collection of essays on contemporary criticism and fiction to be entitled *The Failure of Theory*, will be published by Harvester Press.

CHARLES PEAKE is Emeritus Professor of English Literature at the University of London. He published the comprehensive critical study *James Joyce, the Citizen and the Artist* in 1980. In addition to James Joyce and the modern novel, his main interests lie in the area of eighteenth century literature, notably Jonathan Swift, Defoe, and Richardson. He has contributed a number of articles to journals and periodicals.

C. GEORGE SANDULESCU holds degrees from the Universities of Bucharest, Leeds, and Essex. His interests are equally divided between twentieth century fiction, with special emphasis on James Joyce, and present-day theories of language, with special focus on Discourse Analysis. He edited *Language for Special Purposes* (Paris: Didier, 1973), published *The Joycean Monologue* (Colchester: A Wake Newslitter Press, 1979), and has contributed articles on both language and literature to scholarly journals. During the academic years 1983–84 and 1985–86 he was visiting professor of English at the University of Turin, Italy. He is a member of the editorial board of *Etudes Irlandaises* (University of Lille), and Director of the Princess Grace Irish Library of the Principality of Monaco.

FRITZ SENN has been director of the Zurich James Joyce Foundation since its inception in August 1985. He has attended practically all the international James Joyce Symposia since 1967. He is a trustee of the James Joyce Foundation at Tulsa, and European editor of the *James Joyce Quarterly*. In 1984 he published two volumes of essays entitled *Nichts gegen Joyce*, and *Joyce's Dislocutions*. He has lectured extensively in the United States at the Universities of New York, Indiana, Ohio, Hawaii, and Delaware.

FRANCISCO GARCÍA TORTOSA studied modern philology at the University of Salamanca, where he was awarded a B.A. and a Ph.D. He has been an Assistant Teacher at Kingston Polytechnic, London, and at the University of Leeds, as well as lecturing on English philology at the Universities of Salamanca, Santiago de Compostela and Seville. He has been Head of the Departments of English Philology in Santiago de Compostela and in Seville, where he is presently Dean of the Faculty of Philology, and has lectured at universities in Europe and North America. He has published five books and a considerable number of articles in Spanish and foreign periodicals. His research centres mainly on stylistics applied, principally, to modern English literature, and especially James Joyce, although he has also dealt with medieval and Renaissance literature.

DONALD PHILLIP VERENE is Professor and Chairman of the Department of Philosophy at Emory University, Atlanta, Georgia. He has published a number of volumes in the field of philosophy, among which are: *Giambattista Vico's Science of Humanity* (1976), a volume of essays edited with Giorgio Tagliacozzo; *Symbol, Myth, and Culture: Essays and Lectures of Ernst Cassirer 1935–1945* (1979), a volume of Cassirer's unpublished papers; *Vico's Science of Humanity* (1981); and *Hegel's Recollection: A Study of Images in the Phenomenology of Spirit* (1985). He is Editor of the quarterly *Philosophy and Rhetoric*, and Coediter of the yearbook *New Vico Studies*. He organized and directed the international conference on *Vico and Joyce* in Venice in Summer 1985.

INDEX TO QUOTATIONS FROM
ULYSSES

The numbers in the Garland 1984 Edition of *Ulysses* indicate episode, line, and place in line respectively. For all the other editions the numbers indicate page, line (and, occasionally, place in line).

The lower-case letters a, b, c, d, in the third column of this index refer to the top, upper-middle, lower-middle, and bottom portions of the forty-line pages of this book.

The text of the 1986 Bodley Head and Penguin editions have exactly the same line numbers as the Garland edition. The references for the Garland edition are therefore equally valid for the British editions.

Garland 1984	KEY WORD & Type of Change	Page	Bodley Head 1960	Random House 1961	Penguin 1968
1.3:8	by → on	152d	1.4:8	3.3:8	9.3:8
1.5:1	*Introibo* etc	116a	1.6	3.5	9.5
1.6:11	up → out	5a	1.8	3.7	9.6
"	" " "	154b	"	"	"
"	" " "	157b	"	"	"
"	" " "	195b	"	"	"
1.10:10	country → land	154b	1.12	3.11	9.11
"	" " "	157c	"	"	"
1.24:9	low → slow	154b	1.28	3.26	9.25
"	" " "	157d	"	"	"
1.24:9	Chrysostomos.	115d	1.31	3.28	9.27
"	"	179d	"	"	"
"	"	195d	"	"	"
1.79:11	read . . . original	119d	3.31	5.3	11.11
1.86:5	great → grey	151d	4.4	5.14	11.17
1.113:7	breeks	168d	5.3	6.3	12.8
1.128:11	(SPELL)Connolly	154b	5.23	6.21	12.24
1.136:5	Hair on end.	80b	5.31	6.28	12.32
1.194:7	went (DELETE) I	152d	8.1	8.14	14.18
1.206:10	It's	154b	8.16	8.28	14.31
1.240:2	*love's bitter mystery*	30b	9.22	9.23	15.27
1.248:9	slowly, (ADD) wholly,	151d	9.31	9.32	15.35
1.249:5	behind → beneath	151d	9.32	9.33	15.36
1.250:3	alone	151d	9.33	9.34	15.37
1.258:3	pantomime	154b	10.11	10.2	16.8
1.279:1	No (ADD COMMA)	13d	11.6	10.26	16.32
"	" " . "	25a	"	"	"
1.314:5-7	(SWITCH) to and fro	154b	12.15	11.25	17.34
"	" " " "	158d	"	"	"
1.316:5	(SPELL) barbacans	78d	12.17	11.27	17.36
"	" "	161b	"	"	"
1.329:5	haled	152d	13.1	12.1	18.13
1.340:8	said (ADD) thirstily	162c	13.16	12.16	18.24
1.367:4	weird sisters	106c	14.10	13.1	19.13
1.385:4	mouth with fry	151d	14.32	13.23	19.33
1.398:7	paps	154b	15.19	13.37	20.9
1.411:4	could (DELETE) only	154b	16.2	14.12	20.24
"	" " "	159a	"	"	"
1.417:1-6	(ADD SIX ITEMS)	154b	16.9	14.18	20.30
1.428:16	from (ADD) the	151d	16.25	14.32	21.3
1.444:9-11	(ADD THREE ITEMS)	154c	17.10	15.10	21.19
"	" " "	159b	"	"	"
1.481:10	Agenbite of inwit.	79d	18.20	16.7	22.18
"	" " "	192a	"	"	"

Index to quotations from Ulysses

Garland 1984	KEY WORD & Type of Change	Page	Bodley Head 1960	Random House 1961	Penguin 1968
490:4	make (ADD) any	154c	18.29	16.16	22.27
"	" " "	159c	"	"	"
1.513:9	tie (DELETE COMMA)	78a	19.22	16.42	23.13
1.515:11	(DELETE) Agenbite etc	64a	19.25	17.3	23.16
"	" " " "	79d	"	"	"
"	" " " "	191	"	"	"
1.547:9	made (ADD) out	154c	20.31	17.40	24.9
1.562:1	We're	152d	21.19	18.18	24.24
1.602:9	-like → -sweet	154c	23.4	19.23	25.28
"	" " "	159d	"	"	"
1.605:7	He's	154c	23.7	19.26	25.31
"	"	160b	"	"	"
1.614:1	There's	154d	23.17	19.36	26.6
1.628:3	(SPELL) ferule	154d	24.1	20.16	26.20
"	" "	160d	"	"	"
"	" "	161c	"	"	"
1.638:3	the → a	154d	24.13	20.27	26.31
1.680:11	him (ADD COMMA)	78b	26.1	21.37	28.2
1.694:1-2	and lips	151d	26.16	22.9	28.16
1.708:10	(SPELL) *Übermensch*	117c	27.1	22.27	28.32
1.736:1	(DISPLAY OF VERSE)	24c	27.31ff	23.16ff	29.23ff
1.738:1	(SPELL) *Iubilantium*	117c	27.33	23.18	29.25
2.24:2	tissues → tissue	166c	29.6	24.29	30.24
2.32:11	waves → water	165b	29.17	24.39	30.34
2.78:10	waves	165c	31.6	26.7	32.6
2.83:9	waves	165c	31.13	26.13	32.11
2.124:4	tangled → thick	166a	32.27	27.17	33.17
2.139:7	tangled → thick	80b	33.11	27.33	33.32
"	" " "	166a	"	"	"
2.143:10	only true thing	41d	33.17	27.38	33.37
2.255:10	brogues	168d	37.26	31.2	37.1
2.312:7	thirstily	162d	39.33	32.28	38.25
2.343:8	intrigues (DELETE COMMA)	78c	41.8	33.25	39.21
2.344:1	influence (DELETE COMMA)	78c	"	"	"
2.371:9	the → their	166c	42.8:6	34.15:5	40.12:6
2.380:14	All (ADD) human	166d	42.21	34.27	40.24
2.387:8	(SPELL) awhile	167b	42.30	34.35	40.30
3.2:12	to read	171a	45.8	37.3	42.23
3.13:1	(SPELL) *Nach-*	117c	45.22	37.14	42.33
3.15:3	(SPELL) *Neben-*	117c	45.25	37.17	42.35

Garland 1984	KEY WORD & Type of Change	Page	Bodley Head 1960	Random House 1961	Penguin 1968
3.17:1	boots	168d	45.27	37.19	43.2
3.18:3	(DEITALICISE) Los	117a	45.29	37.20	43.3
"	" " "	178a	"	"	"
3.18:4	(DECAP) *demiurgos*	117a	"	"	"
"	" "	178a	"	"	"
3.21:1	*Madeline the mare*	26a	46.2	37.24	43.6
3.23:7	(SPELL) acatalectic	26a	46.4	37.26	43.8
3.24:4	*deline the mare*	27a	"	"	43.9
"	" " "	118b	"	"	"
3.51:4	on → upon	167d	47.5	38.17	43.37
3.79:3-8	(ADD SIX ITEMS)	163b	48.4	39.5	44.29
3.107:13	Marsh's	105b	49.4	39.36	45.20
3.114:2	nimium → amplius	118d	49.13	40.1	45.26
3.141:4	epiphanies (ADD) written	167d	50.14	40.34	46.18
3.151:3ff	(ADD THIRTEEN ITEMS)	27b	50.26	41.3	46.28
"	" " "	163c	"	"	"
3.181:9	February 1904	131b	51.28	41.36	47.20
3.182:13	*Lui, c'est moi.*	118c	51.29	41.38	47.22
3.199:1	(SPELL) Nother	5b	52.16	42.15	47.39
"	" " "	27d	"	"	"
3.227:9	(ADD SIX ITEMS)	163c	53.20	43.8	48.30
3.272:1	(SPELL) barbacans	161b	55.11	44.17	50.3
3.343:7	again	199a	58.5	46.20	52.2
3.358:5	lifting (ADD) again	198b	58.24	46.38	52.17
3.386:2	Adam	163d	59.26	47.28	53.8
3.435:7	that word	30b	61.24	49.5	54.25
"	" "	39b	"	"	"
3.451:9	(ADD FOUR ITEMS)	9b	62.12	49.23	55.4
"	" " "	168a	"	"	"
4.28:3	Curious mice	14c	66.6	55.35	57.32
4.199:3	Bleibtreu-...W.15	130b	72.21	60.25	62.26
4.298:8	(Molly's) cream	71b	76.10	63.14	65.14
4.351:11	(SPELL)metamspychosis	79a	78.5	64.32	66.31
4.489:1	(SPELL) brillantined	79a	83.12	68.24	70.26
"	" "	161c	"	"	"
4.508:12	patiently (DELETE COMMA)	78c	84.3	69.6	71.8
5.111:3	(SPELL) vailed	79a	90.1	74.6	75.23
5.156:6	man. (ADD) Letter.	131b	91.28	75.16	76.31
5.227:1	(SPELL) *Là*	117d	94.14	77.17	78.29
5.245:10	world/word	87c	95.3	77.37	79.10

Index to quotations from Ulysses

Garland 1984	KEY WORD & Type of Change	Page	Bodley Head 1960	Random House 1961	Penguin 1968
6.149:1	(ITALICISE)*Trenchant*	115c	113.12	91.6	92.31
6.150:1	(ITALICISE)*retro-* etc	115c	113.13	91.7	92.32
6.405:10	thought(ADD COMMA)	76d	122.33	98.12	100.5
6.612:6	goner → doner	130a	131.6	104.5	105.36
"	" " "	148c	"	"	"
6.772:10	Well preserved	69c	137.12	108.32	110.21
6.772:13	corpse (ADD COMMA)	69c	"	"	110.22
7.166:10ff	(SPELLING . . .)	17b	154.4	121.13	123.1
7.365:2	out(DELETE COMMA)	76d	161.26	127.8	128.30
7.530:5	answered (DELETE COMMA)	75c	168.9	132.20	133.32
7.568:3	(DELETE LIGATURE)	73c	169.25	133.28	135.5
7.793:8	F (DELETE PERIOD)	74b	178.20	141.3	141.33
7.906:1	(PERIODS . . .)	74b	182.32	144.19	145.8
7.940:9	Miss Kate	75a	184.10	145.22	146.11
7.952:4	said (DELETE COMMA)	75c	184.27	146.1	146.23
7.959:5	cried, (COMMA)	75c	185.4	146.8	146.30
7.967:6	said, (COMMA)	75c	185.13	146.17	147.4
7.981:12	said (DELETE COMMA)	75c	186.2	146.33	147.18
7.1032:1	SOPHIST WALLOPS etc	209d	188.8	148.25	149.12
8.19:2	crucifix (DELETE Q.MARK)	76b	190.23	151.22	151.11
8.119:4	wit(DELETE Q.MARK)	76b	194.19	154.16	154.3
8.258:10	P.: → p:	74a	199.30	158.12	157.35
8.496:7	tinned salmon	131b	209.1	164.40	164.24
8.523:10	beard and bicycle	109b	210.4	165.29	165.15
8.552:1	Yeates and Son	109b	211.4	166.18	166.6
8.623:2	(SPELL) *Lacaus esant*	118a	213.32	168.20	168.6
8.890:13	*Du de la* (DELETE TWO COMMAS)	80c	223.24	175.32	175.22
8.1071:3	Rome (DELETE Q.MARK)	75d	230.15	180.26	180.20
8.1084:3	(SPELL) brillantined	161c	230.32	180.42	180.33
8.1093:8	remark (ADD PERIOD)	75c	231.10	181.10	181.5
8.1110:8	removed (DELETE Q.MARK)	75d	231.30	181.28	181.23
9.16:4	(SPELL) Palice	79a	235.21	184.18	184.17
"	" "	178a	"	"	"
9.52:3	(ADD PLURAL) minds	212a	236.31	185.18	185.18

Garland 1984	KEY WORD & Type of Change	Page	Bodley Head 1960	Random House 1961	Penguin 1968
9.84:3	dagger definitions	102c	238.5	186.13	186.15
9.84:5	Horseness	49c	238.5	186.13	186.15
"	"	103a	"	"	"
9.120:2	*LE DISTRAIT →*				
	Le Distrait	75b	239.18	187.17	187.15
9.132:2	(ADD PLURAL) palms	212a	239.31	187.29	187.27
9.133:10	bloodboltered	105a	240.10	187.31	187.29
9.150:10	*limbo patrum*	105a	240.21	188.10	188.10
9.158:2	Local colour.	102c	241.1	188.19	188.20
9.163:5	Loyola	102c	241.8	188.25	188.25
9.192:3	sirrah	105a	242.12	189.22	189.23
9.193:1	Marry	105a	242.12	189.24	189.24
9.195:1	Go to	105a	242.16	189.26	189.26
9.228:11	genius makes no mistakes	122a	243.21	190.22	190.22
"	" " " " "	133d	"	"	"
9.279:1	Yogibogeybox	89d	245.17	191.37	191.37
9.290:10	is gathering	101d	245.32	192.10	192.12
9.294:3	Remember.	102d	246.5	192.14	192.17
9.306:12	Miss Mitchell	75a	246.20	192.28	192.30
9.423:13	love the daughter	31b	250.27	195.35	196.2
9.426:1	(SPELL) *grandp*	28b	250.30	195.38	196.4
"	*grandp* (ADD 5 DOTS)	28b	"	"	"
"	grandp (ADD 43 ITEMS) love etc	5b	"	"	"
"	" " " " " "	9c	"	"	"
"	" " " " " "	28c	"	"	"
"	" " " " " "	32c	"	"	"
"	" " " " " "	39c	"	"	"
"	" " " " " "	54a	"	"	"
"	" " " " " "	67b	"	"	"
"	" " " " " "	129d	"	"	"
"	" " " " " "	149b	"	"	"
"	" " " " " "	178b	"	"	"
"	" " " " " "	192d	"	"	"
"	" " " " " "	212c	"	"	"
9.432:3	image	32a	250.31	195.39	196.5
9.432:11	thing genius	211a	250.32	195.39	196.5
9.500:1	(*Gloria in excelsis Deo.*)	209c	253.20	197.34	198.3
9.577:4	Saint(DELETE 3 HYPHENS)	69c	256.21	200.11	200.14
9.599:2	*Guardian* (ADD PERIOD)	212c	257.13	200.34	200.36
"	*Guardian.* (ADD) Last year.	"	"	"	"

Index to quotations from Ulysses

Garland 1984	KEY WORD & Type of Change	Page	Bodley Head 1960	Random House 1961	Penguin 1968
9.620:7	stay(ADD 2 HYPHENS)	69c	258.4	201.16	201.19
9.631:8	(SPELL) conjugial	212c	258.19	201.30	201.31
9.641:1	Cours (DELETE TWO HYPHENS)	69c	258.32	201.41	202.4
9.760:4	(ADD PLURAL) depths	212a	263.14	205.11	205.20
9.762:1	theolologico-	102d	263.17	205.13	205.23
9.773:4	Monk	104c	263.30	205.24	205.34
9.778:7	gorebellied	105a	263.3	205.30	206.1
9.803:10	stayed (ADD) with her	212d	265.2	206.19	206.28
9.811:8	*Eglintonus*	104c	265.12	206.29	206.37
9.842:7	incertitude	197b	266.19	207.26	207.32
9.843:11	only true thing	89c	266.21	207.28	207.34
9.848:1	*Amplius.* etc	102d	266.26	207.33	207.38
9.900:1	MAGEEGLINJOHN	104d	268.21	209.9	209.14
9.938:8	meacock	105a	269.29	210.17	210.11
9.939:4	(SPELL) -*timoru*-	189b	269.31	210.19	210.12
"	" "	199b	"	"	"
9.1017:1	Judge	104c	272.28	212.27	212.18
9.1020:12	mature man	205b	272.30	212.30	212.21
9.1025:3	Cuck	104c	273.3	212.36	212.26
9.1029:3	to create	171a	273.9	212.41	212.30
9.1063:1	variorum	206b	274.20	213.39	213.28
9.1070:2	Eclecticon	104c	274.29	214.5	213.35
9.1073:9	Bleibtreu	130b	274.33	214.9	213.38
9.1108:10	discussion	102d	276.7	215.7	214.36
9.1123:2ff	(ADD EXTRA DOTS & Q.MARKS)	75d	276.23	215.23	215.14
9.1125:1	Puck	104c	276.26	215.26	215.16
9.1129:7	Eg Lin Ton	104c	276.31	215.31	215.21
9.1131:10	Abbey Theatre	106d	277.1	215.34	215.24
9.1140:8	he → eh	212d	277.12	216.1	215.32
9.1164:4	book (. . .) Homer	1a	278.5	216.27	261.20
10.89:3	(CAP) Tobacconist	74c	283.26	221.19	220.29
"	" "	80d	"	"	"
10.100:9	lying → lie	81a	284.6	221.32	221.3
10.183:3&5	(SWITCH) just & homely	174a	287.11	224.7	223.16
10.623:2	Crushed → Crished	81b	303.19	236.26	235.28
10.634:9	spat → puked	81c	303.34	236.40	236.1
"	" " "	131b	"	"	"
10.635:15	it (ADD COMMA)	81d	304.2	236.41	236.3
10.652:1ff	(PERIODS . . .)	74b	304.21	237.17	236.20
10.819:10	sanded (ADD) tired	82b	311.2	242.9	241.14
10.928:4	Hugh C. Love	74b	315.5	245.8	244.13

243

Garland 1984	KEY WORD & Type of Change	Page	Bodley Head 1960	Random House 1961	Penguin 1968
10.930:11	(DECAP) ford of hurdles	74c	315.9	245.11	244.16
10.995:2	long John	74b	317.26	247.4	246.11
10.997:5	long John	74b	317.28	247.26	246.13
10.1017:5	long John	74b	318.18	247.28	246.33
10.1021:8	long John	74b	318.24	247.32	246.37
10.1026:14	long John	74b	318.31	247.38	247.5
10.1027:4	long John	74b	318.32	247.38	247.5
10.1044:2	(CAP) Panama	74c	319.15	248.14	247.22
10.1216:6	*dernier cri*	75b	326.8	253.13	252.22
10.1220:8	(DEITALICISE) soubrette	75a	326.13	253.17	252.26
10.1250:3	(DEITALICISE) cortège	75a	327.20	254.11	253.19
11.passim	(DECAP) miss	74d	328 ff	256 ff	254 ff
11.87:4	Wine's antiques	205d	331.28	258.10	256.33
11.88:1	Carroll's	205d	331.29	258.11	256.34
11.267:2	*élite*	75b	338.12	263.1	261.31
11.903:12	p.: → P:	74a	361.30	280.22	279.14
11.1071:12	young (ADD Q. MARK)	77a	368.5	285.11	284.3
11.102:8	(SWITCH) dying etc	193d	369.11	286.6	284.35
11.1115:5	repassed → reposed	82d	369.29	286.21	285.10
11.1263:1	envisaged (ADD) battered	205c	375.5	290.20	289.11
11.1263:2	(ADD PLURAL) candlesticks	205c	"	"	"
12.106:3	varieties	206b	380.16	294.39	293.7
12.504:11	pisser Burke	74b	395.18	305.40	304.7
12.612:4	Hard → Hand	82d	399.25	309.1	307.6
12.621:5	terracotta → terra cotta	83b	400.3	309.11	307.16
12.996:2	begob (DELETE COMMA)	77d	414.13	319.28	317.36
12.996:6	myself (DELETE COMMA)	77d	"	"	"
12.1008:11	(SPELL) O'Molloy's	83b	414.28	319.42	318.11
12.1028:15	done (DELETE COMMA)	77d	415.18	320.22	318.33
12.1101:11	stones (ADD COMMA)	78a	418.6	322.23	320.34
12.1163:8	what's → what	83b	420.15	324.11	322.23
12.1360:8	everywhere (DELETE Q. MARK)	76a	427.28	329.30	328.6
12.1485:9	opposite of hatred	38d	432.25	333.14	331.24
12.1489:11	Universal love	29c	432.32	333.21	331.29

244

Index to quotations from Ulysses

Garland 1984	KEYWORD & Type of Change	Page	Bodley Head 1960	Random House 1961	Penguin 1968
12.1490:4	Wyse (ADD PERIOD)	76b	432.33	333.22	331.30
12.1490:5	(CAP) Isn't	"	"	"	"
12.1490:9	told (DELETE Q. MARK)	"	"	"	"
12.1491:12	his motto. Love	29d	433.2	333.25	331.33
12.1493:1	Love (...) love	29d	433.4	333.27	331.34
12.1574:9	Bloom (...) Sinn Fein	106d	436.6	335.39	334.8
12.1624:4	" " "	"	438.4	337.18	335.23
12.1633-34	(SWITCH DIALOGUE LINES)	83c	438.15-17	337.29-31	335.32-33
13.917:13	to (ADD COMMA)	68d	484.28	372.4	369.28
14.1.1	Deshil	208a	499.24	393.1	380.21
14.234:11	horn (ADD COMMA)	69d	508.33	389.34	387.11
14.235:2	while (ADD COMMA)	69d	"	"	"
14.297:5	(CAP) She	70b	511.14	391.27	389.2
14.683:10	not → note	69a	526.15	402.29	399.35
14.1052:6	alas, → alas!	70c	540.28	413.14	410.11
14.1052:12	past!) (DELETE COMMA)	70c	"	"	"
14.1055:7	(SPELL) baisemoins	70c	540.32	413.18	410.14
14.1066:6	luckpenny	5d	541.12	413.30	410.26
14.1066:6	sustained on	153c	542.32	414.37	411.31
14.1390:7	(DECAP) word	74d	533.34	422.42	419.31
14.1459:3	(SPELL) atitudes	69b	556.23	424.41	421.29
14.1582:1	(SPELL) dog-gone	71d	561.13/14	428.16	425.5
15.3:7	flimsy → grimy	193b	561.30	429.4	425.18
15.6:10	coal → coral	192d	562.2	429.7	425.21
15.77:1	*Vidi* etc	120d	564.3	431.15	427.7
15.84:1	(DEITALICISE) Altium etc	120d	564.9	431.22	427.11
15.248:6	*elder in Zion*	72a	568.31	437.13	430.29
15.700:1	Harold's cross bridge	72b	581.24	454.12	440.24
15.991:2	Bleibtreu (...) W.13	130b	590.25	464.31	447.14
15.3594:5	*Le distrait* → The distrait	75b	665.26	558.21	504.8
15.4161:10	a silent word	38c	681.3	579.30	515.36
15.4190:3	*Love's bitter mystery.*	30b	681.32	581.3	516.24
"	" " "	41d	"	"	"
15.4192	The word	30b	682.2	581.5	516.26
"	" "	37d	"	"	"
"	" "	54b	"	"	"
"	" "	89b	"	"	"
15.4197	Prayer	89b	682.5	581.10	516.29

Garland 1984	KEY WORD & Type of Change	Page	Bodley Head 1960	Random House 1961	Penguin 1968
15.4203	I loved you	41b	682.11	581.18	516.35
16.294:2	was it? (ADD COMMA)	131a	715.4	621.5	541.11
16.612:13	yes, ay, or no	188a	726.34	629.34	550.9
16.1260:10	L. Boom	120b	751.31	647.41	568.20
16.1262:7	" "	"	.33	.43	.21
16.1274:10	Boom	"	752.15	648.15	568.34
16.1295:4	indication	205a	753.7	648.39	569.17
16.1352:5	whore	201d	755.16	650.23	571.3
16.1355:6	of her. (ADD 6 ITEMS)	201c	755.20	650.26	571.6
16.1411:11	bosom	201d	757.28	652.9	572.28
16.1453:7	sovereign (ADD 6 ITEMS)	200c	759.12	653.13	573.33
17.98:12	(SPELL) indiction	60c	780.8	669.1	589.15
"	" " "	203d	"	"	"
17.99:4	MXMIV → MCMIV	60c	780.9	669.2	589.16
"	" " " "	204b	"	"	"
17.154:1	(CAP) Lisle	74c	782.16	670.27	591.5
17.165:10	filter	161d	782.30	671.4	591.18
"	"	215b	"	"	"
17.217:13	variety	206b	785.1	672.25	592.37
17.232:7	adhered (ADD COMMA)	78a	785.20	673.1	593.14
17.238:4	water (ADD COMMA)	78a	785.28	673.7	593.21
17.284:11	a shoot	72c	787.27	674.27	595.2
17.315:5	breakfasts (ADD COMMA)	71a	789.1	675.25	595.35
17.365:10	cream (...) Molly	71b	791.2	677.6	597.19
17.661:6	(SPELL) spilikins	79b	802.32	686.2	606.27
17.665:10	variety	206b	803.6	686.8	606.33
17.733:1	(ADD) By juxtaposition.	130d	806.1	688.10	609.3
17.734:3	(SPELL) entituled	79b	806.2	688.11	609.4
17.1043:8	lattiginous	162b	819.11	698.23	619.20
17.1202:3	(SPELL) pilosity	161d	825.23	703.14	624.13
17.1358:6	inverted volumes	136d	832.7	708.12	629.9
17.1413:7	secret document	136d	834.10	709.38	630.30
17.1472:3	Fry's	131c	836.25	711.28	632.25
17.1491:6	(SPELL) ungual	162a	837.16	712.9	633.13
17.1700:5	Bleibtreu (...) W.15	130b	845.31	718.16	639.19
17.1869:2	Rudolph	130c	852.20	723.18	644.17
17.2259:9	(SPELL) entituled	79b	868.17	735.21	656.20
18.196:14	it (love)	29c	879.1	743.24	664.23
18.229:5	up → U p	74a	880.9	744.21	665.20

Index to quotations from Ulysses

Garland 1984	KEY WORD & Type of Change	Page	Bodley Head 1960	Random House 1961	Penguin 1968
18.255:11	(ITALICISE) *Irish*	75b	881.9	745.9	666.10
18.619:12	theyre → there	79c	895.11	755.24	676.26
18.814:14	morning → moaning	79c	902.26	760.41	682.6
18.939:1	plaice → place	79c	907.16	764.17	685.25
18.1595:2	posadas	135a	932.24	782.40	704.12
18.1600:13	yellow houses	135a	932.32	783.4	704.18